grzimek's
Student Animal Life Resource

• • • •

grzimek's
Student Animal Life Resource

• • • •

Birds
volume 2

Ducks to Auks

THOMSON

GALE

Detroit • New York • San Francisco • San Diego • New Haven, Conn. • Waterville, Maine • London • Munich

THOMSON

GALE

Grzimek's Student Animal Life Resource
Birds

Project Editor
Melissa C. McDade

Editorial
Julie L. Carnagie, Madeline Harris,
Heather Price

Indexing Services
Synapse, the Knowledge Link
Corporation

Rights and Acquisitions
Sheila Spencer, Mari Masalin-Cooper

Imaging and Multimedia
Randy Bassett, Michael Logusz, Dan
Newell, Chris O'Bryan, Robyn Young

Product Design
Tracey Rowens, Jennifer Wahi

Composition
Evi Seoud, Mary Beth Trimper

Manufacturing
Wendy Blurton, Dorothy Maki

LIBRARY OF CONGRESS CATALOGING-IN-PUBLICATION DATA

Grzimek's student animal life resource. Birds / Melissa C. McDade, project editor.
    p. cm.
    Includes bibliographical references and index.
    ISBN 0-7876-9235-2 (set hardcover : alk. paper) — ISBN 0-7876-9236-0
(volume 1) — ISBN 0-7876-9237-9 (volume 2) — ISBN 0-7876-9238-7 (volume 3)
— ISBN 0-7876-9239-5 (volume 4) — ISBN 0-7876-9240-9 (volume 5)
    1. Birds—Juvenile literature. I. Grzimek, Bernhard. II. McDade, Melissa C.
QL673.G79 2005
598—dc22
                                               2004015729

ISBN 0-7876-9402-9 (21-vol set), ISBN 0-7876-9235-2 (Birds set),
ISBN 0-7876-9236-0 (v.1), ISBN 0-7876-9237-9 (v.2), ISBN 0-7876-9238-7 (v.3),
ISBN 0-7876-9239-5 (v.4), ISBN 0-7876-9240-9 (v.5)

This title is also available as an e-book
Contact your Thomson Gale sales representative for ordering information.

Printed in Canada
10 9 8 7 6 5 4 3 2 1

Contents

BIRDS: VOLUME 3

BIRDS: VOLUME 5

Reader's Guide

Grzimek's Student Animal Life Resource: Birds offers readers comprehensive and easy-to-use information on Earth's birds. Entries are arranged by taxonomy, the science through which living things are classified into related groups. Order entries provide an overview of a group of families, and family entries provide an overview of a particular family. Each entry includes sections on physical characteristics; geographic range; habitat; diet; behavior and reproduction; animals and people; and conservation status. Family entries are followed by one or more species accounts with the same information as well as a range map and photo or illustration for each species. Entries conclude with a list of books, periodicals, and Web sites that may be used for further research.

ADDITIONAL FEATURES

Each volume of *Grzimek's Student Animal Life Resource: Birds* includes a pronunciation guide for scientific names, a glossary, an overview of birds, a list of species in the set by biome, a list of species by geographic location, and an index. The set has 640 full-color maps, photos, and illustrations to enliven the text, and sidebars provide additional facts and related information.

NOTES

The classification of animals into orders, families, and even species is not a completed exercise. As researchers learn more about animals and their relationships, classifications may change. In some cases, researchers do not agree on how or whether to make a change. For this reason, the heading "Number of species" in the introduction of an entry may read "About 36 species" or "34 to 37 species." It is not a question of whether some animals exist or not, but a question of how they are classified. Some researchers are more likely to "lump" animals into the same species classification, while others may "split" animals into separate species.

Grzimek's Student Animal Life Resource: Birds has standardized information in the Conservation Status section. The IUCN Red List provides the world's most comprehensive inventory of the global conservation status of plants and animals. Using a set of criteria to evaluate extinction risk, the IUCN recognizes the following categories: Extinct, Extinct in the Wild, Critically Endangered, Endangered, Vulnerable, Conservation Dependent, Near Threatened, Least Concern, and Data Deficient. These terms are defined where they are used in the text, but for a complete explanation of each category, visit the IUCN web page at http://www.iucn.org/themes/ssc/redlists/RLcats2001booklet.html.

ACKNOWLEDGEMENTS

Special thanks are due for the invaluable comments and suggestions provided by the *Grzimek's Student Animal Life Resource: Birds* advisors:

- Mary Alice Anderson, Media Specialist, Winona Middle School, Winona, Minnesota
- Thane Johnson, Librarian, Oklahoma City Zoo, Oklahoma City, Oklahoma
- Debra Kachel, Media Specialist, Ephrata Senior High School, Ephrata, Pennsylvania
- Nina Levine, Media Specialist, Blue Mountain Middle School, Courtlandt Manor, New York
- Ruth Mormon, Media Specialist, The Meadows School, Las Vegas, Nevada

COMMENTS AND SUGGESTIONS

We welcome your comments on *Grzimek's Student Animal Life Resource: Birds* and suggestions for future editions of this work. Please write: Editors, *Grzimek's Student Animal Life Resource: Birds*, U•X•L, 27500 Drake Rd., Farmington Hills, Michigan 48331-3535; call toll free: 1-800-877-4253; fax: 248-699-8097; or send e-mail via www.gale.com.

Pronunciation Guide for Scientific Names

Acanthisitta chloris uh-kan-thuh-SIT-tuh KLOR-is

Acanthisittidae uh-kan-thuh-SIT-tuh-dee

Acanthiza chrysorrhoa uh-KAN-thih-zuh KRIH-soh-ROH-uh

Acanthizidae uh-kan-THIZ-uh-dee

Accipitridae ak-sip-IT-ruh-dee

Aceros cassidix AH-ser-uhs KAS-sid-iks

Acridotheres tristis AK-rid-uh-THER-eez TRIS-tis

Actenoides concretus ak-TEN-oi-deez con-CREE-tuhs

Actinodura sodangorum AK-tin-uh-DYOOR-uh soh-dan-GOH-rum

Actophilornis africanus ak-tuh-FIL-or-nis AF-rih-kan-uhs

Aechmophorus occidentalis ek-MOH-for-uhs OK-sih-DEN-tal-is

Aegithalidae ee-jih-THAL-uh-dee

Aegithina tiphia ee-JIH-thin-uh TIF-ee-uh

Aegotheles insignis ee-GO-thel-eez IN-sig-nis

Aegothelidae ee-go-THEL-uh-dee

Agelaioides badius ah-jeh-LAY-oid-eez BAD-ee-uhs

Agelaius phoeniceus ah-jeh-LAY-ee-uhs fee-nih-SEE-uhs

Aix sponsa AKS SPON-suh

Ajaia ajaja ah-JAH-ee-uh AH-jah-juh

Alaemon alaudipes al-EE-mon ah-LAUD-ih-peez

Alaudidae ah-LAUD-uh-dee

Alcedinidae al-sed-IN-uh-dee

Alcidae AL-suh-dee

Amytornis striatus am-IT-or-nis stry-AH-tuhs

Anas platyrhynchos AH-nuhs PLA-tee-RIN-koz

Anatidae ah-NA-tuh-dee

Andigena hypoglauca an-DIH-jin-uh HI-poh-GLO-kuh

Anhima cornuta AN-him-uh KOR-nyoo-tuh

Anhimidae an-HIM-uh-dee

Anhinga anhinga AN-hin-guh AN-hin-guh

Anseriformes an-ser-uh-FORM-eez

Anthus spragueii AN-thuhs SPRAG-ee-eye

Aphelocoma californica uh-fel-uh-KOH-muh kal-uh-FORN-
   ik-uh

Apodidae a-POD-uh-dee

Apodiformes a-pod-uh-FORM-eez

Aptenodytes forsteri ap-ten-uh-DIE-teez FOS-ter-eye

Apterygidae ap-ter-IJ-uh-dee

Apteryx australis AP-ter-iks au-STRA-lis

Ara macao AR-uh MUH-kow

Aramidae ar-UH-muh-dee

Aramus guarauna AR-uh-muhs GWAR-aw-nuh

Ardea herodias AR-dee-uh hir-OH-dee-uhs

Ardeidae ar-DEE-uh-dee

Arenaria interpres ar-en-AIR-ee-uh IN-ter-preez

Artamidae ar-TAM-uh-dee

Artamus cyanopterus AR-tam-uhs SIGH-an-OP-ter-uhs

Astrapia mayeri as-truh-PEE-uh MAY-er-eye

Atrichornis rufescens a-TRIK-or-nis ROO-fehs-sens

Atrichornithidae a-trik-or-NITH-uh-dee

Attagis gayi AT-uh-jis GAY-eye

Auriparus flaviceps aw-RIP-ar-uhs FLAV-uh-seps

Balaeniceps rex bal-EEN-uh-seps REX

Balaenicipitidae BAL-een-uh-sip-IH-tuh-dee

Balearica regulorum BAL-ih-AR-ik-uh reg-YOO-lor-um

Batis capensis BAT-is KAP-en-sis

Bombycilla cedrorum bom-bih-SILL-uh SEED-roh-rum

Bombycillidae bom-bih-SILL-uh-dee

Botaurus stellaris BOH-tor-uhs STEL-lar-is

Branta canadensis BRAN-tuh kan-uh-DEN-sis

Bubo sumatranus BYOO-boh SOO-mah-TRAN-uhs

Bucconidae buck-ON-uh-dee

Bucerotidae byoo-ser-UH-tuh-dee

Bucorvus leadbeateri BYOO-kor-vuhs LED-bet-er-eye

Buphagus erythrorhynchus BYOO-fag-uhs eh-RITH-roh-RIN-kuhs

Burhinidae bur-HIN-uh-dee

Callaeas cinerea cal-LEE-uhs sin-EAR-ee-uh

Callaeidae cal-LEE-uh-dee

Calypte anna kuh-LIP-tee AN-nuh

Campephagidae kam-pee-FAJ-uh-dee

Campephilus principalis KAM-pee-FIL-uhs PRIN-sih-PAL-is

Campylorhamphus trochilirostris KAM-pie-luh-RAM-fuhs TRO-kil-ih-ROS-tris

Campylorhynchus brunneicapillus KAM-pie-luh-RIN-kuhs BROO-nee-kap-ILL-uhs

Capitonidae kap-ih-TON-uh-dee

Caprimulgidae kap-rih-MUL-juh-dee

Caprimulgiformes kal-rih-mul-juh-FORM-eez

Caprimulgus indicus KAP-rih-MUL-juhs IN-dih-kuhs

Caprimulgus vociferus KAP-rih-MUL-juhs voh-SIF-er-uhs

Carduelis tristis KAR-doo-lis TRIS-tis

Cariama cristata KAR-ee-ah-muh KRIS-tah-tuh

Cariamidae kar-ee-AH-muh-dee

Casuariidae kas-oo-ar-EYE-uh-dee

Casuarius casuarius kas-oo-AR-ee-uhs kas-oo-AR-ee-uhs

Cathartidae kath-ART-uh-dee

Cephalopterus ornatus SEFF-uhl-OP-ter-uhs AWR-nah-tuhs

Cercomacra cinerascens SIR-koh-MAK-ruh si-NEAR-ass-enz

Certhia americana SIR-thee-uh uh-mer-uh-kAN-uh

Certhiidae sirth-EYE-uh-dee

Chaetura pelagica KEE-tur-uh peh-LAJ-ik-uh

Chalcoparia singalensis kal-kuh-PAIR-ee-uh sin-GAHL-en-sis

Chamaea fasciata kam-EE-uh fah-she-AH-tuh

Chamaepetes unicolor kam-ee-PEET-eez YOO-nih-KUH-luhr

Charadriidae kar-ad-RYE-uh-dee

Charadriiformes kar-ad-rye-uh-FORM-eez

Charadrius vociferus kar-ad-REE-uhs voh-SIF-er-uhs

Chionidae ky-ON-uh-dee

Chionis minor KY-on-is MY-ner

Chiroxiphia linearis ky-roh-ZIF-ee-uh lin-EE-air-is

Chlamydera maculata klam-EE-der-uh mak-yoo-LAH-tuh

Chlidonias niger klih-DON-ee-uhs NY-jer

Cicinnurus regius sih-SIN-yoor-uhs RAY-jee-uhs

Ciconia ciconia SIK-uh-nee-uh SIK-uh-nee-uh

Ciconiidae sik-uh-NYE-uh-dee

Ciconiiformes sik-uh-nee-uh-FORM-eez

Cinclidae SIN-kluh-dee

Cinclosoma punctatum sin-cluh-SOH-muh PUNK-tah-tum

Cinclus cinclus SIN-kluhs SIN-kluhs

Cinclus mexicanus SIN-kluhs MEK-sih-KAN-uhs

Cinnyris asiaticus SIN-ny-ris AY-zhi-AT-ik-uhs

Cissa chinensis SIS-suh CHIN-en-sis

Cisticola juncidis sis-tuh-KOH-luh JUNK-id-is

Climacteridae kly-mak-TER-uh-dee

Climacteris rufa kly-MAK-ter-is ROO-fuh

Colibri coruscans KOH-lee-bree KOR-us-kans

Coliidae kol-EYE-uh-dee

Coliiformes kol-eye-uh-FORM-eez

Colinus virginianus KOL-eye-nuhs ver-JIN-ee-an-nuhs

Colius striatus KOL-ee-uhs stry-AH-tuhs

Columba livia KUH-lum-buh LIV-ee-uh

Columbidae kuh-LUM-buh-dee

Columbiformes kuh-lum-buh-FORM-eez

Coracias garrulus kor-UH-see-uhs GAR-oo-luhs

Coraciidae kor-uh-SIGH-uh-dee

Coraciiformes kor-uh-sigh-uh-FORM-eez

Coracina typica kor-uh-SEE-nuh TIP-ik-uh

Corvidae KOR-vuh-dee

Corvus corax KOR-vuhs KOR-aks

Corythaeola cristata kor-ih-thee-OH-luh KRIS-tah-tuh

Corythaixoides concolor kor-ih-THAKS-oi-deez CON-kuh-luhr

Cotinga cayana KOH-ting-guh KAY-ah-nuh

Cotingidae koh-TING-guh-dee

Cracidae KRA-suh-dee

Cracticidae krak-TIK-uh-dee

Cracticus torquatus KRAK-tik-uhs TOR-kwah-tuhs

Crax globulosa KRAKS glob-yoo-LOH-suh

Crex crex CREKS CREKS

Cuculidae kyoo-KYOO-luh-dee

Cuculiformes kyoo-kyoo-luh-FORM-eez

Cuculus canorus KYOO-kyoo-luhs KAN-or-uhs

Cyanocitta cristata SIGH-an-uh-SIT-tuh KRIS-tah-tuh

Cyclarhis gujanensis SIGH-klar-is GOO-jan-en-sis

Cygnus olor   SIG-nuhs OH-lor

Cymbirhynchus macrorhynchos SIM-bih-RIN-kuhs ma-crow-RIN-kuhs

Cypsiurus parvus sip-SIH-yoor-uhs PAR-vuhs

Dacelo novaeguineae DAY-sel-oh NOH-vee-GIN-ee-ee

Dendrocolaptidae den-droh-koh-LAP-tuh-dee

Dendroica kirtlandii DEN-droy-kuh KIRT-land-ee-eye

Dendropicos goertae   den-droh-PEE-kuhs GER-tee

Dicaeidae die-SEE-uh-dee

Dicaeum ignipectus DIE-see-um IG-nih-PEK-tuhs

Dicruridae die-KRU-ruh-dee

Dicrurus ludwigii DIE-kru-ruhs LOOT-vig-ee-eye

Dicrurus paradiseus DIE-kru-ruhs par-uh-DIE-see-uhs

Diomedea cauta eremite DIE-uh-MED-ee-uh CAW-tuh ER-ih-mite

Diomedea immutabilis DIE-uh-MED-ee-uh im-myoo-TUH-bil-is

Diomedeidae die-uh-med-EYE-dee

Donacobius atricapillus don-uh-KOH-bee-uhs ay-trih-kap-ILL-uhs

Drepanididae dre-pan-ID-uh-dee

Drepanorhynchus reichenowi DRE-pan-uh-RIN-kuhs RYE-keh-now-eye

Dromadidae droh-MAD-uh-dee

Dromaiidae droh-MAY-uh-dee

Dromaius novaehollandiae DROH-may-uhs NO-vee-hol-LAND-ee-ee

Dromas ardeola DROH-muhs ar-dee-OH-luh

Drymodes brunneopygia dry-MOH-deez BROO-nee-oh-PIJ-ee-uh

Dulidae DYOO-luh-dee

Dulus dominicus DYOO-luhs duh-MIN-ih-kuhs

Dumetella carolinensis   dum-uh-TELL-uh kar-uh-LINE-en-sis

Eclectus roratus EK-lek-tuhs ROH-rat-uhs

Egretta ibis EE-gret-uh EYE-bis

Emberizidae em-ber-IZ-uh-dee

Epthianuridae ep-thy-an-YOOR-uh-dee

Epthianura tricolor ep-thy-an-YOOR-uh TRY-kuh-luhr

Eremophila alpestris ER-em-uh-FIL-uh al-PES-tris

Esacus magnirostris EH-sak-uhs MAG-nuh-ROS-tris

Estrilda astrild   ES-tril-duh AS-trild

Estrildidae   es-TRIL-duh-dee

Eudyptes chrysolophus   YOO-dip-teez krih-soh-LOH-fuhs

Eupetidae   yoo-PET-uh-dee

Euplectes orix   YOO-plek-teez OR-iks

Eupodotis caerulescens   yoo-pod-OH-tis see-ROO-less-sens

Eurylaimidae   yoo-rih-lay-IM-uh-dee

Eurypyga helias   yoo-RIH-pij-uh HEE-lee-uhs

Eurypygidae   yoo-rih-PIJ-uh-dee

Eurystomus orientalis   yoo-rih-STOH-muhs or-ih-EN-tal-is

Falco peregrinus   FAL-koh PEHR-eh-GRIN-uhs

Falco rusticolis   FAL-koh rus-TIH-kol-is

Falconidae   fal-KON-uh-dee

Falconiformes   fal-kon-uh-FORM-eez

Ficedula basilanica   fih-SEH-duh-luh bas-ill-AN-ik-uh

Formicariidae   for-mih-kar-EYE-uh-dee

Fratercula arctica   frah-TER-kuh-luh ARK-tik-uh

Fregata magnificens   FREH-gah-tuh mag-NIH-fih-sens

Fregatidae   freh-GAH-tuh-dee

Fringilla coelebs   frin-JILL-uh SEE-lebz

Fringillidae   frin-JILL-uh-dee

Fulmarus glacialis   FULL-mar-uhs glay-SHE-al-is

Furnariidae   fur-nar-EYE-uh-dee

Furnarius rufus   fur-NAR-ee-uhs ROO-fuhs

Galbula pastazae   GAL-bull-uh PAS-tah-zee

Galbula ruficauda   GAL-bull-uh roo-fee-KAW-duh

Galbulidae   gal-BULL-uh-dee

Gallicolumba luzonica   gal-ih-KUH-lum-buh loo-ZON-ik-uh

Galliformes   gal-uh-FORM-eez

Gallinago nigripennis   gal-uh-NAY-go NY-gruh-PEN-is

Gavia immer   GAV-ee-uh IM-mer

Gavia stellata   GAV-ee-uh STEL-lah-tuh

Gaviidae   gav-EYE-uh-dee

Gaviiformes   gav-eye-uh-FORM-eez

Geococcyx californiana   GEE-oh-COCK-siks kal-uh-FORN-uh-kuh

Glareola pratincola   glar-ee-OH-luh prat-in-KOH-luh

Glareolidae   glar-ee-OH-luh-dee

Glaucis hirsuta   GLO-kis her-SOO-tuh

Grallina cyanoleuca   GRAL-line-uh SIGH-an-uh-LYOO-kuh

Grallinidae gral-LINE-uh-dee

Gruidae GROO-uh-dee

Gruiformes groo-uh-FORM-eez

Grus canadensis GROOS kan-uh-DEN-sis

Grus japonensis GROOS jap-ON-en-sis

Gymnogyps californianus JIM-nuh-jips kal-uh-FORN-uh-kuhs

Haematopodidae hee-muh-toh-POD-uh-dee

Haematopus unicolor hee-muh-TOH-puhs YOO-nih-KUH-luhr

Harpactes oreskios hahr-PAK-teez or-es-KEE-uhs

Heliornis fulica hee-LEE-or-nis FUL-ik-uh

Heliornithidae hee-lee-or-NITH-uh-dee

Hemiprocne coronata HEMI-prok-nee koh-roh-NAH-tuh

Hemiprocnidae hemi-PROK-nuh-dee

Himantopus himantopus hih-MAN-tuh-puhs hih-MAN-tuh-puhs

Himatione sanguinea hih-MAY-shun-ee san-GWIN-ee-uh

Hirundinidae hir-un-DIN-uh-dee

Hirundo pyrrhonota HIR-un-doh pir-uh-NOH-tuh

Hirundo rustica HIR-un-doh RUS-tik-uh

Hydrobatidae hi-droh-BAT-uh-dee

Hydrophasianus chirurgus hi-droh-fay-SEE-an-uhs KY-ruhr-guhs

Hypocolius ampelinus hi-poh-KOL-ee-uhs am-peh-LINE-uhs

Hypothymis azurea hi-poh-THY-mis az-YOOR-ee-uh

Hypsipetes madagascariensis hip-sih-PEET-eez mad-uh-GAS-kar-EE-en-sis

Icteria virens ik-TER-ee-uh VY-renz

Icteridae ik-TER-uh-dee

Icterus galbula IK-ter-uhs GAL-bull-uh

Indicator archipelagicus in-dih-KAY-ter AR-kih-peh-LAJ-ik-uhs

Indicatoridae in-dih-kay-TER-uh-dee

Irena puella eye-REEN-uh poo-ELL-uh

Irenidae eye-REEN-uh-dee

Jacanidae juh-KAN-uh-dee

Jynx torquilla JINKS tor-KWILL-uh

Lagopus lagopus LAG-uh-puhs LAG-uh-puhs

Laniidae lan-EYE-uh-dee

Lanius ludovicianus lan-ee-uhs LOO-doh-vih-SHE-an-uhs

Laridae LAR-uh-dee

Larus saundersi   LAR-uhs SON-ders-eye

Laterallus jamaicensis   lat-er-ALL-uhs ja-MAY-sen-sis

Leipoa ocellata   LYE-poh-uh os-ELL-ah-tuh

Liosceles thoracicus   lye-OS-sel-eez tho-RAS-ik-uhs

Lonchura punctulata   LON-chur-uh punk-TOO-lah-tuh

Loxia curvirostra   LOK-see-uh KUR-vih-ROS-truh

Macrocephalon maleo   ma-crow-SEFF-uh-lon MAL-ee-oh

Macronyx ameliae   MA-cron-iks am-EEL-ee-ee

Maluridae   mal-YOOR-uh-dee

Malurus splendens   MAL-yoor-uhs SPLEN-denz

Megaceryle alcyon   MEG-uh-ser-EYE-lee al-SIGH-on

Megapodiidae   meg-uh-pod-EYE-uh-dee

Megalaima haemacephala   meg-uh-LAY-muh hee-muh-SEFF-ah-luh

Melanocharis versteri   mel-uh-NOH-kar-is VER-ster-eye

Meleagris gallopavo   mel-ee-AY-gris gal-uh-PAY-voh

Melichneutes robustus   mel-ik-NOO-teez ro-BUHS-tuhs

Meliphagidae   mel-ih-FAJ-uh-dee

Melospiza melodia   mel-uh-SPY-zuh meh-LOH-dee-uh

Menura alberti   MEN-yoor-uh AL-bert-eye

Menuridae   men-YOOR-uh-dee

Meropidae   mer-OP-uh-dee

Meropogon forsteni   mer-uh-POH-gon FOR-sten-eye

Merops apiaster   MER-ops ay-PEE-as-ter

Mesitornis variegata   meh-SIT-or-nis VAIR-ree-uh-GAH-tuh

Mesitornithidae   meh-sit-or-NITH-uh-dee

Microeca fascinans   my-CROW-ek-uh FAS-sin-ans

Mimidae   MIH-muh-dee

Mirafra javanica   MIR-af-ruh jah-VAH-nik-uh

Mniotilta varia   ny-OH-til-tuh VAIR-ee-uh

Moho bishopi   MOH-hoh BISH-up-eye

Mohua ochrocephala   MOH-hyoo-uh OH-kruh-SEFF-ah-luh

Momotidae   moh-MOH-tuh-dee

Momotus momota   MOH-moh-tuhs MOH-moh-tuh

Monarchidae   mon-ARK-uh-dee

Montifringilla nivalis   mon-tih-frin-JILL-uh NYE-val-is

Morus bassanus   MOR-uhs BASS-an-uhs

Motacilla cinerea   moh-tuh-SILL-uh sin-EAR-ee-uh

Motacillidae   moh-tuh-SILL-uh-dee

Muscicapidae   mus-kih-KAP-uh-dee

Muscicaps striata MUS-kih-kaps stry-AH-tuh

Musophagidae mus-oh-FAJ-uh-dee

Musophagiformes mus-oh-faj-uh-FORM-eez

Mycteria americana mik-TER-ee-uh uh-mer-uh-KAN-uh

Nectariniidae nek-tar-in-EYE-uh-dee

Neodrepanis coruscans nee-oh-DREH-pan-is KOR-us-kans

Neophron percnopterus NEE-oh-fron perk-NOP-ter-uhs

Nesomimus macdonaldi NEZ-oh-MIH-muhs mak-DON-uld-eye

Nonnula ruficapilla NON-nuh-luh roo-fih-kap-ILL-uh

Notharchus macrorhynchos NOTH-ark-uhs ma-crow-RIN-kuhs

Nothocercus bonapartei NOTH-uh-SER-kuhs BOH-nuh-PART-eye

Nucifraga caryocatactes NYOO-sih-FRAG-uh KAR-ee-oh-KAT-ak-teez

Numenius americanus nyoo-MEN-ee-uhs uh-mer-uh-KAN-uhs

Numida meleagris NYOO-mid-uh mel-ee-AY-gris

Numididae nyoo-MID-uh-dee

Nyctea scandiaca NIK-tee-uh skan-DEE-uh-kuh

Nyctibiidae nik-tih-BYE-uh-dee

Nyctibius griseus nik-TIB-ee-uhs GRIS-ee-uhs

Oceanites oceanicus OH-shih-NYE-teez OH-shih-AN-uh-kuhs

Odontophoridae OH-don-tuh-FOR-uh-dee

Opisthocomidae op-is-thuh-KOM-eh-dee

Opisthocomiformes op-is-thuh-kom-eh-FORM-eez

Opisthocomus hoazin op-is-thuh-KOM-uhs HOH-ah-sin

Oriolidae or-ih-OH-lu-dee

Oriolus oriolus or-ih-OH-luhs or-ih-OH-luhs

Ortalis vetula OR-tal-is VET-uh-luh

Orthonychidae or-thuh-NIK-uh-dee

Orthonyx temminckii OR-thon-iks TEM-ink-ee-eye

Otididae oh-TID-uh-dee

Otis tarda OH-tis TAR-duh

Otus asio OH-tuhs AS-ee-oh

Oxyruncidae ok-sih-RUN-kuh-dee

Oxyruncus cristatus OK-sih-RUN-kuhs KRIS-tah-tuhs

Pachycephala pectoralis pak-ih-SEFF-ah-luh pek-TOR-al-is

Pachycephalidae pak-ih-seff-AL-uh-dee

Pachyramphus aglaiae   PAK-ih-RAM-fuhs ag-LAY-ee-ee

Pandion haliaetus   PAN-die-on HAL-ee-ee-tuhs

Parabuteo unicinctus   par-uh-BYOO-tee-oh YOO-nih-SINK-tuhs

Paradisaeidae par-uh-die-SEE-uh-dee

Pardalotidae par-duh-LOT-uh-dee

Pardalotus striatus par-duh-LOT-uhs stry-AH-tuhs

Paridae PAR-uh-dee

Parulidae par-YOOL-uh-dee

Parus major PAR-uhs MAY-jur

Passer domesticus   PASS-er doh-MES-tuh-kuhs

Passerculus sandwichensis pass-ER-kyoo-luhs SAND-wich-en-sis

Passeridae pass-ER-uh-dee

Passeriformes pass-er-uh-FORM-eez

Pelecanidae pel-uh-KAN-uh-dee

Pelecaniformes   pel-uh-kan-uh-FORM-eez

Pelecanoides urinatrix pel-uh-KAN-oi-deez yoor-in-AY-triks

Pelecanoididae pel-uh-kan-OI-duh-dee

Pelecanus erythrorhynchos pel-uh-KAN-uhs eh-RITH-roh-RIN-kuhs

Pelecanus occidentalis   pel-uh-KAN-uhs ok-sih-DEN-tal-is

Pericrocotus igneus per-ih-CROW-kot-uhs IG-nee-uhs

Petroicidae pet-ROY-kuh-dee

Phacellodomus ruber fay-sell-uh-DOH-muhs ROO-ber

Phaethon lepturus FEE-thon LEPT-yoor-uhs

Phaethontidae fee-THON-tuh-dee

Phalacrocoracidae fal-uh-crow-kor-AY-suh-dee

Phalacrocorax carbo   fal-uh-crow-cor-aks KAR-boh

Pharomachrus mocinno far-uh-MAK-ruhs MOH-sin-noh

Phasianidae fay-see-AN-uh-dee

Philepittidae fil-uh-PIT-tuh-dee

Phoenicopteridae FEE-nih-kop-TER-uh-dee

Phoenicopteriformes   FEE-nih-KOP-ter-uh-FORM-eez

Phoenicopterus ruber FEE-nih-KOP-ter-uhs ROO-ber

Phoeniculidae FEE-nih-KYOO-luh-dee

Phoeniculus purpureus fee-NIH-kyoo-luhs purh-PURH-ee-uhs

Phyllastrephus scandens   FIL-uh-STRE-fuhs SKAN-denz

Phylloscopus borealis FIL-uh-SKOH-puhs BOHR-ee-al-is

Phytotoma raimondii fye-toh-TOH-muh RAY-mund-ee-eye

Phytotomidae fye-toh-TOH-muh-dee

Picathartes oreas PIK-uh-THAR-teez OR-ee-uhs

Picoides borealis PIK-oy-deez BOHR-ee-al-is

Picidae PIS-uh-dee

Piciformes pis-uh-FORM-eez

Pinguinus impennis PIN-gwin-uhs IM-pen-is

Pipra filicauda PIP-ruh fil-eh-KAW-duh

Pipridae PIP-ruh-dee

Pitangus sulphuratus PIT-an-guhs sul-FUR-ah-tuhs

Pitohui kirhocephalus PIT-oo-eey kir-uh-SEFF-ah-luhs

Pitta angolensis PIT-tuh an-GOH-len-sis

Pitta sordida PIT-tuh SOR-dih-duh

Pittidae PIT-tuh-dee

Pityriasis gymnocephala pit-ih-RYE-uh-sis jim-nuh-SEFF-ah-luh

Plectoryncha lanceolata PLEK-tuh-RIN-kuh LAN-see-oh-LAH-tuh

Plectrophenax nivalis PLEK-troh-FEN-aks NYE-val-is

Ploceidae ploh-SEE-uh-dee

Ploceus cucullatus PLOH-see-uhs kyoo-KYOO-lah-tuhs

Ploceus philippinus PLOH-see-uhs fil-ih-PINE-uhs

Podargidae pod-AR-juh-dee

Podargus strigoides POD-ar-guhs STRI-goy-deez

Podiceps cristatus POD-ih-seps KRIS-tah-tuhs

Podicipedidae pod-ih-sih-PED-uh-dee

Podicipediformes pod-ih-sih-ped-uh-FORM-eez

Poecile atricapilla PEE-suh-lee ay-trih-kap-ILL-uh

Pogoniulus chrysoconus po-go-NYE-uh-luhs KRIS-oh-KON-uhs

Polioptila caerulea poh-lih-OP-til-uh see-ROO-lee-uh

Polyborus plancus pol-ih-BOHR-uhs PLAN-kuhs

Pomatostomidae poh-may-tuh-STOH-muh-dee

Pomatostomus temporalis poh-may-tuh-STOH-muhs tem-PER-al-is

Prionops plumatus PRY-on-ops PLOO-mah-tuhs

Procellariidae pro-sell-ar-EYE-uh-dee

Procellariiformes pro-sell-ar-eye-uh-FORM-eez

Promerops cafer PRO-mer-ops KAF-er

Prunella modularis proo-NELL-uh mod-YOO-lar-is

Prunellidae proo-NELL-uh-dee

Psaltriparus minimus sol-TRI-par-uhs MIN-ih-muhs

Psittacidae sit-UH-suh-dee

Psittaciformes sit-uh-suh-FORM-eez

Psittacula krameri sit-UH-kuh-luh KRAY-mer-eye

Psittacus erithacus SIT-uh-kuhs eh-RITH-uh-kuhs

Psittirostra cantans SIT-uh-ROS-truh KAN-tanz

Psophia crepitans SOH-fee-uh KREP-ih-tanz

Psophiidae soh-FYE-uh-dee

Pterocles namaqua TER-oh-kleez nah-MAH-kwuh

Pteroclididae ter-oh-KLID-uh-dee

Pterocliformes ter-oh-cluh-FORM-eez

Pterocnemia pennata ter-ok-NEE-mee-uh PEN-ah-tuh

Ptilonorhynchidae TIL-on-oh-RIN-kuh-dee

Ptilonorhynchus violaceus TIL-on-oh-RIN-kuhs vee-o-LAY-see-uhs

Ptiloris victoriae TIL-or-is vik-TOR-ee-ee

Ptyonoprogne rupestris TY-on-oh-PROG-nee ROO-pes-tris

Puffinus puffinus PUFF-in-uhs PUFF-in-uhs

Pycnonotidae pik-noh-NOH-tuh-dee

Pycnonotus barbatus pik-noh-NOH-tuhs BAR-bat-uhs

Rallidae RALL-uh-dee

Ramphastidae ram-FAS-tuh-dee

Ramphastos toco RAM-fas-tuhs TOH-coh

Raphidae RAF-uh-dee

Raphus cucullatus RAF-uhs kyoo-KYOO-lah-tuhs

Recurvirostra americana re-CURV-ih-ROS-truh uh-mer-uh-KAN-uh

Recurvirostridae re-CURV-ih-ROS-truh-dee

Remizidae rem-IZ-uh-dee

Rhabdornis mysticalis RAB-dor-nis mis-TIH-kal-is

Rhabdornithidae rab-dor-NITH-uh-dee

Rheidae REE-uh-dee

Rhinocryptidae RYE-noh-KRIP-tuh-dee

Rhinoplax vigil RYE-noh-plaks VIH-jil

Rhipidura albicollis rip-ih-DYOOR-uh ahl-bih-KOLL-is

Rhipidura leucophrys rip-ih-DYOOR-uh LYOO-kuh-frees

Rhipiduridae rip-ih-DYOOR-uh-dee

Rhynochetidae rye-noh-KEE-tuh-dee

Rhynochetos jubatus rye-noh-KEE-tuhs JOO-bat-uhs

Rostratula benghalensis ros-TRAT-uh-luh ben-GOL-en-sis

Rostratulidae ros-trat-UH-luh-dee

Rupicola rupicola roo-pih-KOH-luh roo-pih-KOH-luh

Sagittariidae saj-ih-tar-EYE-uh-dee

Sagittarius serpentarius saj-ih-TAR-ee-uhs ser-pen-TAR-ee-uhs

Sarcoramphus papa sar-KOH-ram-fuhs PAH-pah

Sarothrura elegans sar-oh-THROO-ruh EL-eh-ganz

Saxicola torquata sax-ih-KOH-luh TOR-kwah-tuh

Sayornis phoebe SAY-ro-nis FEE-bee

Schetba rufa SKET-buh ROO-fuh

Scolopacidae skoh-loh-PAY-suh-dee

Scopidae SKOH-puh-dee

Scopus umbretta SKOH-puhs UM-bret-tuh

Semnornis ramphastinus SEM-nor-nis ram-FAS-tin-uhs

Sialia sialis sigh-AL-ee-uh SIGH-al-is

Sitta canadensis SIT-tuh kan-uh-DEN-sis

Sitta europaea SIT-tuh yoor-uh-PEE-uh

Sittidae SIT-tuh-dee

Smithornis capensis SMITH-or-nis KAP-en-sis

Somateria spectabilis soh-muh-TER-ee-uh spek-TAB-ih-lis

Sphecotheres vieilloti sfek-UH-ther-eez VYE-ill-oh-eye

Spheniscidae sfen-IS-kuh-dee

Sphenisciformes sfen-is-kuh-FORM-eez

Spheniscus magellanicus SFEN-is-kuhs maj-eh-LAN-ik-uhs

Sphyrapicus varius sfir-AP-ik-uhs VAIR-ee-uhs

Steatornis caripensis stee-AT-or-nis kar-IH-pen-sis

Steatornithidae stee-at-or-NITH-uh-dee

Stercorarius parasiticus ster-koh-RARE-ee-uhs par-uh-SIT-ik-uhs

Stiltia isabella STILT-ee-uh IZ-uh-BELL-uh

Strigidae STRIJ-uh-dee

Strigiformes strij-uh-FORM-eez

Struthio camelus STROO-thee-oh KAM-el-uhs

Struthionidae stroo-thee-ON-uh-dee

Struthioniformes stroo-thee-on-uh-FORM-eez

Sturnidae STURN-uh-dee

Sturnus vulgaris STURN-uhs VUL-gar-is

Sula nebouxii SUL-uh NEB-oo-ee-eye

Sulidae SUL-uh-dee

Sylviidae sil-VYE-uh-dee

Syrrhaptes paradoxus SIR-rap-teez PAR-uh-DOKS-uhs

Taeniopygia guttata tee-nee-uh-PIJ-ee-uh GUT-tah-tuh

Terpsiphone viridis terp-SIF-oh-nee VIR-id-is

Thamnophilus doliatus THAM-nuh-FIL-uhs dol-EE-ah-tuhs

Thinocoridae thin-uh-KOR-uh-dee

Threskiornis aethiopicus THRES-kih-OR-nis EE-thi-OH-pi-kuhs

Threskiornithidae thres-kih-or-NITH-uh-dee

Timaliidae tim-al-EYE-uh-dee

Tinamidae tin-AM-uh-dee

Todidae TOH-duh-dee

Todus multicolor TOH-duhs MULL-tee-KUH-luhr

Tragopan satyra TRAG-uh-pan SAT-eye-ruh

Trichoglossus haematodus TRIK-uh-GLOS-uhs HEE-muh-TOH-duhs

Trochilidae trok-ILL-uh-dee

Troglodytes aedon trog-luh-DIE-teez EE-don

Troglodytes troglodytes trog-luh-DIE-teez trog-luh-DIE-teez

Troglodytidae trog-luh-DIE-tuh-dee

Trogonidae troh-GON-uh-dee

Trogoniformes troh-gon-uh-FORM-eez

Turdidae TUR-duh-dee

Turdus migratorius TUR-duhs my-gruh-TOR-ee-uhs

Turnicidae tur-NIS-uh-dee

Turnix sylvatica TUR-niks sil-VAT-ik-uh

Turnix varia TUR-niks VAIR-ee-uh

Tyrannidae tie-RAN-uh-dee

Tyto alba TIE-toh AHL-buh

Tytonidae tie-TON-uh-dee

Upupa epops UP-up-uh EE-pops

Upupidae up-UP-uh-dee

Uria aalge YOOR-ee-uh AHL-jee

Vanellus vanellus vah-NELL-uhs vah-NELL-uhs

Vangidae VAN-juh-dee

Vireo atricapillus VIR-e-oh ay-trih-kap-ILL-uhs

Vireonidae vir-e-ON-uh-dee

Volatinia jacarina vol-uh-TIN-ee-uh jak-uh-REE-nuh

Zenaida macroura ZEN-ay-duh ma-crow-YOOR-uh

Zosteropidae zos-ter-OP-uh-dee

Zosterops japonicus ZOS-ter-ops jap-ON-ik-uhs

Words to Know

A

Acacia: A thorny tree, or any of several trees, shrubs, or other plants of the legume family that tend to be ornamental.

Adaptation: Any structural, physiological, or behavioral trait that aids an organism's survival and ability to reproduce in its existing environment.

Adaptive evolution: Changes in organisms over time that allow them to cope more efficiently with their biomes.

Adaptive shift: An evolutionary process by which the descendants of an organism adapt, over time, to ecological niches, or natural lifestyles, that are new to that organism and usually filled in other places by much different organisms.

Aftershaft: The secondary feather that branches from the base of the main feather.

Algae: Tiny plants or plantlike organisms that grow in water and in damp places.

Alpine: Used to refer to the mountainous region of the Alps, or to describe other areas related to mountains.

Altitude: The height of something in relation to the earth's surface or sea level.

Altricial: Chicks that hatch at an early developmental stage, often blind and without feathers.

Anisodactyl: Toe arrangement with three toes pointing forward and one toe facing backward.

Anting: A behavior birds use to interact with ants, either by rolling in an ant hill or placing ants into their feathers.

Aphrodisiac: Anything that intensifies or arouses sexual desires.

Aquatic: Related to water.

Arachnid: Eight-legged animals, including spiders, scorpions, and mites.

Arboreal: Living primarily or entirely in trees and bushes.

Arthropod: A member of the largest single animal phylum, consisting of organisms with segmented bodies, jointed legs or wings, and exoskeletons.

Asynchronous hatching: A situation in which the eggs in a nest hatch at different times, so that some chicks (the older ones) are larger and stronger than others.

Australasia: Region consisting of Australia, New Zealand, New Guinea, and the neighboring islands of the South Pacific.

Avian: Relating to birds.

Aviary: Large enclosure or cage for birds.

B

Barb: Stiff filament that forms the framework of a feather.

Bib: Area under the bill of a bird, just above the breast.

Biodiversity: Abundance of species in a particular biome or geographical area.

Biparental: Both male and female of the species incubate, feed, and fledge their young.

Bower: Shady, leafy shelter or recess.

Brackish: Water that is a mix of freshwater and saltwater.

Bromeliads: A family of tropical plants. Many bromeliads grow high on the branches and trunks of trees rather than in the soil.

Brood: Young birds that are born and raised together.

Brood parasite: An animal species, most often a bird, in which the female lays its own eggs in the nests of other bird species. The host mother raises the chick as if it were her own. This behavior has also been observed in fish.

Brushland: Habitat characterized by a cover of bushes or shrubs.

Burrow: Tunnel or hole that an animal digs in the ground to use as a home.

C

Cache: A hidden supply area.

Camouflage: Device used by an animal, such as coloration, allowing it to blend in with the surroundings to avoid being seen by prey and predators.

Canopy: The uppermost layer of a forest formed naturally by the leaves and branches of trees and plants.

Cap: Patch on top of bird's head.

Carcass: The dead body of an animal. Vultures gather around a carcass to eat it.

Carnivore: Meat-eating organism.

Carrion: Dead and decaying animal flesh.

Caruncle: A genetically controlled outgrowth of skin on an animal, usually for dominance or mating displays.

Casque: A horny growth on the head of a bird resembling a helmet.

Cavity: Hollow area within a body.

Churring: Referring to a low, trilled, or whirring sound that some birds make.

Circumpolar: Able to live at the North and South Pole.

Clutch: Group of eggs hatched together.

Collagen: A type of protein formed within an animal body that is assembled into various structures, most notably tendons.

Colony: A group of animals of the same type living together.

Comb: Fleshy red crest on top of the head.

Coniferous: Refers to evergreen trees, such as pines and firs, that bear cones and have needle-like leaves that are not shed all at once.

Coniferous forest: An evergreen forest where plants stay green all year.

Continental margin: A gently sloping ledge of a continent that is submerged in the ocean.

Convergence: In adaptive evolution, a process by which unrelated or only distantly related living things come to resemble one another in adapting to similar environments.

Cooperative breeding: A social organization of breeding where several birds (not just the parents) feed a group of hatchlings.

Courtship: Behaviors related to attracting a mate and preparing to breed.

Courtship display: Actions of a male and female animal that demonstrate their interest in becoming or remaining a pair for breeding.

Covert: Term derived from the word for something that is concealed, and used to describe the small feathers that cover the bases of the larger feathers on a bird's wing and tail.

Crèche: A group of young of the same species, which gather together in order to better avoid predators.

Crepuscular: Most active at dawn and dusk.

Crest: A group of feathers on the top or back of a bird's head.

Critically Endangered: A term used by the IUCN in reference to a species that is at an extremely high risk of extinction in the wild.

Crop: A pouch-like organ in the throat where crop milk is produced.

Crop milk: A cheesy, nutritious substance produced by adult pigeons and doves and fed to chicks.

Crown: Top of a bird's head.

Cryptic: To be colored so as to blend into the environment.

D

Deciduous: Shedding leaves at the end of the growing season.

Deciduous forest: A forest with four seasons in which trees drop their leaves in the fall.

Decurved: Down-curved; slightly bent.

Defensive posture: A position adopted to frighten away potential predators.

Deforestation: Those practices or processes that result in the change of forested lands to non-forest uses, such as human settlement or farming. This is often cited as one of the major causes of the enhanced greenhouse effect.

Distal: Away from the point of attachment.

Distraction display: Behaviors intended to distract potential predators from the nest site.

Diurnal: Refers to animals that are active during the day.

Domesticated: Tamed.

Dominant: The top male or female of a social group, sometimes called the alpha male or alpha female.

Dormant: Not active.

Dorsal: Located in the back.

Dung: Feces, or solid waste from an animal.

E

Ecological niche: The role a living creature, plant or animal, plays in its community.

Ecotourist: A person who visits a place in order to observe the plants and animals in the area while making minimal human impact on the natural environment.

Elevation: The height of land when measured from sea level.

Endangered: A term used by the U.S. Endangered Species Act of 1973 and by the IUCN in reference to a species that is facing a very high risk of extinction from all or a significant portion of its natural home.

Endemic: Native to or occuring only in a particular place.

Epiphyte: Plant such as mosses that grows on another plant but does not depend on that host plant for nutrition.

Estuary: Lower end of a river where ocean tides meet the river's current.

Eucalyptus: Tall, aromatic trees.

Evolve: To change slowly over time.

Extinct: A species without living members.

Extinction: The total disappearance of a species or the disappearance of a species from a given area.

Eyespot: Colored feathers on the body that resemble the eyes of a large animal, which function in helping to frighten away potential predators.

F

Family: A grouping of genera that share certain characteristics and appear to have evolved from the same ancestors.

Feather tract: Spacing of feathers in a pattern.

Feces: Solid body waste.

Fermentation: Chemical reaction in which enzymes break down complex organic compounds into simpler ones. This can make digestion easier.

Fledgling: Bird that has recently grown the feathers necessary to fly.

Flightless: Species that have lost the ability to fly.

Flock: A large group of birds of the same species.

Forage: To search for food.

Frugivore: Animal that primarily eats fruit. Many bats and birds are frugivores.

G

Gape: The width of the open mouth.

Genera: Plural of genus.

Generalist feeder: A species that eats a wide variety of foods.

Genus (pl. genera): A category of classification made up of species sharing similar characteristics.

Granivore: Animal that primarily eats seeds and grains.

Grassland: Region in which the climate is dry for long periods of the summer, and freezes in the winter. Grasslands are characterized by grasses and other erect herbs, usually without trees or shrubs, and occur in the dry temperate interiors of continents.

Gregarious: Used to describe birds that tend to live in flocks, and are very sociable with other birds. The word has come to be used to describe people who are very outgoing and sociable, as well.

H

Habitat: The area or region where a particular type of plant or animal lives and grows.

Hallux: The big toe, or first digit, on the part of the foot facing inwards.

Hatchling: Birds that have just hatched, or broken out of the egg.

Hawking: Hunting for food by sitting on a perch, flying out and capturing the food, and returning to the perch to eat.

Heath: Grassy and shrubby uncultivated land.

Herbivore: Plant eating organism.

Heterodactyl: With toes pointed in opposite directions; usually with first and second inner front toes turned backward and the third and fourth toes turned forward.

Homeotherm: Organism with stable independent body temperature.

Host: A living plant or animal from which a parasite takes nutrition

I

Igapó: Black waters of the Amazon river area.

Incubation: Process of sitting on and warming eggs in order for them to hatch.

Indicator species: A bird or animal whose presence reveals a specific environmental characteristic

Indigenous: Originating in a region or country.

Insectivore: An animal that eats primarily insects.

Introduced: Not native to the area; brought in by humans.

Invertebrate: Animal lacking a spinal column (backbone).

Iridescent: Having a lustrous or brilliant appearance or quality.

IUCN: Abbreviation for the International Union for Conservation of Nature and Natural Resources, now the World Conservation Union. A conservation organization of government agencies and nongovernmental organizations best known for its Red Lists of threatened an

K

Keel: A projection from a bone.

Keratin: Protein found in hair, nails, and skin.

Kleptoparasite: An individual that steals food or other resources from another individual.

L

Lamellae: Plural of lamella; comb-like bristles inside a flamingos bill.

Larva (pl. larvae): Immature form (wormlike in insects; fishlike in amphibians) of an organism capable of surviving on its own. A larva does not resemble the parent and must go through metamorphosis, or change, to reach its adult stage.

Lek: An area where birds come to display courtship behaviors to attract a mate (noun); to sing, flutter, hop and perform other courtship behaviors at a lek (verb).

Lerp: Sugary lumps of secretions of psillid insects, small plant-sucking insects living on Eucalyptus trees.

Lichen: A complex of algae and fungi found growing on trees, rocks, or other solid surfaces.

Litter: A layer of dead vegetation and other material covering the ground.

M

Mandible: Upper or lower part of a bird's bill; jaw.

Mangrove: Tropical coastal trees or shrubs that produce many supporting roots and that provide dense vegetation.

Mantle: Back, inner-wing, and shoulder area.

Mesic: Referring to any area that is known to be wet or moist.

Midstory: The level of tropical forests between ground level (understory) and treetops (overstory).

Migrate: To move from one area or climate to another as the seasons change, usually to find food or to mate..

Mixed-species flock: A flock of birds that includes multiple species.

Mobbing: A group of birds gathering together to defend themselves from another large bird by calling loudly and flying at the intruder.

Molt: The process by which an organism sheds its outermost layer of feathers, fur, skin, or exoskeleton.

Monogamous: Refers to a breeding system in which a male and a female mate only with each other during a breeding season or lifetime.

Montane forest: Forest found in mountainous areas.

Mutualism: A relationship between two species where both gain something and neither is harmed.

N

Nape: Back part of the neck.

Near Threatened: A category defined by the IUCN suggesting that a species could become threatened with extinction in the future.

Nectar: Sweet liquid secreted by the flowers of various plants to attract pollinators (animals that pollinate, or fertilize, the flowers).

Neotropical: Relating to a geographic area of plant and animal life east, south, and west of Mexico's central plateau that includes Central and South America and the West Indies.

Nest box: A small, human-made shelter intended as a nest site for birds. Usually a rectangular wooden box with a round entrance hole.

Nestling: Young bird unable to leave the nest.

New World: Made up of North America, Central America, and South America; the western half of the world.

Niche: A habitat with everything an animal needs.

Nictating membranes: Clear coverings under the eyelids that can be moved over the eye.

Nocturnal: Occuring or active at night.

O

Omnivore: A plant- and meat- eating animal.

Opportunistic feeder: One that is able to take advantage of whatever food resources become available.

Overstory: The level of tropical forests nearest treetops.

P

Palearctic: The area or subregion of Europe, Africa, and the Middle East, that is north of the Tropic of Cancer, and the area north of the Himalayas mountain range.

Pampas: Open grasslands of South America.

Parasite: An organism that lives in or on a host organism and that gets its nourishment from that host.

Pelagic: To live on the open ocean.

Permafrost: Permanently frozen lands.

Plain: Large expanse of land that is fairly dry and with few trees.

Plumage: Feathers of a bird.

Pneumatic: Air-filled cavities in the bones of birds.

Poisonous: Containing or producing toxic materials.

Pollen: Dust-like grains or particles produced by a plant that contain male sex cells.

Pollinate: To transfer pollen from the male organ to the female organ of a flower.

Polyandry: A mating system in which a single female mates with multiple males.

Polygamy: A mating system in which males and females mate with multiple partners.

Polygynous lek: A mating system in which several males display together for the attention of females. A female, after watching the displaying males, may mate with one or more males in the lek.

Polygyny: A mating system in which a single male mates with multiple females.

Precocial: Young that hatch at an advanced stage of development, with feathers and able to move.

Predator: An animal that eats other animals.

Preen: To clean and smooth feathers using the bill.

Preen gland: A gland on the rear of most birds which secretes an oil the birds use in grooming.

Prey: Organism hunted and eaten by a predator.

Primary forest: A forest characterized by a full-ceiling canopy formed by the branches of tall trees and several layers of smaller trees. This type of forest lacks ground vegetation because sunlight cannot penetrate through the canopy.

Promiscuity: Mating in which individuals mate with as many other individuals as they can or want to.

Pupae: Plural of pupa; developing insects inside cocoon.

Q

Quill: Hollow feather shaft.

R

Rainforest: An evergreen woodland of the tropics distinguished by a continuous leaf canopy and an average rainfall of about 100 inches (250 centimeters) per year.

Raptor: A bird of prey.

Regurgitate: Eject the contents of the stomach through the mouth; to vomit.

Resident: Bird species that do not migrate.

Retrices: Plural of retrix; paired flight feathers of the tail, which extend from the margins of a bird's tail.

Rictal bristles: Modified feathers composed mainly of the vertical shaft.

Riparian: Having to do with the edges of streams or rivers.

Riverine: Located near a river.

Roe: Fish eggs.

Roost: A place where animals, such as bats, sit or rest on a perch, branch, etc.

S

Savanna: A biome characterized by an extensive cover of grasses with scattered trees, usually transitioning between areas dominated by forests and those dominated by grasses and having alternating seasonal climates of precipitation and drought.

Scavenger: An animal that eats carrion.

Scrub forest: A forest with short trees and shrubs.

Secondary forest: A forest characterized by a less-developed canopy, smaller trees, and a dense ground vegetation found on the edges of fores

Sedentary: Living in a fixed location, as with most plants, tunicates, sponges, etc. Contrast with motile.

Semi-precocial: To be born in a state between altricial and precocial. Semi-precocial chicks can usually leave the nest after a few days.

Sequential polyandry: A mating system in which a female mates with one male, leaves him a clutch of eggs to tend, and then mates with another male, repeating the process throughout the breeding season.

Serial monogamy: Mating for a single nesting then finding another mate or mates for other nestings.

Serrated: Having notches like a saw blade.

Sexual dichromatism: Difference in coloration between the sexes of a species.

Sexual dimorphism: Differences in size and in shapes of body or body parts between sexes of a species.

Sexually mature: Capable of reproducing.

Sheath: Tubular-shaped covering used to protect a body part.

Snag: A dead tree, still standing, with the top broken off.

Social: Species in which individuals are found with other individuals of the same species.

Solitary: Living alone or avoiding the company of others.

Specialist feeder: A species that eats only one or a few food items.

Species: A group of living things that share certain distinctive characteristics and can breed together in the wild.

Squab: Young pigeons and doves.

Steppe: Wide expanse of semiarid relatively level plains, found in cool climates and characterized by shrubs, grasses, and few trees.

Sternum: The breastbone.

Subalpine forest: Forest found at elevations between 9,190 and 10,500 feet (2,800 and 3,200 meters).

Sub-canopy: Below the treetops.

Subordinate: An individual that has lower rank than other, dominant, members of the group.

Subspecies: Divisions within a species based on significant differences and on genetics. Subspecies within a species look different from one another but are still genetically close to be considered separate species. In most cases, subspecies can interbreed and produc

Subtropical: Referring to large areas near the tropics that are not quite as warm as tropical areas.

Syndactyly: A condition in which two bones (or digits) fuse together to become a single bone.

Syrinx (pl. syringes): Vocal organ of birds.

T

Taiga: Subarctic wet evergreen forests.

Tail coverts: The short feathers bordering the quills of the long tail feathers of a bird. They may be over-tail or under-tail (i.e., top or bottom).

Tail streamer: A central part of a bird's tail that is longer than other parts.

Talon: A sharp hooked claw.

Taxonomy: The science dealing with the identification, naming, and classification of plants and animals.

Temperate: Areas with moderate temperatures in which the climate undergoes seasonal change in temperature and moisture. Temperate regions of the earth lie primarily between 30 and 60° latitude in both hemispheres.

Terrestrial: Relating to the land or living primarily on land.

Territorial: A pattern of behavior that causes an animal to stay in a limited area and/or to keep certain other animals of the same species (other than its mate, herd, or family group) out of the

Tetrapod: Any vertebrate having four legs or limbs, including mammals, birds, reptiles, and others.

Thermal: Rising bubble of warm air.

Thicket: An area represented by a thick, or dense, growth of shrubs, underbrush, or small trees.

Threat display: A set of characteristic motions used to communicate aggression and warning to other individuals of the same species.

Threatened: Describes a species that is threatened with extinction.

Torpor: A short period of inactivity characterized by an energy-saving, deep sleep-like state in which heart rate, respiratory rate and body temperature drop.

Tropical: The area between 23.5° north and south of the equator. This region has small daily and seasonal changes in temperature, but great seasonal changes in precipitation. Generally, a hot and humid climate that is completely or almost free of frost.

Tundra: A type of ecosystem dominated by lichens, mosses, grasses, and woody plants. It is found at high latitudes (arctic tundra) and high altitudes (alpine tundra). Arctic tundra is underlain by permafrost and usually very wet.

U

Understory: The trees and shrubs between the forest canopy and the ground cover.

V

Vertebra (pl. vertebrae): A component of the vertebral column, or backbone, found in vertebrates.

Vertebrate: An animal having a spinal column (backbone).

Vocalization: Sound made by vibration of the vocal tract.

Vulnerable: An IUCN category referring to a species that faces a high risk of extinction.

W

Wattle: A fold of skin, often brightly colored, that hangs from the throat area.

Wetlands: Areas that are wet or covered with water for at least part of the year and support aquatic plants, such as marshes, swamps, and bogs.

Wingbars: Stripes of coloration on the wing.

Wingspan: The distance from wingtip to wingtip when the wings are extended in flight.

X

Xeric forest: Forest adapted to very dry conditions.

Z

Zygodactyl: Two pairs of toes, with two toes pointing forward and two toes facing backward.

Getting to Know Birds

FEATHERS

It is easy to tell that an animal is a bird. If it has feathers, it is one of the more than 8,600 kinds of birds in the world. Birds can also be recognized by their bills, wings, and two legs, but feathers are what make them different from every other animal.

First feathers

Scientists are not sure when feathers first appeared on animals. They might have begun as feather-like scales on some of the dinosaurs. In 1861, fossils of a feathered animal, *Archaeopteryx* (ar-key-OP-tuh-rix), were found in Germany. These are the first animals known to scientists that were covered with feathers. These crow-sized animals with heads like lizards lived on the Earth about 150 million years ago.

How birds use different types of feathers

Feathers in most birds' wings and tail help them fly. Each of these flight feathers has a stiff shaft that goes from one end to the other. Flight feathers are light, but they are surprisingly strong. Birds that can fly can escape enemies and get to food sources and nesting places they wouldn't be able to walk to.

Feathers have many other uses in addition to flight. The outer feathers on a bird's body give it color and shape and help to waterproof the bird. Outer feathers with patterns are useful for camouflaging some birds, and colorful feathers send messages. For example, male birds show off their bright feathers to impress females or wave them as warnings to others. Downy inner feathers trap air to keep the bird warm.

Archaeopteryx is the first animal known to be covered with feathers. (© François Gohier/Photo Researchers, Inc. Reproduced by permission.)

Scientists have names for different types of feathers and also for groups of feathers according to where they grow on a bird's body.

Flight

Most birds' bodies are built for flight. Air sacs in their chests and hollow bones keep them light. They have powerful chest muscles that move their wings. The wing and tail feathers are tough, and birds can turn some of them for steering. A bird usually shuts its wing feathers to trap the air as its wings go down. This lifts the bird into the air and pushes it forward. Then, as it raises the wings, it fans the feathers open to let the air through.

How birds fly depends somewhat on the shape of their wings. Vultures and seabirds have long, narrow wings that are great for soaring high on air currents or gliding over the ocean. Songbirds have short, broad wings that are made for flapping as the birds fly among trees. Falcons have narrow, pointed wings that curve backward. These wings help them fly fast and steer well. But all birds flap their wings at times and glide at other times, depending on what they are doing and how the wind is blowing.

Some birds use their wings in unusual ways. Hummingbirds can flap their wings about fifty times every second. This allows them to hover at one spot as they lap nectar from flowers. Flipper-like wings help penguins to "fly" through the water, and even ostriches use their wings to keep their balance as they run.

The wing of a bird is rounded on top and flat on the bottom, similar to the wing of an airplane. This shape is what gives the bird the lift it needs to stay up in the air.

Birds take off and land facing the wind. Small birds (up to the size of pigeons) can jump up from the ground and fly right off into the air. Larger birds have to jump off something high or run along the ground or the water to get going.

BIRDS' BODIES

Different, but the same

A 400-pound (181-kilogram) ostrich may seem very different from a tiny bee hummingbird that weighs less than an ounce (about 2 grams). But all birds have many things in common besides having feathers. They have bills, two legs, a backbone, they are warm-blooded (keep an even body temperature), and they lay hard-shelled eggs.

Body shapes

Birds have many different shapes. Wading birds such as flamingos have long necks and long legs. Eagles have short necks and legs. But both kinds of birds are able to find their food in the water. Falcons and penguins have sleek, torpedo-shaped bodies that are perfect for catching speedy prey. Turkeys' heavier bodies are just right for their quiet lives in the forest searching for acorns and insects.

Bill shapes

Bird bills come in a wide variety of shapes. They use their bills to gather food, build nests, fix their feathers, feed their young, attract mates, and attack their enemies. The type of food a bird eats depends on its bills' shape. For example, the sturdy bills of sparrows are good for cracking seeds, and hawks' hooked beaks are perfect for tearing up prey.

Legs and feet

Bird legs and feet fit their many different lifestyles. For example, hawks have sharp talons for hunting and ducks have webbed feet to help them swim. Some of the birds that spend most of their lives in the air or on the water are not good at walking. Most birds have four toes, but some have three, and ostriches have only two.

BIRDS' SENSES

Sight

For most birds, sight is their best sense. They can see much better than humans, and they can see in color, unlike many mammals.

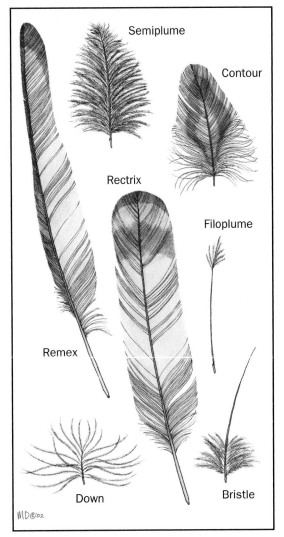

A bird's stiffest feathers are the remex feathers of the wing and the retrix feathers of the tail. The outside of a bird's body is covered with contour feathers that give the body shape and waterproof the bird. Underneath the contour feathers are the semiplume and down feathers that help keep the bird warm. Filoplumes lie alongside the contour feathers and help the bird tell if its feathers are in place. Some birds have bristles around their beaks that allow them to feel insects in the air. (Illustration by Marguette Dongvillo. Reproduced by permission.)

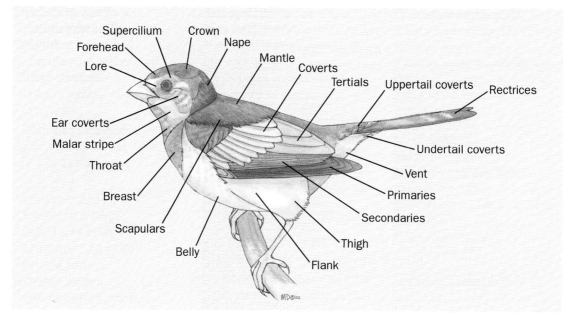

A bird's eyes are big and are usually set on the sides of its head. The eyes focus independently, so that the bird sees two different things at the same time. This gives the bird a very wide view and helps it to watch for predators in most directions. Most birds cannot roll their eyes, but they can turn their heads farther around than mammals can. Owls and other birds of prey have forward-facing eyes that usually work together. This helps them judge distance as they swoop down on prey.

Hearing

Birds have a good sense of hearing—they can hear about as well as mammals. The sound goes in through a little opening near each eye. The holes are usually covered with feathers. They lead to the bird's middle and inner ear, which are very sensitive to sounds. Because owls hunt at night, hearing is especially important to them. Some owls have a disc of stiff feathers on the face. The disc catches sounds, such as the squeaks of a mouse, and leads them to the ears.

Touch

Birds have many nerve endings, which shows that they have a good sense of touch. They can also feel pain, hot, and cold.

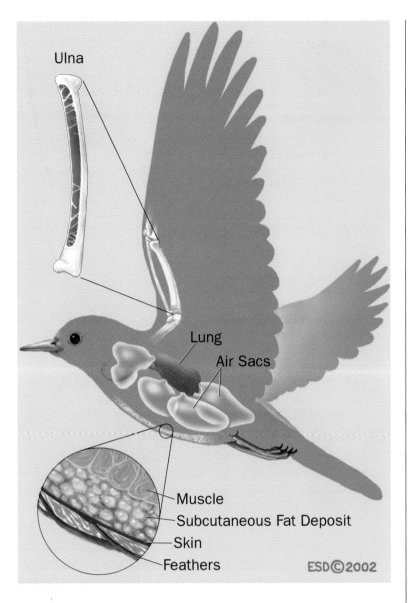

Ulna

Lung

Air Sacs

Muscle
Subcutaneous Fat Deposit
Skin
Feathers

ESD©2002

Birds' bodies have adaptations for flight, including air sacs in the chest and hollow bones to keep them light, and strong chest muscles. (Illustration by Emily Damstra. Reproduced by permission.)

Some long-billed birds have very sensitive bills and can feel their prey in muddy water.

Smell and taste

Most birds' sense of smell seems to be poorly developed. But kiwis, turkey vultures, and several other birds are able to find food by sniffing it. Although birds do not have many taste buds on their tongues, they can often taste well enough to avoid eating harmful foods.

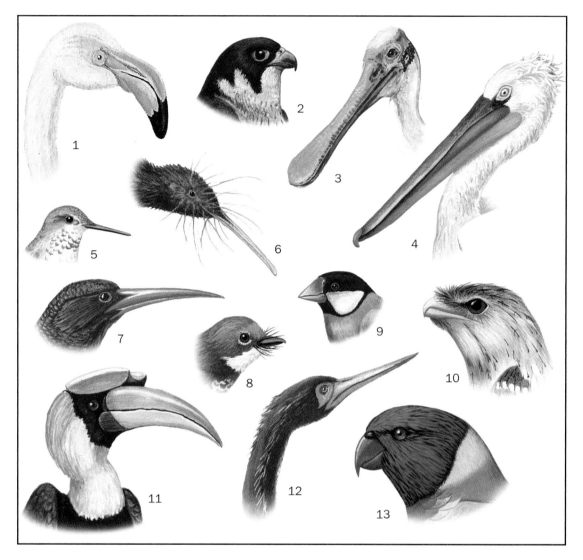

Bills are different shapes and sizes for different eating methods: 1. The greater flamingo filters microorganisms from water; 2. A peregrine falcon tears its prey; 3. Roseate spoonbills sift water for fish; 4. The Dalmation pelican scoops fish in its pouch; 5. Anna's hummingbird sips nectar; 6. The brown kiwi probes the soil for invertebrates; 7. The green woodhoopoe probes bark for insects; 8. Rufous flycatchers catch insects; 9. Java sparrows eat seeds; 10. Papuan frogmouths catch insects; 11. The bicornis hornbill eats fruit; 12. American anhingas spear fish; 13. Rainbow lorikeets crack nuts. (Illustration by Jacqueline Mahannah. Reproduced by permission.)

Organs and muscles

Birds have many of the same organs that humans have, but they have special features that help with flight and keep them light. Their biggest, strongest muscles control their wings. Birds

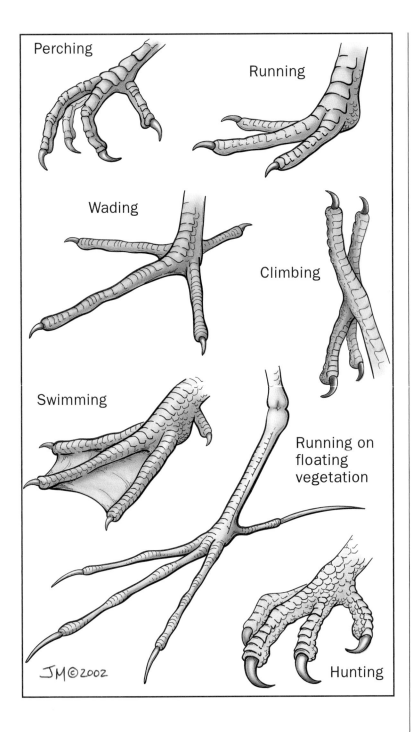

Perching

Running

Wading

Climbing

Swimming

Running on floating vegetation

Hunting

JM©2002

The number of toes, and the arrangement of their toes and feet fit birds' different lifestyles. (Illustration by Jacqueline Mahannah. Reproduced by permission.)

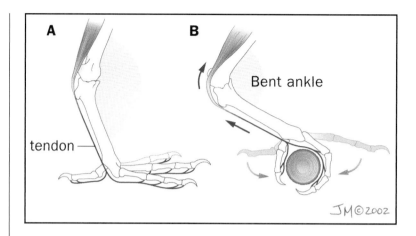

do not have a heavy jaw with teeth to grind their food. Instead, it is ground up in a muscular stomach called a gizzard, and they swallow gravel to help with the grinding. To get the energy they need for flight, birds digest their food quickly. Their fast digestion also keeps them from being weighed down for long by the food they have eaten.

Skeleton

A birds' skeleton is strong, even though it light. Many of the bones are hollow, and some of them are joined together to give the skeleton extra strength. (Loons and other diving birds have some solid bones to help the birds sink in the water.) The breastbone, or sternum, of a flying bird has a part called the keel. The bird's big flight muscles are attached to the keel. What looks like a backward-bending knee on a bird is really its ankle. The bird's knee is hidden high up inside its body feathers.

Body temperature

Birds are warm-blooded, which means their bodies stay at an even temperature no matter how warm or cold it is outside. They make their own heat from the food that they eat. Some birds cope with cold weather by growing extra feathers or a layer of fat, fluffing their feathers to trap more air, and huddling together with other birds. When birds can't find enough food to keep warm, they fly to warmer places. In hot weather, they cool down by panting, swimming in cool water, sitting in the shade, and raising their wings to catch a breeze.

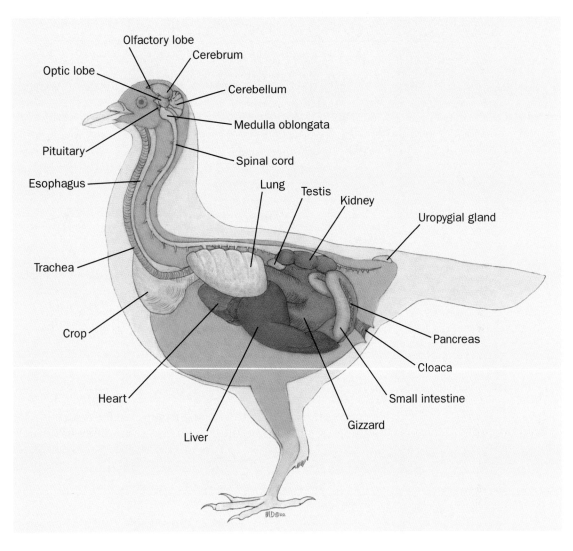

Labels on illustration:
Olfactory lobe
Cerebrum
Optic lobe
Cerebellum
Medulla oblongata
Pituitary
Spinal cord
Esophagus
Lung
Testis
Kidney
Uropygial gland
Trachea
Crop
Heart
Pancreas
Cloaca
Small intestine
Liver
Gizzard

FAMILY LIFE

Singing

Singing is one of the most important ways that songbirds communicate. Birds do not sing just because they are happy. Instead, a male songbird sings to say that he "owns" a certain territory, and he warns birds of the same species to stay away. Songbirds do not have to see each other to know who is nearby. Birds can recognize the songs of their neighbors, because each bird of the same species sounds a little different. Male birds show off to females by singing the most complicated songs they can. Often the best singers are the strongest, healthiest males.

Though birds may look different on the outside, they have the same organs on the inside. (Illustration by Marguette Dongvillo. Reproduced by permission.)

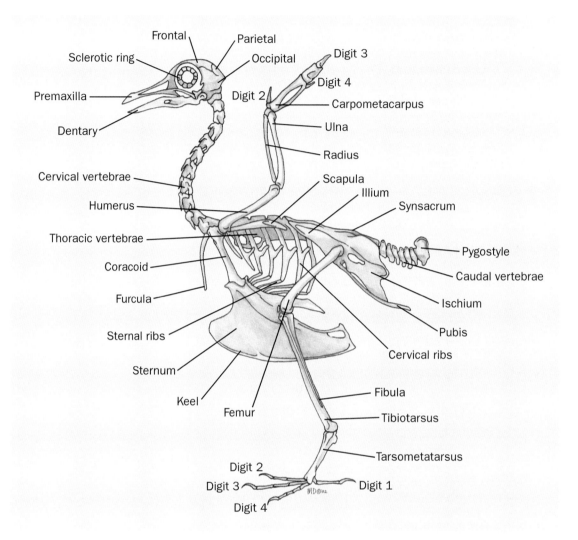

Frontal
Parietal
Occipital
Digit 3
Sclerotic ring
Digit 4
Digit 2
Premaxilla
Carpometacarpus
Dentary
Ulna
Radius
Cervical vertebrae
Scapula
Illium
Synsacrum
Humerus
Thoracic vertebrae
Pygostyle
Coracoid
Caudal vertebrae
Furcula
Ischium
Sternal ribs
Pubis
Sternum
Cervical ribs
Keel
Fibula
Femur
Tibiotarsus
Tarsometatarsus
Digit 2
Digit 3
Digit 1
Digit 4

MD©02

Birds have a strong, light skeleton. (Illustration by Marguette Dongvillo. Reproduced by permission.)

When a female songbird hears her mate singing, her brain tells her body to make hormones (special chemicals). These hormones make eggs start to grow inside her body.

Other ways birds communicate

Singing is just one of the many ways that birds communicate with each other. They have warning calls that tell other birds that a predator is nearby. They chirp to say, "I am here, where are you?" And young birds sometimes beg noisily to be fed. At breeding time, birds have a variety of courtships displays that ask, "Will you be mine?" and state, "We belong together." These include bowing, flight displays, and calling together. Male birds

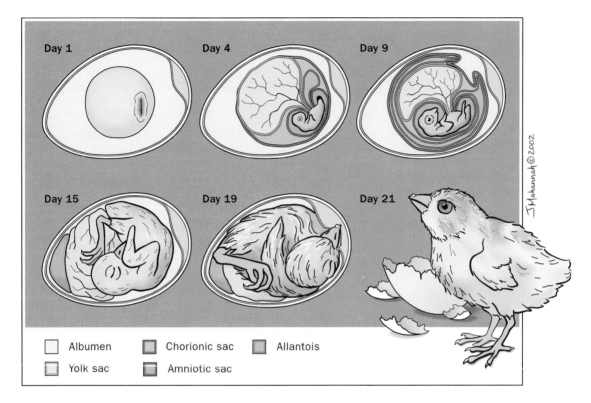

Albumen

Yolk sac

Chorionic sac

Amniotic sac

Allantois

parade and show off bright feathers or blow up colorful throat sacs to impress females.

Nests

When a bird has found a mate, it is nest-building time. Birds lay their hard-shelled eggs where they can be protected from predators and rain. There are many different kinds of nests. Some birds lay their eggs right on the ground or on the sides of cliffs, some use tree holes or burrows, and some weave complicated stick nests. A few kinds of birds even bury their eggs in mounds of soil and leaves.

Eggs and hatching

Eggs come in many different sizes and colors. Those laid on the ground usually have camouflage colors, and eggs laid in hidden places are often white. The female bird usually incubates the eggs (keeps them warm), especially if she has duller, harder-to-see feathers than the male. Sometimes males and females take turns, and occasionally the males incubate by themselves. Some birds, such as cowbirds, lay their eggs in the nests of other bird species and let the other birds incubate them.

An egg is a perfect package for the chick developing inside it. The albumen (egg white) and yolk provide all the food and water it needs, and are used up as the bird develops. Air moves in and out through hundreds of tiny holes in the shell. Waste from the developing chick is stored in a sac called the allantois (uh-LAN-tuh-wus). The chorionic (kor-ee-AHN-ik) sac lines the inside of the shell, and the amniotic sac surrounds the chick. Time spent in the egg is different for each species, but for this chick, feathers have started to grow by Day 15, and the chick begins making noises by Day 19. There is a little egg tooth on the tip of the chick's bill that it uses to break out of the shell on Day 21. (Illustration by Jacqueline Mahannah. Reproduced by permission.)

Growth of young birds

There are two main types of newly hatched birds. Young chickens, ducks, geese, turkeys, and ostriches are precocial (pre-KOH-shul). Precocial chicks are covered with down feathers and can run or swim after their parents soon after hatching. Before long, they learn to find their own food, but the parents usually protect them for a while longer. Altricial (al-TRISH-ul) birds are helpless when they hatch. Songbirds, seabirds, owls, parrots, and woodpeckers are some of the altricial birds. They are naked, blind, and weak, and they need to be fed by adults at least until they leave the nest.

HABITATS, HABITS, AND PEOPLE

Surviving in a habitat

In order to live in a habitat, birds need food, water, and shelter (such as a hedge to hide in). At breeding time, they also need a place to raise their young. Many different kinds of birds can live in the same habitat because they eat different foods and nest in different places. Some birds, such as crows, can often adapt to changes in their habitat, but other birds are very particular and have to leave if something changes.

Staying alive and keeping fit

Birds have to have their feathers in flying shape at all times so that they can escape predators. Well-cared-for feathers are also necessary for keeping the birds warm and waterproof. Birds often have to stop what they are doing and take time out to fix their messed-up feathers. Sometimes they start with a bath. But they always finish by preening. To preen, the birds nibble along each feather to remove dirt and tiny pests. Most birds also get oil on their beaks from a gland near their tails. They spread the oil on each feather and straighten it by zipping it through their beaks. The oil keeps the feathers from drying out and waterproofs them. When a feather gets too worn, it either falls out or gets pushed out by a new feather growing in its place.

Migration

Migration is one way birds cope with natural changes in their habitats. When the weather gets cold and insects get scarce in fall, for example, insect-eating birds fly to warmer places where

Arctic Tern

Sooty Shearwater

Wandering Albatross

Seabirds have some of the longest migrations. The arctic tern migrates about 25,000 miles (40,000 kilometers) round-trip each year. The sooty shearwater breeds around New Zealand and the southern tip of South America and migrates in the spring to the northern Pacific and Atlantic Oceans. The wandering albatross moves around the Earth from west to east over the oceans south of the tips of the southern continents. (Illustration by Emily Damstra. Reproduced by permission.)

they will be able to find the food they need. Their bodies are programmed to tell them that when the days start getting shorter, they have to eat more so they will have enough fuel for the journey. They follow the same migration routes year after year, and they know the general direction they should go and where to stop. The migrating birds are guided by the stars and by the direction the sun moves across the sky. Birds have a built-in compass and are able to follow magnetic fields in the earth. Some birds also rely on landmarks such as rivers and mountains to follow, and some may use sounds and smells to help them find their way.

Birds and people

Birds are some of the most visible wild animals on Earth, and they play an important part in people's lives. Humans learned about flight from birds, they eat birds and their eggs, and they keep birds as pets. They appreciate the way birds eat insect pests and weed seeds, and they enjoy watching and listening to birds. Sometimes people kill the birds that eat fish or destroy their crops. People have also harmed birds unintentionally by polluting their habitats or turning them into farms and cities.

Humans now take the disappearance of birds from an area as a warning—there may be harmful poisons in the air or water. Many people are working hard to preserve natural places for birds and all wild animals. They are also having some success with fixing habitats that have been destroyed, but fixing them is much harder than preserving them in the first place.

FOR MORE INFORMATION

Books

Johnson, Jinny. *Children's Guide to Birds.* New York: Simon & Schuster, 1996.

MacKay, Barry Kent. *Bird Sounds.* Mechanicsburg, PA: Stackpole Books, 2001.

Markle, Sandra. *Outside and Inside Birds.* New York: Bradbury Press, 1994.

Perrins, Christopher M. *The Illustrated Encyclopedia of Birds.* New York: Prentice Hall Press, 1990.

Proctor, Noble S., and Patrick J. Lynch. *Manual of Ornithology, Avian Structure and Function.* New Haven, CT: Yale University Press, 1993.

Reid, Struan. *Bird World.* Brookfield, CT: The Millbrook Press, 1991.

Rupp, Rebecca. *Everything You Never Learned About Birds.* Pownal, VT: Storey Communications, Inc., 1995.

Sibley, David Allen, Chris Elphick, and John B. Dunning, Jr., eds. *National Audubon Society: The Sibley Guide to Bird Life & Behavior.* New York: Alfred A. Knopf, 2001.

Taylor, Kim. *Flight.* New York: John Wiley & sons, Inc., 1992.

Periodicals

Able, Kenneth P. "The Concepts and Terminology of Bird Navigation." *Journal of Aviation Biology* 32 (2000): 174–182.

Berger, Cynthia. "Fluffy, Fancy, Fantastic Feathers." *Ranger Rick* (January 2001): 2–10.

Greij, Eldon. "Happy Returns: Landing Safely Is Every Bit as Tricky as Flying." *Birders World* (February 2003): 58–60.

Kerlinger, Paul. "How High? How High a Bird Flies Depends on the Weather, the Time of Day, Whether Land or Water Lies Below—and the Bird." *Birder's World* (February 2003): 62–65.

Miller, Claire. "Guess Where They Nest." *Ranger Rick* (March 1996): 19–27.

Pennisi, Elizabeth. "Colorful Males Flaunt Their Health." *Science* (April 4, 2003): 29–30.

Web sites

"Act for the Environment." National Wildlife Federation. http://www.nwf.org/action/ (accessed on May 3, 2004).

"All About Birds." Cornell Lab of Ornithology. http://www.birds.cornell.edu/programs/AllAboutBirds/ (accessed on May 3, 2004).

American Bird Conservancy. http://www.abcbirds.org (accessed on May 3, 2004).

American Ornithologists' Union. http://www.aou.org (accessed on May 3, 2004).

"Bird and Wildlife Information Center." National Audubon Society. http://www.audubon.org/educate/expert/index.html (accessed on May 3, 2004).

BirdLife International. http://www.birdlife.net (accessed on May 3, 2004).

"Birdlife Worldwide." Birdlife International. http://www.birdlife.net/worldwide/index.html (accessed on May 3, 2004).

National Audubon Society. http://www.Audubon.org (accessed on May 3, 2004).

National Wildlife Federation. http://www.nwf.org (accessed on May 3, 2004).

The Nature Conservancy. http://nature.org (accessed on May 3, 2004).

order

CHAPTER

PHYSICAL CHARACTERISTICS

Waterfowl, including ducks, geese, and swans, vary greatly in size and weight. The smallest is the tropical pygmy-goose, which weighs just 10 ounces (269 grams) and stands 12 inches (30 centimeters) tall. The largest is the trumpeter swan, which stands at 72 inches (183 centimeters) and weighs more than 38 pounds (17 kilograms). Screamers are large birds, standing 30 to 37 inches (76 to 95 centimeters) and weighing anywhere from 6 to 88 pounds (3 to 40 kilograms). Their wingspan is 5.6 feet (170 centimeters).

These birds have compact bodies with long necks and full webbing between the three forward-pointing toes. The lower bill is flat while the upper is cone-shaped with a sort of nail at the tip. Waterfowl are unable to glide but can fly quickly with their necks outstretched. Five species are flightless, including three of the four species of steamer-ducks, the Auckland Island teal, and the Campbell Island teal. Screamers look like geese but they have a small, chicken-like head. Their feathers are gray or greenish-black, with some white on the head and neck, fading into the forewing. The screamer has a feathered "horn" on the front top of its head, and its eyes range from yellow to orange. Screamers, like waterfowl, have webbing between their toes.

Ducks, swans, and geese have broad wings that come to a point. Feather coloration varies from the white of most swans to the brown of many geese to the bright patterns of many northern ducks. Male coloration is more vibrant than that of females. Geese and swans molt, shed their feathers, once a year

phylum

class

subclass

● **order**

monotypic order

suborder

family

while ducks molt twice each year. During the molting season, waterfowl are flightless except for the magpie goose. Screamers molt gradually and so are never rendered flightless.

GEOGRAPHIC RANGE

Screamers are found only in South America, whereas ducks, geese, and swans are found throughout the world except in the Arctic region.

HABITAT

Waterfowl and screamers can be found in virtually any wetland as long as there is sufficient food available. Screamers inhabit tropical and subtropical wetlands such as marshes, swamps, and lagoons. They also are found on savannas, a tropical plant environment made up of shrubs, trees, and grasses, and the flood plains of tropical forests. Some waterfowl are found in saltwater environments outside of breeding season.

DIET

The herbivorous, plant-eating, screamer and waterfowl eat mostly leaves, flowers, and seeds of aquatic vegetation. They also small fish, insects, and plankton.

BEHAVIOR AND REPRODUCTION

Most waterfowl are active during the day and seek the safety of shelter at night. When not nesting, they are social birds and gather in groups during the winter months. These groups can reach up to three thousand birds. When nesting, though, they prefer to be alone for the most part. Screamers are solitary, alone, nesters as well.

Screamers build their nests out of weeds and sticks and choose sites close to the water. A seasonally monogamous, one mate per season, bird, screamers often return to the same nest for many seasons, and some use the same nest for life. Both sexes build and defend the nest. They lay two to seven eggs, which parents will take turns incubating, warming, for forty-two to forty-five days. They cover the eggs with weeds if they must both leave the nest. New chicks are tended to for just a couple days, and they are ready for flight by eight to ten weeks. They are completely independent by fourteen weeks of age.

Screamers get their name for the loud vocalizations used to defend territory and to call out to one another. Their screams can be heard from a distance of 1.9 miles (3 kilometers).

Some species of waterfowl build their nests near the water, while others nest more than a mile from the waters' edge. Those that nest far away are surface-feeding ducks that can walk without difficulty. Most nest on the ground while others build their homes in trees. The nest is made of whatever can be found around the site, and shortly before the eggs are laid, females pluck the soft down from their undersides and line the nest with it. Clutch, number of eggs laid, sizes vary greatly, from two to twenty-two. Incubation lasts from twenty-two to forty days, and with the exception of a few species, males do not assist in this duty. Chicks are born with a covering of down that becomes water repellent as it rubs against the mother's feathers. Ducklings feed independently the first day. Ducks care for their young until they are able to fly, between forty to seventy days. Geese and swans care for their young until the following spring.

Predators of waterfowl and screamers include red fox, coyote, weasel and mink, crow, owl, raccoon, badger, skunk, magpie, and skuas.

DUCKS, GEESE, SWANS, SCREAMERS AND PEOPLE

Humans hunt waterfowl as a food source, and waterfowl are domesticated for their eggs, liver, and meat. Eiders are raised for their feathers, which are used in comforters, sleeping bags, and pillows.

CONSERVATION STATUS

Six species of Anseriformes are listed as Extinct, no longer existing, and another fourteen are listed as Endangered, facing a very high risk of extinction in the wild in the near future. Twelve are listed as Vulnerable, facing a high risk of extinction in the wild in the medium-term future, and eight are listed as Near Threatened, in danger of becoming threatened with extinction. The reasons for the threats to these populations are habitat destruction, human hunting and collecting, and toxic poisoning due to modern agricultural methods.

FOR MORE INFORMATION

Books:

Burnie, David, and Don E. Wilson, eds. *Smithsonian Institution Animal: The Definitive Visual Guide to the World's Wildlife.* New York: DK Publishing, 2001.

LeMaster, Richard. *Waterfowl Identification: The LeMaster Method.* Mechanisburg, PA: Stackpole Books, 1996.

Miller, Sara Swan. *From Swans to Screamers.* New York: Scholastic Library Publishing, 2000.

Smith, Christopher. *Field Guide to Waterfowl and Upland Birds.* Belgrade, MT: Wilderness Adventures Press, Ltd., 2000.

Wexo, John. *Ducks, Geese, and Swans (Zoobook Series).* Poway, CA: Wildlife Education, Ltd., 2001.

Periodicals:

"No Swansong in the Chesapeake Bay—Spectrum—Mute Swan Killing Stopped." *Environment* (December 2003): 7.

Quick, Suzanne. "Plan to End Protection of Mute Swans Raise Flaps." *Milwaukee Journal Sentinel Online* (May 16, 2004). Online at http://www.jsonline.com/news/state/may04/229949.asp (accessed on May 27, 2004).

Web sites:

"Anseriformes." *The Chaffee Zoo.* http://www.chaffeezoo.org/animals/anseriformes.html (accessed on May 27, 2004).

Ducks Unlimited. http://www.ducks.org (accessed on May 27, 2004).

Howard, Laura. "Family Anhimidae." *Animal Diversity Web.* http://animaldiversity.ummz.umich.edu/site/accounts/information/Anhimidae.html (accessed on May 27, 2004).

Howard, Laura. "Family Anitidae." *Animal Diversity Web.* http://animaldiversity.ummz.umich.edu/site/accounts/information/Anatidae.html (accessed on May 27, 2004).

Howard, Laura. "Order Anseriformes." *Animal Diversity Web.* http://animaldiversity.ummz.umich.edu/site/accounts/information/Anseriformes.html (accessed on May 27, 2004).

"USFWS Drops Mute Swan Killing Plan." *The Humane Society of the United States.* http://www.hsus.org/ace/19328 (accessed on May 27, 2004).

Waterfowl USA. http://www.waterfowlusa.org (accessed on May 27, 2004).

DUCKS, GEESE, AND SWANS
Anatidae

Class: Aves

Order: Anseriformes

Family: Anatidae

Number of species: 147 species

phylum

class

subclass

order

monotypic order

suborder

△ family

PHYSICAL CHARACTERISTICS

Anatids (members of the family Anatidae) are medium to extra-large birds with stocky bodies, webbed feet, and a flat bill. Coloring varies but is primarily brown with white, black, and metallic green accents. The smallest species stands 13 inches (33 centimeters) and weighs no more than 0.5 pounds (0.2 kilograms) while the largest grows up to 6 feet (1.8 meters) in length and weighs up to 49 pounds (22.5 kilograms).

GEOGRAPHIC RANGE

Found on all continents except Antarctica.

HABITAT

Anatids need water. Some require fast-flowing streams; others prefer rainforests, tundra, or even the lava fields of volcanoes. Marshland is another common habitat for these birds.

DIET

Despite the fact that most geese, ducks, and swans require water bodies for survival, not all species eat aquatic food. Some species are vegetarian and eat primarily seeds, roots, leaves, and stems. Others eat insects, and still others thrive almost exclusively on aquatic invertebrates (water animals without backbones). Some anatids favor plankton and algae (AL-jee).

BEHAVIOR AND REPRODUCTION

Nearly half of all anatids migrate (move from region to region, seasonally), and most of those that don't tend to wander over a wide area to remain near a plentiful water supply.

Anatids are known for their flock formations, which experts believe may help them in locating food as well as protect them from predators, animals that hunt them for food. Aside from humans, primary predators include red foxes, badgers, raccoons, coyotes, skunks, weasels, minks, owls, skuas, American crows, and black-billed magpies.

Anatids use their ritualized displays to help keep family groups close, convey information about reproductive status, defend territory or mates, and establish pair bonds. They communicate via sounds as well, with whistles, quacks, and honks. They spend a great deal of time in the water, preening themselves. Anatids use their bills to waterproof their feathers with oil secreted from a gland near their eyes. Waterfowl are social and live in flocks of up to several hundred thousand birds.

Although most anatids are monogamous (muh-NAH-guh-mus; have only one mate), some have several mating partners each season. Those species that are monogamous stay paired for one season, several seasons, or even for life. Breeding season varies depending on region. Courtship displays include vocalization as well as specific swimming patterns and movements. Almost all anatids mate on the water. Nests are then built on land in areas with dense vegetation. Nests are often lined with feathers. Usually the female builds the nest while the male defends her and their territory.

Eggs are laid over a twenty-four-hour period, and average clutch sizes range from four to thirteen eggs. Incubation (warming sufficiently for hatching) lasts from twenty-two to forty days and is done by the female. With a few species exceptions, males also don't help care for their young. Some anatid species lay their eggs in other females' nests. Within hours of hatching, chicks follow their mother on food outings and are often accompanied by their father, who protects his brood from predators. Chicks stay with mothers for five to ten weeks and are ready to mate around the age of one to three years.

MAKE WAY FOR DUCKLINGS

In May 2004, a mallard duck hatched thirteen ducklings in the courtyard of Christopher Farms Elementary School in Virginia. Prior to their hatching, school officials were not even aware of the nest.

According to an article written by journalist Mary Reid Barrow and printed in *The Virginian Pilot,* the mother was able to fly in and out but the babies were stuck inside the courtyard in the center of the school. Teachers and others got behind the mother, who repeatedly circled with her ducklings in front of the main doors, and edged all fourteen ducks through the school via the main hallway and out the door.

The family went straight for a nearby pond without another problem.

DUCKS, GEESE, SWANS, AND PEOPLE

Anatids and humans have a long history of interaction. Humans have domesticated (tamed) a number of species and have hunted waterfowl almost since the beginning of humankind. Waterfowl hunting is a huge source of revenue in the United States, with outdoor stores selling millions of dollars worth of hunting gear. Also, waterfowl play an important role in keeping the balance of wetland ecosystems.

CONSERVATION STATUS

Six species are Extinct, died out. Four are Critically Endangered, facing an extremely high risk of extinction; nine are Endangered, facing a very high risk of extinction; and twelve species are listed as Vulnerable, facing a high risk of extinction. The greatest threats to these birds are overhunting and wetland drainage. When wetlands are drained, waterfowl can no longer breed there. Pollution from industry also threatens birds in rivers and streams.

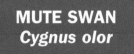

Mute swan *(Cygnus olor)*

Resident　　Breeding　　Nonbreeding

MUTE SWAN
Cygnus olor

Physical characteristics: This large, white bird weighs anywhere from 14.6 to 33 pounds (6.6 to 15 kilograms) and measures 4 to 5.3 feet (1.3 to 1.6 meters) in length. Its neck is S-shaped, and the bill is orange with a black base. Wingspan measures 7 to 8 feet (2.1 to 2.4 meters). Males and females look alike except males are larger.

Geographic range: Found in central and northern Europe. The mute swan winters in northern Africa, the Near East, and to northwest India and Korea. It has been introduced into the United States.

Habitat: Mute swans require water with plenty of vegetation, such as lagoons, marshes, lakes, and canals.

Diet: Mute swans eat aquatic vegetation, including grass and seeds. They also feed on invertebrates, insects, aquatic worms, and small amphibians. Mute swans do not dive but reach under the water with their long necks and grab food.

Behavior and reproduction: Mute swans get their name for their silence. Only when they're mad will they hiss. This bird is territorial and will fight to the death to defend its home range, which can encompass up to 10 acres (4 hectares). Unlike most anatids, mute swans do not migrate in large flocks. Mute swans fly at a rate of 50 to 55 miles per hour (80.5 to 88.5 kilometers per hour).

Mute swans do not mate for life, but do usually maintain a pair bond for one breeding season. These birds build their large nests in March and April, and the nests are made of vegetation lined with feathers and down. Nests are built in the reeds surrounding water or on floating mats. Clutch size is usually five to seven eggs, sometimes as large as twelve. Incubation lasts thirty-six to thirty-eight days. Chicks (also called cygnets; SIG-nuts) are born with grayish-brown feathers that will turn white within twelve months. The tiny birds stay in the nest only for about an hour. Cygnets ride under parents' wings or on their backs. By the next mating season, parents chase away their young. Mute swans don't usually breed before the age of three years. They oldest known mute swan in the wild was nineteen years.

Mute swans and people: Mute swans have been known to knock down jet-skiers, and they can be dangerous to small children. They will attack people who get too close to their nests. These birds were saved from extinction due to hunting in Britain when people began domesticating them. The mute swan is the most common swan and is often seen in parks. It is a symbol of love and purity.

Conservation status: Not threatened. In fact, the population of this swan is on the rise. ■

Canada goose (*Branta canadensis*)

Resident   Breeding   Nonbreeding

CANADA GOOSE
Branta canadensis

Physical characteristics: This is a large goose with a solid black neck. The head is also black, but there is a white band running underneath the chin. The Canada goose weighs 4.5 to 14.4 pounds (2 to 6.5 kilograms) and stands 21.7 to 43.3 inches (55 to 110 centimeters) tall. Its bill is black, as are its feet. The plumage (feathers) is various shades of brown. Adults lose their feathers and become flightless for three to four weeks each summer until their feathers regrow.

Geographic range: Found in most of Canada and in the United States.

Habitat: The Canada goose feeds in grassland and open marshes. Like other waterfowl, it requires a permanent body of water in which to live.

Diet: Canada geese eat a variety of grasses by pulling them from the ground with their bills. They also feed on corn, wheat, and rice.

The mostly herbivorous, eating plant material, bird also eats aquatic vegetation.

Behavior and reproduction: Canada geese migrate slowly in a V-shaped formation, and you know they're above by their loud honking. Each formation is comprised of a number of smaller family groups, and if you watch them land, you'll see the families break off into their individual units. This species can be aggressive and will attack if threatened. These geese are vocal, and pairs will "talk" with one another so quickly that it sounds as if all the sound is coming from just one bird. Babies have a particular raspy call they use to summon their parents.

Canada geese mate for life. They build their nests from grasses and other available vegetation and line them with cattail down. Nests are usually near water. Females lay four to seven eggs and incubate them for twenty-five to thirty days. Within one day of hatching, goslings are led to water by their mother. Canada geese parents often gather goslings into groups and look after them communally. Goslings fly for the first time between forty and eighty-six days, and are ready to mate between two and three years. The average lifespan in the wild is fifteen to twenty years.

Canada geese mate in pairs for life. These geese fly together during courting, before they mate for the season. (Jack A. Barrie/Bruce Coleman Inc. Reproduced by permission.)

A group of flying geese is called a gaggle. A group of geese on the ground is called a skein (skayn).

Canada geese and people: More than most anatids, this species is tolerant of humans. While this has endeared the bird to some, it has been a source of irritation for others. Canada geese like to live in habitats such as golf courses, and their presence is of concern to country clubs and the like. Some humans enjoy feeding these geese, while others prefer hunting them.

Conservation status: Canada geese are not threatened. ■

Mallard (*Anas platyrhynchos*)

Resident   Breeding   Nonbreeding

MALLARD
Anas platyrhynchos

Physical characteristics: Mallards weigh between 1.7 and 3.5 pounds (750 to 1,580 grams) and measure 19.7 to 25.6 inches (50 to 65 centimeters) long. The head of the male is metallic green and the chest is brown. Feet are orange.

Geographic range: Without doubt the most abundant duck, there are approximately ten million mallards in North America and millions more in Eurasia, Europe, and Asia.

Habitat: Mallards live in the shallow, calm waters of wetlands, including marshes, bays, and even city ponds. They prefer to have the protection of some vegetative cover.

Diet: Mallards eat fish, amphibians, and invertebrates. They also on plant parts and eat insects and worms. They eat by dipping their heads beneath the water's surface or by upending, but rarely do they dive.

Behavior and reproduction: Mallards are territorial and become very aggressive when their space is intruded upon. A migratory bird, mallards are among the first to return to breeding grounds in the spring.

Males and females search for nesting ground together. The female lays eight to twelve eggs in her ground nest. Incubation lasts twenty-seven to twenty-eight days, during which the male leaves the female to join a new flock. Ducklings fly between the age of fifty and sixty days and are ready to breed at one year. Mallards are seasonally monogamous, have just one mate per season, and have been known to breed with other species.

Mallards are vocal. The male makes soft sounds while the female quacks so loudly that her call can be heard from miles away. Hawks prey on eggs, but adult mallards are preyed upon primarily by human hunters.

Mallards and people: Mallards are popular with humans because of their beautiful coloration and for their abundant numbers. In Canada, 50 percent of all ducks are mallards. This species is highly tolerant of human activity, which is why public parks are popular habitats. People not only hunt adult mallards for their meat, but also harvest their eggs.

Conservation status: Mallards are common, and not threatened. The Hawaiian subspecies are rare. ■

Mallards live in the shallow, calm waters of wetlands, including marshes, bays, and even city ponds. These birds migrate, and are some of the first to return to breeding grounds in the spring. (© Manfred Danegger/OKAPIA/ Photo Researchers, Inc. Reproduced by permission.)

King eider (Somateria spectabilis)

Breeding   Nonbreeding

KING EIDER
Somateria spectabilis

Physical characteristics: Weighs 3.3 to 4.4 pounds (1.5 to 2 kilograms) and measures 17 to 25 inches (43 to 63 centimeters) in length. Male has a blue, yellow, and white head. Bill is bright orange and yellow and develops from a "shield" from the top of the face.

Geographic range: King eiders live on the Arctic coasts. They winter off the coast of Iceland, Norway, Kuril and Aleutian Islands, and as far south as California and Long Island (New York).

Habitat: Lives in oceans and other saltwater areas. Breeds on land in Arctic freshwater wetlands.

Diet: King eiders eat mostly mussels, sand dollars, squid and small fish. They dive (sometimes as deep as 150 feet, or 50 meters) and up-end (put their heads under while their back end stays out of the water) to retrieve food. They also eat tundra vegetation.

Grzimek's Student Animal Life Resource

Behavior and reproduction: Eiders migrate in a straight line. They are seasonally monogamous, and the male leaves the female midway through incubation. Females lay four to five eggs into holes in the ground that have little lining. Incubation lasts twenty-two to twenty-four days. Ducklings are ready to breed at three years.

King eiders and people: This duck is hunted for food and game, and its down is among the highest quality available, used to make pillows and comforters.

Conservation status: The king eider is common throughout its range. ■

The king eider is hunted for food and sport. Its down, fine feathers, is used to fill pillows and comforters. (© B. Randall/ VIREO. Reproduced by permission.)

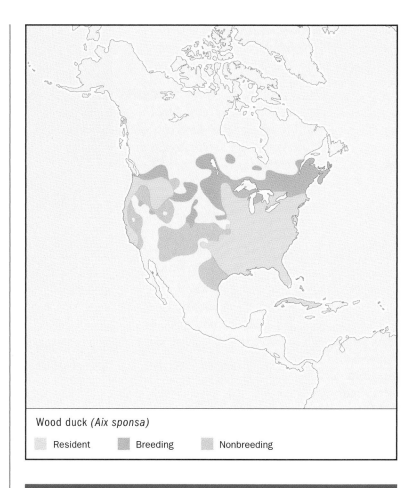

Wood duck *(Aix sponsa)*

☐ Resident ☐ Breeding ☐ Nonbreeding

WOOD DUCK
Aix sponsa

Physical characteristics: The male is more colorful than the female, with a metallic green crest and crown surrounding his purple face. Throat is white; tail is square. The body of both sexes is various shades of brown. Measures 17 to 20 inches (43 to 51 centimeters) and weighs about 1.3 pounds (0.6 kilograms).

Geographic range: Found in eastern North America from the southern tip of Florida to northern Nova Scotia, west across Quebec and Ontario to the southern tip of Texas.

Habitat: Wood ducks live in woodland streams and pools, river valleys, swamps and marshlands, and lakes.

Diet: Wood ducks feed primarily on aquatic vegetation. They also eat water and land invertebrates as well as berries, nuts, and seeds.

Behavior and reproduction: This duck migrates to Cuba, the Bahamas, and Mexico for the winter. It is territorial and will defend its range, which is about 24 acres (9.7 hectares) per breeding pair. Wood ducks are vocal, especially during migration.

Pairs form in the fall and are seasonally monogamous. The female lays anywhere from six to fifteen eggs in nests that are actually holes in tree trunks or former woodpecker holes. Incubation lasts twenty-eight to thirty-seven days, and the male leaves just a few days before ducklings hatch. Young leave the nest within two days and are ready to mate at one year. Snapping turtles are the primary predators of eggs and ducklings.

The wood duck is found in eastern North America, and migrates to Cuba, the Bahamas, and Mexico for the winter. (Robert J. Huffman/Field Mark Publications. Reproduced by permission.)

Wood ducks and people: Humans overhunted and destroyed habitats of the wood duck almost to extinction in the early 1900s. The hunting season was declared closed in 1918, which allowed for repopulation.

Conservation status: The white-winged wood duck is considered Endangered, and the black-billed wood duck is Vulnerable due to habitat destruction. ◼

FOR MORE INFORMATION

Books:

Burk, Bruce. *Waterfowl Studies: Geese and Swans.* Vol. 3. Atglen, PA: Schiffer Publishing, 1999.

Hehner, Mike, Chris Dorsey, and Greg Breining. *North American Game Birds (Hunting and Fishing Library Series).* Chanhassen, MN: Creative Publishing International, 2002.

Shurtleff, Lawton L., and Christopher Savage. *The Wood Duck and the Mandarin: The Northern Wood Ducks.* Berkeley, CA: University of California Press, 1996.

Sibley, David Allen, Chris Elphik, and John B. Dunning, eds. *The Sibley Guide to Bird Life and Behavior.* New York: Knopf Publishing Group, 2001.

Periodicals:

Barrow, Mary Reid. "School Helps Duck Family, and Students Get an Education." *The Virginian Pilot* (May 16, 2004).

Web sites:

"The Birdhouse Network: Wood Duck." Lab of Ornithology. http://birds.cornell.edu/birdhouse/bird_bios/speciesaccounts/wooduc.html (accessed on May 25, 2004).

Canada Goose Conservation Society. http://www.cgcs.demon.co.uk/ (accessed on May 25, 2004).

Howard, L. "Anatidae." Animal Diversity Web. http://animaldiversity.ummz.umich.edu/site/accounts/information/Anatidae.html (accessed May 25, 2004).

"King Eider." Enature. http://www.enature.com/fieldguide/showSpeciesFT.asp?fotogID=548&curPageNum=1&recnum=BD0675 (accessed on May 25, 2004).

"Mute Swan." Tropical Birds of Paradise. http://www.auburnweb.com/paradise/birds/mute_swan.html (accessed on May 25, 2004).

"Nature: Wood Duck." Texas Parks and Wildlife Department. http://www.tpwd.state.tx.us/factsheets/birds/wood_duck/wood_duck.htm (accessed on June 1, 2004).

SCREAMERS
Anhimidae

Class: Aves

Order: Anseriformes

Family: Anhimidae

Number of species: 3 species

PHYSICAL CHARACTERISTICS

Screamers are large, goose-like birds that swim well and live in and near fresh water. They have a horn-like projection on top of their heads, and a short, downcurved bill. Their legs are long and thick, and their feet are only shallowly webbed. Wings are long and broad, which makes them able to soar well. They weigh 5 to 7 pounds (2 to 3 kilograms) and measure 28 to 36 inches (71 to 92 centimeters) long.

Each wing has a sharp, spur-like outgrowth of bone. These spurs, which are used as weapons, are covered with keratin, the same material that makes up hair and fingernails. Body coloration is black or gray on top with lighter hues below.

GEOGRAPHIC RANGE

Screamers are found in South America, from Venezuela and Colombia to Uruguay and northern Argentina.

HABITAT

Screamers live in swamps, marshes, lagoons, and lakes as well as flood plains, meadows, and savannas (tropical or subtropical plant communities characterized by low trees and shrubs as well as grasses and herbs).

DIET

Screamers are vegetarian birds that feed on aquatic plants and seeds. They do not dive for food.

phylum

class

subclass

order

monotypic order

suborder

▲ **family**

BEHAVIOR AND REPRODUCTION

Screamers remain in their breeding range year-round and are somewhat social. Outside the breeding season, they tend to flock together. And though they swim well, screamers mostly live on land. Their long toes make them able to walk on aquatic vegetation and floating mats. Screamers got their name because of their very loud vocalizations.

Screamers are solitary nesters that build their nests out of vegetation, weeds, and sticks on or near the water. The female lays two to seven spotted eggs, and incubation (warming sufficient for hatching) lasts forty-two to forty-five days. Parents take turns incubating, and the male helps care for newborns. Chicks leave the nest within a few days. Babies first fly at ten to twelve weeks, and they no longer require parental care around twelve to fourteen weeks.

Screamers are seasonally monogamous (muh-NAH-guh-mus; having just one mate each year). The expected life span in the wild is eight to ten years. Predators include skunks, weasels, and red fox.

SCREAMERS AND PEOPLE

Though sometimes hunted for food, screamers are more likely to be captured and tamed. They adapt easily to captivity and can be kept with chickens. They walk around freely at South American parks and zoos.

CONSERVATION STATUS

The northern screamer is listed by the IUCN as Near Threatened, at risk of becoming threatened. Although it is not in immediate peril, its numbers have drastically fallen in recent years due to habitat destruction.

Horned screamer (Anhima cornuta)

Resident

HORNED SCREAMER
Anhima cornuta

Physical characteristics: The horned screamer measures 34 to 37 inches (86 to 94 centimeters) long. Its body is greenish black with a white belly. A "horn" protrudes from its forehead.

Geographic range: Found in the Amazonian regions of Venezuela, the Guianas, Colombia, Ecuador, Peru, Bolivia, and Brazil.

Habitat: The horned screamer lives in wetlands of tropical forests such as lakes, swamps, and marshes. It is found at altitudes up to 3,300 feet (1,100 meters).

The horned screamer lives in wetlands of tropical forests such as lakes, swamps, and marshes. (© T. McNish M./VIREO. Reproduced by permission.)

Diet: Horned screamers eat aquatic vegetation.

Behavior and reproduction: This bird has a distinctive set of calls that can be heard for miles. It swims or walks on vegetation while feeding, and likes to rest in shrubs and trees rather than on the ground.

Screamers build floating nests of plants and vegetation. The female lays two eggs, which are incubated by both parents. Both parents also care for the young.

Horned screamers and people: These birds are tamed and kept as pets. They are also hunted for their meat.

Conservation status: Horned screamers are not considered to be threatened. ■

FOR MORE INFORMATION

Books:

Bird, David M. *The Bird Almanac: A Guide to Essential Facts and Figures of the World's Birds.* Buffalo, NY: Firefly Books, 2004.

Hilty, Steven L. *Birds of Venezuela,* 2nd ed. Princeton, NJ: Princeton University Press, 2003.

Sibley, David Allen, Chris Elphik, and John B. Dunning, eds. *The Sibley Guide to Bird Life and Behavior.* New York: Knopf Publishing Group, 2001.

Web sites:

Howard, L. "Anhimidae." Animal Diversity Web. http://animaldiversity.ummz.umich.edu/site/accounts/information/Anhimidae.html (accessed on June 1, 2004).

CHICKEN-LIKE BIRDS
Galliformes

Class: Aves
Order: Galliformes
Number of families: 5 families

order

PHYSICAL CHARACTERISTICS

Galliformes are medium to large in size, with a stocky body, small head, and short wings. Quails are the smallest species, weighing less than 1 ounce (20 grams) and measuring just 5 to 6 inches (12 to 15 centimeters). The wild turkey weighs 17 to 22 pounds (8 to 10 kilograms), and the domesticated turkey bred for eating can weigh up to 44 pounds (20 kilograms). The green peafowl measures up to 98 inches (250 centimeters) in length.

Galliformes have short bills that usually curve downward to assist in pecking plant material from the ground. Their feet are big and strong—so strong that they can move heavy branches or stone. Some galliform tails are one-third the size of their total body length. Both sexes are often brown or black, but the males of a few species are incredibly colorful.

GEOGRAPHIC RANGE

Galliformes are found on every continent except Antarctica.

HABITAT

Gallinaceous birds enjoy a wide variety of habitats: forests, mountains, farmland, semideserts, and savannas (plant communities characterized by shrubs and low trees as well as grasses and herbs).

DIET

The chicken-like birds eat nuts, seeds, and parts of plants. Their large feet help them move branches and stones to discover food other animals could not access. Chicks eat insects and larvae (LAR-vee; immature stage for some insects) during their first few weeks of life.

Galliformes regularly swallow small stones to help the digestive process. The rocks help break down nuts and seed coverings as well as the tough fibers that make up green vegetation. These birds don't drink much water, but a few species visit salt licks, where they eat clay soil that gives them required minerals.

BEHAVIOR AND REPRODUCTION

Social behavior varies among species. Many species are solitary (lone) or spend the year in pairs. Other species spend the nonbreeding season feeding together in larger groups.

Males are territorial. Because their vivid colorations make them easy to spot, some species move only when threatened, preferring to spend the majority of their time sitting still. Most species do not migrate. In fact, they rarely leave the area in which they were born. A few do migrate (travel seasonally from region to region), however.

Galliformes are terrestrial (land-based) and are not built for long-distance flight. They are better equipped to make strong, short bursts of flight. When threatened, they are more likely to run away than fly. When they do take flight, most species cannot fly high above the ground.

Gallinaceous birds bathe by squatting in shallow pits and beating their wings. This dusts their feathers and removes parasites.

Breeding habits vary throughout the order. Those species in which there is little physical difference between the male and female tend to be monogamous (having just one mate), whereas those in which the males are more colorful are polygynous (one male, many females). Males have many physical traits used to attract females, including bright colors, shaped tail feathers, and other distinct markings. Some have combs (fleshy red crests on top of the head) and eyebrows. One family—the curassows—has a colorful knob on the beak that gets larger as the bird ages.

Vocalizations play an important role in courtship displays and territorial rituals. They are also used to communicate with a mate. In some species, the calls can be heard for up to 4 miles (6.4 kilometers).

The family known as megapodes do not need to sit on their eggs to incubate (keep warm for hatching to occur) them.

The male builds a large mound of sand or vegetation and digs into it. The female lays her eggs in the burrow, and it's up to the male to regulate the temperature of the nest, sometimes for up to eleven months until the egg hatches. In monogamous (muh-NAH-guh-mus) pairs, where each bird mates with just one other bird, both parents help care for the young.

For those species that do incubate their eggs with their own body heat, incubation time varies from seventeen days to four weeks. Clutch sizes vary from seven to twenty eggs.

Young are born with their eyes open, able to feed somewhat independently within a few hours of hatching. Hatchlings are born with colors aimed at helping them stay hidden, but those first downy feathers are replaced with brighter colors as the bird matures. Offspring leave their parents at around one year of age.

Predators include red foxes, striped skunks, chipmunks, squirrels, raccoons, snakes, and crows.

GALLIFORMES AND PEOPLE

As people turned from a hunter-gatherer society into a farming society, they began to domesticate several galliform species. Turkeys, chickens, and guineafowl continue to be an important part of the human diet throughout the globe. The eggs of Galliformes are highly prized, as their high yolk content is a rich protein source.

Because Galliformes are sedentary, not very active, they are easy to shoot, which makes them the most popular hunting birds throughout the world. Every year, tens of millions of Galliformes are raised and released specifically for shooting purposes. In fact, many species have been introduced into other countries for purpose of sport or decoration. These introductions have proved to be a serious threat to the native bird populations, as is habitat destruction and degradation.

CONSERVATION STATUS

Of all the galliform species, 104 are considered Threatened, at risk of extinction, or Near Threatened, could become threatened. Those under the greatest threat are pheasants and partridges. One, possibly two, species has become extinct since 1600. Hunting for adults and eggs is a serious threat to these game birds. Conservation efforts are being made throughout the world to stabilize populations, but habitat destruction is the primary threat. Those species that depend on forests are in the most critical danger, as logging for timber and clear-cutting for agriculture is on the rise.

FOR MORE INFORMATION

Books:

Hehner, Mike, Chris Dorsey, and Greg Breining. *North American Game Birds.* Chanhassen, MN: Creative Publishing International, 2002.

Kaufman, Ken. *Kingbird Highway: The Story of a Natural Obsession That Got a Little Out of Hand.* New York: Houghton Mifflin, 2000.

Periodicals:

Smith, Doug. "Working for Wildlife; Pheasants: Forever or Not?" *Star Tribune* (May 3, 2004).

Web sites:

American Bird Conservancy. http://www.abcbirds.org (accessed on July 13, 2004).

"Galliformes." Earthlife. http://www.earthlife.net/birds/galliformes.html (accessed on June 1, 2004).

National Audubon Society. http://www.audubon.org (accessed on July 13, 2004).

MOUNDBUILDERS
Megapodiidae

Class: Aves

Order: Galliformes

Family: Megapodiidae

Number of species: 22 species

PHYSICAL CHARACTERISTICS

Moundbuilders have big, strong legs and feet. The short bill curves downward, and most moundbuilders look like other galliforms (members of the order Galliformes) in body shape and dull coloring. There are a few species that have patterned plumage (feathers), but in these birds, the patterning helps conceal them from predators.

Moundbuilders weigh between 1.1 and 5.5 pounds (0.5 to 2.5 kilograms) and measure 11 to 27 inches (28 to 70 centimeters) in length.

GEOGRAPHIC RANGE

Primarily in Australia and New Guinea as well as on islands throughout the southeastern Pacific and Southeast Asia.

HABITAT

Moundbuilders must live in regions where climate conditions encourage the decomposition of organic matter, and so they prefer tropical and subtropical rainforests. Only the malleefowl and the Australian brush-turkey can be found in habitats outside the rainforest.

DIET

Most of what moundbuilders eat comes from the forest floor. These birds feed on fallen fruits, seeds, ants, scorpions, and even small snakes. Although most of this food gets eaten as the birds dig through forest leaf-litter, they do seek out specific types of food, fruit being one of these.

CAUGHT ON FILM

For the first time ever, the threatened Vanuatu (van-wah-TOO) megapode was captured on film by Dr. Mark O'Brien in December 2003. O'Brien, a researcher from the Royal Society for the Protection of Birds, had visited the Pacific nation of Vanuatu so that he could work with the chief in an effort to determine a way that islanders could still harvest eggs, but in a sustainable way.

According to a press release posted on Birdlife.org, only 2,500 pairs of Vanuatu megapodes remain, and only on the 108 islands of Vanuatu. As a result of O'Brien's visit, the chief initiated a conservation program that included a moratorium (temporary halt) on egg collection that lasted four months. Anyone disobeying the rule was fined $135 or the equivalent in pigs or cattle. And because the species is rarer in the southeastern part of the nation, those communities agreed to a five-year ban on egg collection.

O'Brien acknowledged that another visit to Vanuatu is necessary to learn the effects of the moratorium.

BEHAVIOR AND REPRODUCTION

It's difficult to separate reproduction behavior from other behavior because nearly all aspects of life among moundbuilders revolve around their incubation (keeping eggs warm for hatching) methods. The moundbuilder family is vocal, and calls range from low-pitched and quiet to incredibly loud and wail-like.

Unlike other birds, moundbuilders do not use their body heat to incubate their eggs. Instead, they rely on solar radiation (on beaches), geothermal activity (from soil near volcanic areas), and the decomposition of organic matter (in mounds). Mounds consist of leaf-litter and soil, and adults constantly add fresh material to conserve moisture. Some species dig burrows rather than build mounds, and their eggs are incubated by the sun or geothermal sources (sand, soil). Clutch sizes range from twelve to thirty eggs each season and must incubate for forty-five to seventy days.

Moundbuilders lay their eggs in individual holes deep within the incubation site, and each chick hatches separately, without help from the parents. Chicks dig for two to fifteen hours to reach the surface, and they are completely independent at the time of hatching. This means they leave the site, find food and water, recognize and avoid predators, animals that hunt them for food, and even regulate their own body heat upon birth.

Some moundbuilders are monogamous (muh-NAH-guh-mus; having only one mate) while others are polygynous (puh-LIH-juh-nus; one male, several females). Predators include foxes, birds of prey, dingoes, and wild cats.

MOUNDBUILDERS AND PEOPLE

Humans have traditionally harvested the birds' eggs, which are rich in protein. Although native people have been harvesting eggs for thousands of years, the recent human population growth has proven to be more than the moundbuilder population can sustain, and overharvesting has become a serious problem.

CONSERVATION STATUS

Almost half of the twenty-two species face some level of threat. Six species are listed as Vulnerable by the IUCN, facing a high risk of extinction, dying out, while one is Critically Endangered, facing an extremely high risk of extinction, and another two are Endangered, facing a very high risk of extinction. One species is Near Threatened, at risk of becoming threatened. The main reasons for threat include habitat loss, overharvesting of eggs, and predation by introduced animals.

Malleefowl *(Leipoa ocellata)*

Resident

MALLEEFOWL
Leipoa ocellata

Physical characteristics: Both sexes grow to be around 23.6 inches (60 centimeters) long. Males weigh 4 to 5.5 pounds (1.8 to 2.5 kilograms) while females weigh 3.3 to 4.5 pounds (1.5 to 2 kilograms). Upperparts have a distinct stripe pattern of white, black, and gray. Stripes are made up of spots that resemble eyes, which help to ward off predators.

Geographic range: Found in Australia, primarily in the southern states. Recently rediscovered in the deserts of central Australia.

Habitat: Malleefowl live among eucalyptus (yoo-kah-LIP-tus) trees and the spiny, shrub-like acacia (uh-KAY-shah) woodlands.

Male malleefowls spend up to eleven months each year building their incubation mounds and taking care of them. (© R. Brown/VIREO. Reproduced by permission.)

Diet: The malleefowl feed on plants, especially seeds and fruits. About 20 percent of their diet is comprised of ground-dwelling invertebrates (animals without backbones). They'll drink water if it's available, but don't require it.

Behavior and reproduction: Malleefowl are territorial and pairs will defend their incubation mound. Despite being monogamous, they are solitary (lone) birds, and males will remain near the mound while females wander. These birds rarely fly, but they roost (rest) in the safety of trees.

Malleefowl are ready to mate between the ages of two to four years, and they continue breeding until the age of twenty years or so. Males spend up to eleven months each year building the incubation mounds and tending to them. One mound is used for numerous generations. Females lay two to thirty-four eggs at intervals of two to seventeen days, depending upon the weather. The drier the season, the longer the laying time between eggs. Incubation lasts fifty-five to seventy-seven days, depending on the temperature of the mound. Male malleefowl determine mound temperature by dipping their beaks into the mound. Malleefowl live to be about thirty years old. Foxes and wild cats are the primary predators, and the mortality rate of eggs is very high.

Malleefowl and people: Wheat farming encroaches upon the habitat of the malleefowl, and sheep grazing threatens the malleefowl's food sources.

Conservation status: Classified as Vulnerable due to habitat destruction and the predation of introduced animals. ■

Maleo (*Macrocephalon maleo*)

▨ Resident

MALEO
Macrocephalon maleo

Physical characteristics: Maleos grow to 21.7 inches (55 centimeters) long. Females weigh slightly more (3.3 to 3.9 pounds, or 1.5 to 1.8 kilograms) than males (2.9 to 3.5 pounds, or 1.3 to 1.6 kilograms). This large bird has deep black upperparts and underparts that are white tinged with pink. The head is topped with a black "helmet."

Geographic range: The maleo is found on Sulawesi in Indonesia.

Habitat: Maleos live in tropical forests as well as plantations.

Diet: The maleo feeds on a variety of fruits and seeds. Also eats cockroaches and other invertebrates found on the forest floor.

Behavior and reproduction: The maleo is a shy bird. Monogamous pairs will not leave each other and will defend their burrows from other pairs.

Rather than building a mound out of the soil, this species burrows or tunnels into the soil. Both sexes participate in burrowing and tending to the site. Eggs are laid 4 to 40 inches (10 to 100 centimeters) deep, with ten to twelve days in between each egg. Eggs are five times the size of chicken eggs.

Maleos and people: Natives of Sulawesi have harvested maleo eggs for centuries.

Conservation status: Classified as Vulnerable due to population decline. The increase in human population has caused overharvesting of maleo eggs. ■

FOR MORE INFORMATION

Books:

Jones, Darryl N., et al. *The Megapodes: Megapodiidae.* Oxford, U.K.: Oxford University Press, 1995.

Periodicals:

"Megapode Captured On Film for First Time." *BirdLife International* (December 19, 2003). Online at http://www.birdlife.org/news/news/2003/12/vanuatu_megapode.html (accessed on June 2, 2004).

Web sites:

"Craciformes." Earth Life. http://www.earthlife.net/birds/craciformes. html (accessed on June 2, 2004).

"Mallee Fowl." Earth Sanctuaries Limited. http://www.esl.com.au/ malfowl.htm (accessed on June 2, 2004).

"The Malleefowl." Malleefowl Preservation Group. http://www. malleefowl.com.au/Malleefowl.htm (accessed on June 2, 2004).

CURASSOWS, GUANS, AND CHACHALACAS
Cracidae

Class: Aves
Order: Galliformes
Family: Cracidae
Number of species: 50 species

PHYSICAL CHARACTERISTICS

Length in the cracids (members of the family Cracidae) varies from 16.5 to 36.2 inches (42 to 92 centimeters) and weight is 0.8 to 9.5 pounds (0.4 to 4.3 kilograms). The slim birds are long-legged with short, rounded wings and long tails. Though short, the beak is strong and lightly curved. The feet are similar to those of moundbuilders, with well-developed toes. Plumage (feathers) is black or olive brown to reddish brown, and white marks are scattered throughout. Male curassows of many species have a fleshy knob on the root of the beak or brightly colored areas of naked skin on the head.

GEOGRAPHIC RANGE

These birds are found in south Texas through tropical South America as far as central Argentina. United States is home to only one species, whereas Colombia and Brazil harbor twenty-four and twenty-two species, respectively.

HABITAT

Cracids live in tropical forest regions, plantations, and forested areas where there is a second, lighter growth of vegetation. Although most species prefer the warmth of lowlands, some do live in mountain forests of altitudes above 9,800 feet (3,000 meters).

DIET

Though mainly plant eaters, cracids also feed on insects and other small animals. They enjoy berries and small fruits whole,

WHAT'S SO GREAT ABOUT RAINFORESTS?

Aside from many species of cracids, thousands of other animals live in the tropical rainforests. In fact, half of all the known animals in the world today live in the rainforest. And we're always hearing about the importance of rainforest conservation. What makes the rainforest so special?

Rainforests are home to so many diverse species because these forests are the oldest living ecosystems on the planet. Having escaped the effects of the Ice Age, some rainforests have been around for one hundred million years! When the Ice Age wiped out other living systems, the rainforest continued to thrive, so every living organism within also kept reproducing and evolving. Today, some rainforest species number in the millions.

Though you won't find jungle cats or large animals in the rainforest, it is host to a mind-boggling fifty million species of invertebrates. On a single tree alone in Peru, one scientist found more than fifty different species of ants. Despite these impressive statistics, experts estimate that 137 species of life forms become extinct *every day* in the rainforests, mostly due to logging and cattle ranching.

Like any ecosystem, the rainforest inhabitants have developed so that they depend upon one another for survival. When one species is removed from the system, the effect is ripple-like, and virtually all other species must adapt. In addition to animal life, the rainforest is home to numerous plant species that we have only just begun to recognize as having medicinal use.

but will bite into bigger fruit such as guavas and mangoes. They also eat seeds, soft leaves, and buds. Unlike other Galliformes, cracids won't scratch the forest floor for their food.

BEHAVIOR AND REPRODUCTION

We don't know much about cracid life because they are such shy birds. They seem to live socially in small groups or flocks, and their nests are found in groups. They are vocal birds whose calls are loud and cacophonous (having an unpleasant sound). Some of the mountain forest-dwelling species migrate to lower altitudes during the colder months.

Cracids build their nests in trees or bushes. The nest is a flat platform, usually longer than it is wide and built from twigs, plant stems, leaves, grass, and other similar items. Some of the species are polygamous (puh-LIH-guh-mus; having several mates in one season), but no one is certain about the others. Curassow hens lay two eggs; chachalacas, three; and guans, three to four. Experts believe that only the female incubates (keeps warm before hatching) the eggs. Incubation periods vary from twenty-one to thirty-six days, depending on species.

Newborns are able to leave the nest very soon after birth. They are able to fly, hop, and walk along twigs when just a few days old. Cracids spend a great deal of time in the trees, hopping from branch to branch and walking on twigs. Cracids fall prey to jaguars and other big cats.

CURASSOWS, GUANS, CHACHALACAS AND PEOPLE

Hunters in Latin America value cracids as a rich protein source. However, because the reproduction rate of cracids is so slow, the population cannot withstand intensive hunting pressure. Cracids are greatly affected by habitat destruction. Native tribes use tail and wing feathers for ornamentation.

CONSERVATION STATUS

Cracids are more threatened than any other bird family in the Americas. Twenty-three of the fifty species are threatened with extinction, or close to being threatened with extinction, including 64 percent of curassows (nine species) and 16 percent of the chachalacas (two species). About 50 percent of guans are threatened (twelve species). Primary threats are overhunting and habitat loss.

Plain chachalaca (*Ortalis vetula*)

Resident

PLAIN CHACHALACA
Ortalis vetula

Physical characteristics: The plain chachalaca weighs 15.5 to 28 ounces (440 to 794 grams) and measures 19 to 22.8 inches (48 to 58 centimeters) long. Coloration is olive-brown.

Geographic range: This species is found in Texas, Mexico, and Costa Rica.

Habitat: Plain chachalacas live in lowland forests as well as forests at the base of mountains in Central America. They also dwell in scrub and tall brush vegetation.

Diet: The bulk of their diet is made up of fleshy fruit. They also eat green leaves, shoots, and buds as well as twigs and some insects. Though chachalacas live mostly in trees, they descend to the ground for feeding.

Behavior and reproduction: This social bird has a distinct "cha cha lack, cha cha lack" call which nearby chachalacas sing in chorus. Most humans find it an unpleasant sound.

Nests are built 3.3 to 33 feet (1 to 10 meters) off the ground in trees. Females lay two to four eggs and incubate them for about twenty-five days.

Plain chachalacas and people: Humans may eat plain chachalacas.

Conservation status: These birds are not threatened. ■

Plain chachalacas live mostly in trees, but come to the ground for feeding. (Erwin and Peggy Bauer/Bruce Coleman Inc. Reproduced by permission.)

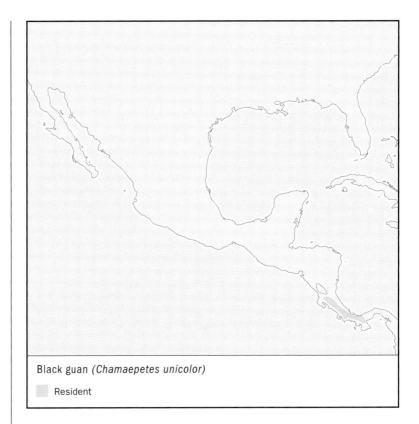

Black guan *(Chamaepetes unicolor)*

Resident

BLACK GUAN
Chamaepetes unicolor

Physical characteristics: Black guans weigh 2.4 to 2.6 pounds (1.1 to 1.2 kilograms) and measure 24 to 27 inches (62 to 67 centimeters) long. The male is entirely black except for a bare blue patch on his face.

Geographic range: Found in western Panama and in Costa Rica.

Habitat: Black guans are found in mountain forests above 3,300 feet (1,000 meters) in southern Central America.

Diet: They eat mostly fruit, but also seeds and some plants. Black guans feed alone, in pairs, or in small groups.

Behavior and reproduction: Outside the breeding season, black guans live alone. They pair off during the breeding season. Females lay two to three eggs and are responsible for incubation (sitting on the eggs).

Black guans and people: There is no known interaction between black guans and humans.

Conservation status: Listed as Near Threatened, not currently threatened, but could become so, by the IUCN due to habitat destruction. ■

Black guans live alone, except for the breeding season, during which they pair off. (Illustration by Brian Cressman. Reproduced by permission.)

Wattled curassow (*Crax globulosa*)

Resident

WATTLED CURASSOW
Crax globulosa

Physical characteristics: This curassow weighs about 5.5 pounds (2.5 kilograms) and measures 32.2 to 35 inches (82 to 89 centimeters) long. The male is black with a white belly and a red globe-like ornamentation above and below the bill. The female has reddish brown belly feathers and a red fleshy area between the beak and face.

Geographic range: The wattled curassow is found from Colombia and western Brazil to Bolivia.

Habitat: This bird prefers the tropical rainforest in the Amazon basin. It rarely leaves the trees except to breed..

Diet: Wattled currasows feed on vegetation and small invertebrates (animals without backbones).

Behavior and reproduction: The wattled curassow whistles softly for four to six seconds at a time. Nothing is known about this bird's reproductive habits in the wild. In captivity, the female lays two eggs.

Wattled currasows and people: These birds are hunted for food, often to the detriment of the bird population.

Conservation status: Listed as Vulnerable, facing a high risk of extinction, by the IUCN. Humans rarely see wattled currasows not only because of the patchy distribution of the species, but because it lives primarily in higher altitudes where there are fewer people. The main threat to the wattled curassow is overhunting. ∎

Wattled currasows live in tropical rainforests in the Amazon River basin. They spend most of their time in the trees, and come down just for breeding. *(Illustration by Brian Cressman. Reproduced by permission.)*

FOR MORE INFORMATION

Books:

Brooks, Daniel M., and Stuart D. Strahl. *Cracids: Status Survey and Conservation Action Plan for Cracids 2000–2004.* Gland, Switzerland: IUCN, 2001.

Kricher, John. *A Neotropical Companion,* 2nd ed. Princeton, NJ: Princeton University Press, 1999.

Web sites:

"About Rainforests: Tropical Rainforest Animals." Kid's Corner, Rainforest Action Network. http://kids.ran.org/kidscorner/rainforests/s06_animals.html (accessed on June 2, 2004).

"Plain Chachalaca." Animals Online. http://www.animals-online.be/birds/hokkos/plain_chachalaca.html (accessed on June 2, 2004).

"Plain Chachalaca." ENature. http://www.enature.com/fieldguide/showSpeciesRECNUM.asp?recnum=bd0640 (accessed on June 2, 2004).

family

CHAPTER

phylum

class

subclass

order

monotypic order

suborder

 family

PHYSICAL CHARACTERISTICS

These chicken-like birds weigh 1.5 to 3.5 pounds (0.7 to 1.6 kilograms) and measure 15.5 to 28.2 inches (40 to 72 centimeters) long. Their bills are short and their legs are strong. Some have small spurs on their legs, while others have a long, sharp spur on each leg. Still others have none at all. The tail is short and points downward. Some guineafowl have wattles that hang from the bottom of their bills. Males are generally larger than females.

Plumage (feathers) varies in color, from black with a brown wave design to black with white wavy lines or white spots. The head is usually bare for the most part, with small patches of feathers on some species. Skin color on the head varies.

GEOGRAPHIC RANGE

Guineafowl are native to Africa and Madagascar.

HABITAT

Though primarily found in rainforests, some guineafowl live in open-country habitats other than the desert, such as grasslands and plains with thickets and brush. Others prefer secondary forests, which are forests that grow after a major disturbance such as logging or fire occurs.

DIET

Some guineafowl eat small invertebrates (animals without backbones) and a variety of plants. Others also eat berries and other fruit in trees as well as bulbs dug up from underground. Flocks will crowd each other in order to eat, but they don't fight with their bills during feeding. Most species need to drink water to thrive.

BEHAVIOR AND REPRODUCTION

Guineafowl live in groups of up to twenty individuals, with the exception of the vulturine guineafowl, which live in flocks of twenty to thirty). These birds roost (rest) in trees during the night and call to one another. Calls vary according to species and are used not only to locate flock members but to warn of intruders. The crested guineafowl has been known to socialize with vervet monkeys. While the monkeys eat from the treetops, the guineafowl feed below on fruit and feces that fall from the trees. Monkeys help protect the birds by warning of danger from above while the birds warn monkeys of danger on the ground. Feeding usually occurs in the early dawn hours.

During breeding, pairs form monogamous (muh-NAH-guh-mus; one male to one female mate) bonds and breed throughout the year. Clutch sizes vary from as few as seven to as many as twenty-three eggs of various colors. Chicks are born with a soft down covering and can usually flutter-fly by the age of two to three weeks.

Guineafowl hide from their predators in trees and thickets. They also will choose to run rather than fly when in danger. Their primary enemies are hawks, owls, and other meat-eating animals. Average life span is unknown.

GUINEAFOWL AND PEOPLE

Guineafowl have been domesticated (tamed) and are a popular "pet" bird known for their ability to keep Lyme disease at bay by eating the ticks that carry it.

CONSERVATION STATUS

The white-breasted guineafowl is listed as Vulnerable, facing a high risk of extinction, due to hunting and habitat destruction. No other species are threatened.

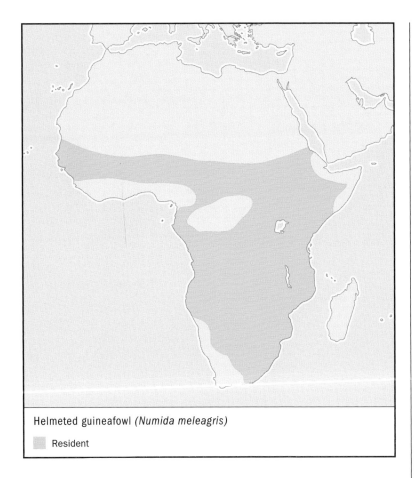

Helmeted guineafowl (*Numida meleagris*)

Resident

HELMETED GUINEAFOWL
Numida meleagris

Physical characteristics: The helmeted guineafowl measures 20 to 25 inches (50 to 63 centimeters) long and weighs 2.5 to 3.5 pounds (1.15 to 1.6 kilograms). Males and females are not noticeably different in size. Plumage is mostly blackish gray with white spots and lines. Head ornamentation varies.

Geographic range: This bird is found in Africa south of the Sahara; one population found north of the Sahara.

Habitat: This guineafowl lives on savannas (tropical and subtropical plant community with some trees and shrubs among grasses and herbs) and in woodlands.

Diet: Helmeted guineafowl find food by pecking into the ground. Their diet consists of 90 percent insects, but also includes berries, seeds, and reptiles. They will eat whatever plants are abundant.

Behavior and reproduction: This guinea is extremely vocal and social. Females make a call that sounds like "Buckwheat!" It lives in flocks of up to thirty-five but sometimes feeds in flocks of up to 1,000. Roosts from sunset to sunup. This species can run up to 20 miles (32.2 kilometers) daily.

Pairs mate for life. The female lays twelve to twenty-three eggs, which she will incubate (keep warm for hatching) for twenty-four to twenty-seven days. The nest is a shallow hole in the ground protected by vegetation. Both parents feed and care for chicks. This guinea's breeding schedule corresponds with rainfall patterns.

Helmeted guineafowl and people: Southern Africa's most popular land gamebird, bird hunted for sport. First domesticated by the ancient Egyptians.

Conservation status: Not threatened, but there has been a recent decline in parts of its range, most likely due to loss of habitat. ■

FOR MORE INFORMATION

Books:

Perrins, Christopher. *Firefly Encyclopedia of Birds.* Richmond Hill, Canada: Firefly Books, 2003.

Sibley, David Allen, Chris Elphik, and John B. Dunning, eds. *The Sibley Guide to Bird Life and Behavior.* New York: Knopf Publishing Group, 2001.

Periodicals:

Smith, Nancy. "Go Ahead, Get Guineas!" *Mother Earth News* (October 1, 2003).

Web sites:

"Guinea Fowl." Honolulu Zoo. http://www.honoluluzoo.org/guineafowl.htm (accessed on June 9, 2004).

"Helmeted Guineafowl." Kenya Birds. http://www.kenyabirds.org.uk/h_gfowl.htm (accessed on June 9, 2004).

family

phylum

class

subclass

order

monotypic order

suborder

△ **family**

PHYSICAL CHARACTERISTICS

Fowls and pheasants measure 6 to 48 inches (15 to 125 centimeters) and weigh 1.5 to 24.2 pounds (0.7 to 11 kilograms). All species have a heavy, round body. Legs and neck are short, head and tail are small (except in a few long-tailed species), and facial ornamentation varies. Coloration of skin and plumage (feathers) also varies, but males are almost always the more colorful sex.

GEOGRAPHIC RANGE

Fowls and pheasants are found throughout North America, Europe, Asia, Africa, and Australasia.

HABITAT

Habitats vary widely for these birds. Some live in mountain regions, others in subtropical forests and rainforests. Still others prefer the grasslands.

DIET

Fowls and pheasants eat vegetation, buds, pine needles, roots, bulbs, seeds, fruits, invertebrates (animals without backbones) such as ants and termites, and berries. Baby snowcocks eat legumes (peas, beans, and lentils).

BEHAVIOR AND REPRODUCTION

Regardless of species, the daily routine of these birds is basically the same. They roost (rest) in trees during the night and descend at dawn for some serious feeding time. After eating for a few hours, they head for cover. The end of the day brings about another feeding frenzy, after which birds call to one another as they prepare to roost for the night.

Because these birds are largely land dwellers, most species don't migrate (travel seasonally from one region to another) much. Species that live in the open grasslands are more social than their forest cousins, possibly to defend themselves against predators. Those social species can be found in flocks of twenty to one hundred individual birds.

Nests are shallow scrapes in the ground, lined with little vegetation and hidden by grasses or rocks. Clutch sizes can be as high as twenty eggs or as few as one. Incubation (keeping warm until hatching) is done by the female, and chicks leave the nest as soon as they hatch. First flight is taken in seven to ten days. Females are ready to mate at one year of age, but males tend to wait until their full adult colors have developed, usually in their second season.

Predators include foxes, ravens, badgers, coyotes, skunks, raccoons, hawks, owls, cats, dogs, and other medium-sized meat-eaters.

FOWLS AND PHEASANTS AND PEOPLE

Phasianidae is arguably the most important bird family to the human population because they are hunted in the wild and raised domestically for their meat and feathers.

CONSERVATION STATUS

Seventy-three species (41 percent of all species) are included on the 2003 IUCN Red List of Threatened Species.

TURKEY TRIVIA

- Ben Franklin wanted the wild turkey to be the national bird, not the bald eagle.
- Despite being so huge, turkeys roost in trees at night.
- Turkeys "dust off" their feathers by rolling in ant hills and decayed logs.
- Male turkeys have beards.
- Forty-nine states have spring wild turkey hunting seasons (Alaska doesn't have any wild turkeys).
- Wild turkeys can run up to 12 miles per hour (19.3 kilometers per hour) for short distances.
- They can fly at 55 miles per hour (88.5 kilometers per hour) for short distances.
- Turkeys see in color.
- Turkeys have heart attacks, as was proven when the U.S. Air Force was doing test runs to break the sound barrier. Wild turkeys nearby dropped dead.

Wild turkey (*Meleagris gallopavo*)

Resident

WILD TURKEY
Meleagris gallopavo

Physical characteristics: Weighs 6.6 to 24.2 pounds (3 to 11 kilograms) and measures 30 to 49 inches (76 to 125 centimeters), with males larger than females. Females are dull in color, but males have bare blue and pink heads, red wattles, and dark plumage with metallic green and bronze highlights. Legs are pink.

Geographic range: Found in Mexico and the United States from Vermont to Florida and west to Washington, Oregon, and California.

Habitat: Though the wild turkey prefers a mix of hardwood forest and grassland, it can survive tropical forest and scrub areas.

Diet: The wild turkey eats leaves, shoots, seeds, buds, fruits, berries, grains, insects, spiders, and sometimes small vertebrates (animals with backbones). It searches for food by picking at the ground.

Behavior and reproduction: Wild turkeys live on home ranges that sometimes overlap. Each range has a male hierarchy as well as a female hierarchy, with the strongest of each sex at the top. They're vocal birds and have a wide variety of calls.

These birds are polygamous (puh-LIH-guh-mus; one male has several female mates). Mating takes place in the spring, and courtship includes strutting and gobbling by the males. Clutch sizes range from eight to fifteen eggs, and females incubate them for twenty-seven to twenty-eight days. Chicks fly for the first time between six and ten days, and they remain with the mother until the springtime. Predators include bobcats, foxes, and great horned owls.

Wild turkeys are vocal—they have a variety of calls that they use. Males gobble during courtship, the time before mating when they attract mates. (John Shaw/Bruce Coleman Inc. Reproduced by permission.)

Wild turkeys and people: These are popular game birds. Towns across America have turkey-calling contests.

Conservation status: Overhunting reduced the population dramatically in the early twentieth century, but careful conservation and management have successfully restored numbers. ■

Willow ptarmigan *(Lagopus lagopus)*

Resident

WILLOW PTARMIGAN
Lagopus lagopus

Physical characteristics: Small grouse weighing 0.9 to 1.8 pounds (0.4 to 0.8 kilograms) and measuring 14 to 17 inches (36 to 43 centimeters). Males have a rust-colored head and upperparts and a bright red "comb" over the eyes that is larger in spring and summer. Females are a little smaller than males, and both sexes are completely white in winter except for a black tail. Feet are covered in feathers, which helps them walk on snow.

Geographic range: The willow ptarmigan (TAR-mih-gun) is found in northern Asia and Europe, from Alaska into Canada.

Habitat: This bird prefers the tundra (treeless plain of arctic and subarctic regions) and the forest's edge as well as moist areas like pond edges and arctic valleys. Likes willow trees.

Diet: This species eats flowers, buds, and insects in the summer, willow and birch buds and twigs in winter, and berries in the fall.

Behavior and reproduction: Willow ptarmigans often sleep in snowbanks in winter, which they get to by flying, rather than walking, so as not to leave tracks for predators to follow. They live in large groups of both sexes in winter. Males are territorial in the spring and vocalize to set boundaries.

The willow ptarmigan is monogamous (muh-NAH-guh-mus; having just one mate) and each pair has its own territory. Nesting starts anywhere from April to June, depending on the latitude. The female lays eight to eleven eggs and incubates them for twenty-two days. Males keep newly hatched chicks warm. Chicks fly at the age of ten to twelve days. Families stay together until the fall.

Willow ptarmigans are hunted by foxes, martens, lynx, and wolves.

Willow ptarmigans and people: Popular hunting birds in the United Kingdom, Scandinavia, Finland, and Russia. Hunted in the United States and managed so that populations are sustainable. The willow ptarmigan is the Alaska state bird, and is the focus of stories, toys, and art in arctic cultures.

Conservation status: This bird is not threatened. ■

Willow ptarmigans are reddish during the summer, and turn white for the winter, except for a black tail. The colors help them blend in with their environment during the different seasons. (© JLM Visuals. Reproduced by permission.)

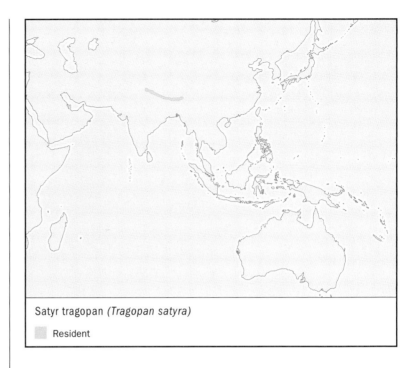

Satyr tragopan (*Tragopan satyra*)

Resident

SATYR TRAGOPAN
Tragopan satyra

Physical characteristics: Weighs 2.2 to 4.6 pounds (1 to 2.1 kilograms) and measures 22 to 28 inches (57 to 72 centimeters). Females are slightly smaller than males. Males have dark red underparts with blue facial skin. Brown plumage covers the lower back and rump.

Geographic range: The satyr tragopan lives in the central and eastern Himalayas.

Habitat: This bird lives in mountain forests at altitudes ranging between 5,900 and 14,100 feet (1,800 and 4,300 meters).

Diet: Eats bulbs, roots, and leaves as well as insects, sprouts, and seeds.

Behavior and reproduction: Unlike most pheasants, the satyr tragopan spends a great deal of time in the trees, and is most active during the day. Reported to be shy in the wild, these birds live in pairs or sometimes larger family groups. Males vocalize in what is

The male satyr tragopan has a brightly colored "bib" that he expands during the breeding season to attract a mate. (Illustration by Emily Damstra. Reproduced by permission.)

considered to be a wail at dawn from April to June, a sign that breeding season is about to begin.

These birds are monogamous. Nests are made of sticks as high as 20 feet (6 meters) in trees. Clutch size is two to three eggs, and they are incubated for twenty-eight days.

Satyr tragopans and people: Himalayan forest conservation campaigns use this bird as a central figure.

Conservation status: Not currently listed as threatened by the IUCN. The satyr tragopan is still hunted in Nepal. ■

FOR MORE INFORMATION

Books:

Green-Armitage, Stephen. *Extraordinary Pheasants.* New York: Harry N. Abrams, 2002.

Madge, Steve, et al. *Pheasants, Partridges, and Grouse: A Guide to the Pheasants, Partridges, Quails, Grouse, Guineafowl, Buttonquails, and Sandgrouse of the World.* Princeton, NJ: Princeton University Press, 2002.

Web sites:

"Gobble, Gobble, Gobble." Wisconsin Department of Natural Resources. http://www.dnr.state.wi.us/org/caer/ce/eek/critter/bird/wildturkey. htm (accessed on June 9, 2004).

"Ptarmigans." Hinterland's Who's Who. http://www.hww.ca/hww2.asp?pid=1&id=64&cid=7 (accessed June 9, 2004).

"Satyr-tragopan." Brno Zoo. http://www.zoobrno.cz/english/galery/gal_satyr_e.htm (accessed on June 9, 2004).

"Wild Turkey." Bowhunting. http://www.bowhunting.net/NAspecies/nasturk2.htm#top (accessed on June 9, 2004).

"Wild Turkey." The Waldron Village News. http://www.waldronmi.com/wildlife/wild_turkey.htm (accessed on June 9, 2004).

"Willow Ptarmigan." NatureWorks. http://www.nhptv.org/natureworks/willowptarmagin.htm (accessed on June 9, 2004).

NEW WORLD QUAILS
Odontophoridae

Class: Aves
Order: Galliformes
Family: Odontophoridae
Number of species: 32 species

family
CHAPTER

PHYSICAL CHARACTERISTICS

These small birds have plump bodies and short wings. They weigh 4 to 16 ounces (125 to 465 grams) and measure 7 to 15 inches (17 to 37 centimeters). Males are slightly larger and, in some species, have slightly more dramatic plumage (feather) coloring. Many species have red rings around the eyes, and some have crests on their heads ranging from tiny tufts of hair to long feathers. Quail bills have serrated (sharply notched) edges. Legs are strong to help in running, digging, and scratching.

GEOGRAPHIC RANGE

New World quails are native to North, Central, and South America, though they have been introduced elsewhere.

HABITAT

New World quails occupy a vast array of habitats. Bobwhites live in ranges from grassland to woodland edge while other species prefer the desert. Others are found in mountain, tropical, and subtropical forests. Quail often make their homes on agricultural land.

DIET

New World quails scratch for seeds from grasses, trees, and shrubs. Those who live on agricultural land eat leftover grain seeds as well as corn, wheat, peanuts, and black bean crops. Those birds in tropical forests dig for plant roots, and some species feed on bulbs. Chicks eat mostly invertebrates (animals without backbones).

phylum

class

subclass

order

monotypic order

suborder

▲ **family**

BEHAVIOR AND REPRODUCTION

Nearly every species of New World quail forms coveys (KUH-veez; small flocks). Though experts once thought coveys were family units, it is now believed that covey members are adult pairs as well as helpers from previous clutches (number of birds hatched at one time).

These birds are most active during the day and spend the majority of their time on the ground. Some forest species roost (rest) in trees. Although none of these quail are migratory (travel seasonally from region to region), those that live in mountain regions may move to different altitudes with the seasons.

New World quails call and whistle to each other, with the bobwhite having the most varied calling habits. Predators include birds of prey, weasels, and foxes. Skunks, raccoons, snakes, coyotes, and possums prey on quail eggs.

Reproduction of the quail has not been studied in depth. Though they were once believed to be monogamous (muh-NAH-guh-mus; have only one mate), evidence is proving that theory wrong. At least with the bobwhite, it seems the mating system is flexible, and the birds alternate between monogamy, polygyny (puh-LIH-juh-nee; one male to several females), polyandry (PAH-lee-an-dree; one female to several males), and promiscuity (prah-MISS-kyoo-ih-tee; indiscrimate mating where individuals mate with as many other individuals as they want).

Clutch size varies with the species, with tropical and forest birds having smaller clutches of three to six eggs. Nests are bowl-like and built on the ground. Sometimes vegetation is used to cover the nest for safety purposes. Though not well described for many species, incubation (warmth sufficient for hatching) takes sixteen to thirty days. Chicks are able to leave the nest within hours of hatching and begin to fly in less than two weeks. Twenty to fifty percent of all chicks die from predation.

NEW WORLD QUAILS AND PEOPLE

Most species are hunted for sport or food.

CONSERVATION STATUS

Conservation status varies. Those living in mild-weather regions and grasslands are common and not threatened. Forest species also seem to adapt well to human impact and are maintaining their populations. The status of the Latin American species is difficult to assess because research into their status has been minimal. The bearded woo-partridge, for example, was considered Critically Endangered, facing an extremely high risk of extinction, in 1995 but has been recategorized as Vulnerable, facing a high risk of extinction, due to the discovery of several small and separate populations.

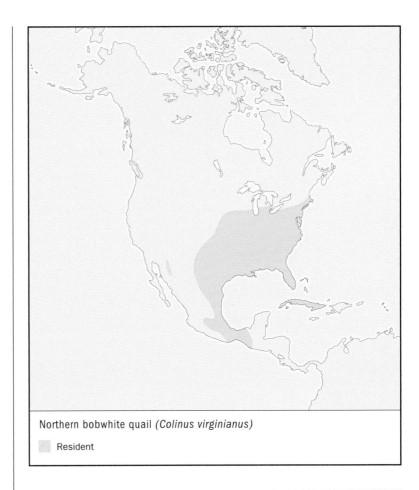

Northern bobwhite quail *(Colinus virginianus)*

☐ Resident

NORTHERN BOBWHITE QUAIL
Colinus virginianus

Physical characteristics: This is one of the smaller Galliformes, weighing just 4 to 8 ounces (129 to 233 grams) and measuring a mere 8 to 10 inches (20 to 25 centimeters). Females are smaller than males. Adult males have white throats and stripes on their faces; females have cream-colored faces and throats. Wings of the males also have distinct black markings which females lack.

Geographic range: Found from southern New England west through Ontario, Canada to southeastern Minnesota. Found also in eastern Florida and Wyoming, western Kansas, and Oklahoma southward throughout parts of Mexico. Introduced species are found on

Caribbean Islands, Washington, Oregon, Hawaii, British Columbia, New Zealand, Italy, Germany, and Cuba.

Habitat: Rather than pure grassland, the northern bobwhite prefers pine savannas (tropical or subtropical plant communities characterized by trees and shrubs among herbs and grass cover). It also lives in clearings of forested areas and in farmland. In the southeastern United States, this bird lives in pine savannas that are actually maintained and grown just for them. What is important is that habitats contain low-growing brush and vegetation, which is important for food as well as protection from predation.

Diet: They eat mostly seeds, but also fruits, invertebrates, and green leafy materials. About 85 percent of their diet is vegetation, while 15 percent is animal. They do, however, survive on whatever is abundant given the weather and climate conditions. Females eat more insects than do males because they need more protein to produce healthy eggs.

Behavior and reproduction: Behavior of this species is similar to that of the rest of the family. The bobwhite has more calls than other species: one for food location, two parental calls, eleven to warn of danger, four pertaining to group movement, and six sexual. After breeding season, coveys change members and either grow larger or smaller. During this time, some birds travel nearly 60 miles

(100 kilometers). Coveys are comprised of ten to thirty individual birds whose home ranges vary in size depending on quality of habitat.

Bobwhites are believed to have a flexible mating system. Unmated males make the famous "bob-white!" call that can be heard for great distances. Males engage in courtship displays that include puffing out their chests and exhibiting their feathered wings. The head lowers and is moved from side to side to ensure that the female notices his fine markings and coloring. Pairs begin forming in January, and nests are built in shallow bowls on the ground. Vegetation and dead grasses are used to cover and camouflage the nests. Clutch sizes average twelve to fourteen eggs, and they are laid at a rate of one per day. Incubation lasts twenty-three to twenty-four days and is performed by both parents, and if one mate dies, the other will take over.

Chicks leave the nests with the adults within hours of hatching and will fly within fourteen days. Both parents care for the young. Hatching success varies, but is rarely higher than 40 percent. Bobwhite females have been known to lay new clutches and renest as many as four times if necessary. Annual survival of chicks is typically less than 30 percent. Predators include hawks and other birds of prey, snakes, weasels, foxes, raccoons, coyotes, and possums. When threatened, coveys will disperse suddenly in all directions, which often startles intruders so that none of the birds are caught.

Northern bobwhites and people: This species is widely hunted and raised for food. Conservation of the bobwhite is a primary concern because this particular hunting industry turns a huge profit.

Conservation status: Though this population is widespread and common, there has been a steady decline in numbers throughout recent years, primarily in the eastern United States. Conservationists believe this to be the result of reforestation, loss of habitat, and intensification of agricultural practices. Some populations have decreased by as much as 90 percent. The masked bobwhite, a subspecies, is considered Endangered in the United States and is the focus of management and conservation programs in many areas.   ∎

FOR MORE INFORMATION

Books:

Guthery, Fred S. *On Bobwhites*. College Station, TX: Texas A & M University Press, 2001.

Perrins, Christopher. *Firefly Encyclopedia of Birds*. Richmond Hill, Canada: Firefly Books, 2003.

Sibley, David Allen, Chris Elphik, and John B. Dunning, eds. *The Sibley Guide to Bird Life and Behavior.* New York: Knopf Publishing Group, 2001.

Web sites:

Chumchal, M. *"Colinus virginianus."* Animal Diversity Web. http://animaldiversity.ummz.umich.edu/site/accounts/information/Colinus_virginianus.html (accessed on June 10, 2004).

"Northern Bobwhite." ENature. http://www.enature.com/fieldguide/showSpeciesSH.asp?curGroupID=1&shapeID=964&curPageNum=20&recnum=BD0167 (accessed on June 10, 2004).

"Wildlife in Connecticut: Bobwhite." Connecticut Department of Environmental Protection. http://dep.state.ct.us/burnatr/wildlife/factshts/bwhite.htm (accessed on June 10, 2004).

monotypic order
CHAPTER

phylum

class

subclass

order

● **monotypic order**

suborder

family

PHYSICAL CHARACTERISTICS

The hoatzin (watt-ZEEN) is a medium-size bird measuring 24.5 to 27.5 inches (62 to 70 centimeters) and weighing 1.4 to 1.9 pounds (650 to 850 grams). Its face is bright blue and without feathers. It has thick eyelashes above bright red eyes. The bill is short and gray. The head is topped by a fan-shaped crest of long feathers that resembles a punk haircut. Neck is long and buff colored, as is the tip of the tail. Underparts are chestnut colored, upperparts are bronze and olive.

Very young hoatzins have two claws on each wing. These claws allow them to climb back up to the nests if they have been forced by predators to suddenly vacate the nest to seek shelter.

GEOGRAPHIC RANGE

Hoatzins are found in South America.

HABITAT

Hoatzins live in vegetation bordering water such as swamps, lakes, lagoons, streams, and rivers. Large populations can be found along the Amazon and Orinoco River systems. Hoatzins never live in altitudes above 1,640 feet (500 meters).

DIET

These herbivores (plant eaters) feed on little else than tree leaves. They like young leaves and shoots as well as flowers and buds. They eat throughout the day, with especially long feeding periods at sunrise and sunset. Hoatzins enjoy leaves from more than fifty plant species.

Hoatzins have stomachs similar to those of cows in that they ferment (break down for easier digestion) their food. In other birds with multi-chambered stomachs, fermentation usually occurs in the hindgut (end of the digestive system). But hoatzins have particularly large crops (pouches that resemble stomachs where food is held) containing enzymes that attack food and break it down. The remaining fatty acids are absorbed through the crop wall and used as energy. These bacteria become a source of protein, carbon, and other nutrients. The crop also breaks down toxins present in a number of the plant leaves eaten by hoatzins.

BEHAVIOR AND REPRODUCTION

Hoatzins live in units that include a monogamous (muh-NAH-guh-mus; one male to one female mate) pair and up to

Hoatzin *(Opisthocomus hoazin)*

Resident

five nonbreeding helpers that are still around from the previous year's nesting efforts. This species is territorial, and all members of the social unit defend the territory by vocalizing, chasing trespassers, and fighting off intruders in the air.

During nonbreeding season, hoatzins leave their territory and form temporary flocks of up to 100 birds. The exception to this is when breeding territories result in unusually high reproductive success. These particular territories are defended year round. Hoatzins are noisy and make a variety of calls, including shrieks, hisses, grunts, and growls. Adults are able climbers but not so good at flying. Even so, they can fly up to 380 yards (350 meters) before needing a rest. As much as 80 percent of their time is spent roosting (resting) in trees.

Throughout the breeding season, hoatzins establish territories along waterways. They are colonial (grouped together) nesters, sometimes building as many as twenty-eight nests in

one tree. Nests are actually unlined platforms of twigs on branches 6.5 to 16.5 feet (2 to 5 meters) high. As a rule, nests are built directly above water.

Females can lay one to six eggs, with two eggs being the most common. Eggs are laid after thirty to thirty-one days of incubation (keeping warm for hatching), which is performed by all members of the unit. When more than one egg is laid, incubation begins with the laying of the second egg. Eggs are laid one-and-a-half days to two days apart. Hoatzin chicks are nearly naked at birth, but are covered with down by twenty days. The crop of a newborn is sterile (free of bacteria). Bacteria forms within the first two weeks as adults feed the chicks.

Newborns are cared for continuously by all members of the social unit for the first three weeks of life. If left undisturbed by predators, nestlings will venture from home at two to three weeks of age. If predators approach, young will drop into the water for protection. They swim underwater and use those wing claws to make their way through aquatic vegetation. Once out, however, they will not return to the nest. Young hoatzins are able to fly around fifty-five to sixty-five days. By day 100, they shed their wing claws.

Newborn hoatzins are protected by adults for their first three weeks. They stay in the nest for those three weeks, unless a predator disturbs them. If they're disturbed, they drop into water (they can swim underwater) to escape, and they don't return to the nest again. (© François Gohier/Photo Researchers, Inc. Reproduced by permission.)

Hoatzins breed during the rainy season. Monkeys are the greatest enemies of this bird. In captivity, the hoatzin can live up to thirty years.

HOATZINS AND PEOPLE

The local name given to this bird in Guyana is "stinking pheasant" because the strong odor of the hoatzin is similar to the smell of cow manure. The odor comes from the fatty acids in the crop. The odor prevents the hoatzin from being hunted for its meat, but hoatzin eggs are consumed by some local populations. The meat is used for bait, and feathers are used to make fans. Locals in the Amazon make a soup from the hoatzin to help relieve asthma.

CONSERVATION STATUS

Hoatzins are not threatened. However, conservationists are concerned over the loss of habitat due to industrial pollution and the conversion of land for agricultural use.

FOR MORE INFORMATION

Periodicals:

Brown, Nancy Marie. "What's a Hoatzin?" *Research/Penn State* 27, no. 2 (June 1996). Online at http://www.rps.psu.edu/jun96/hoatzin.html (accessed on June 11, 2004).

Zahler, Peter. "Crazy Like a Hoatzin." *International Wildlife Magazine* (July/August 1997). Online at http://www.nwf.org/internationalwildlife/hoatzin.html (accessed on June 11, 2004).

Web sites:

"Ecotourism is Stressing Animals to Death." Cooltech. http://cooltech.iafrica.com/science/308057.htm (accessed on June 14, 2004).

Grosset, Arthur. "Hoatzin." http://www.arthurgrosset.com/sabirds/hoatzin.html (accessed on June 11, 2004).

Payne, Robert B. "Recent Families, Birds of the World." University of Michigan, Museum of Zoology. http://www.ummz.lsa.umich.edu/birds/Bird_Families_of_the_World.html (accessed on June 11, 2004).

Rainforest Conservation Fund. http://www.rainforestconservation.org (accessed on July 13, 2004).

CRANES, RAILS, AND RELATIVES

Gruiformes

Class: Aves

Order: Gruiformes

Number of families: 11 families

PHYSICAL CHARACTERISTICS

Gruiforms, birds of the order Gruiformes, vary greatly in size. The smallest species, the American black rail, is only 4.7 inches (12 centimeters) high, whereas the Sarus crane, at 5.8 feet (176 centimeters), is the tallest flying bird. Weights in the group also vary tremendously. The American black rail weighs in at only 8 ounces (20 grams), while kori bustards and great bustards have been known to reach weights of more than 40 pounds (18 kilograms), making them among the heaviest flying birds.

Most species of Gruiformes are primarily black, gray, or brown in color, and many species have streaked markings. However, there are some exceptions, including the sunbittern and some rails and cranes. Rails are sometimes greenish or purplish in color. Cranes have black or white feathers, often with distinctive patches of red skin on the head and neck. The sunbittern is a particularly colorful gruiform, with large black and red "eyespots" on its wings—these spots resemble the eyes of a much larger animal and help scare off potential predators.

Bill shape also varies among the gruiforms. Cranes have narrow, medium-length bills that they use to search for invertebrates in soft mud. Trumpeters, which search for food on rainforest floors, have short bills resembling those of chickens. The limpkin has an extremely unusual bill, which bends to the right at its tip. The limpkin's bill is adapted to feeding on apple snails, its primary food.

GEOGRAPHIC RANGE

Gruiformes as a group are found on all the continents except Antarctica, although most gruiform families have a more limited distribution. The kagu is found exclusively on the island of New Caledonia, off the coast of Australia in the Pacific Ocean. Buttonquails are found in portions of Europe, Africa, Asia, and Australia. Mesites are found in Madagascar. Trumpeters are found in the Amazon basin in the northern part of South America. Seriemas are found in central and eastern South America. The sunbittern is found in Central America and South America. The limpkin is found in Central America and South America, as well as parts of Florida and Mexico. Bustards inhabit portions of Africa, southern Europe, south and Southeast Asia, New Guinea, and Australia. Sungrebes are found in Central America, South America, Africa, and south and Southeast Asia. Cranes are found on all continents except Antarctica and South America, although Asia and Africa are particularly rich in species. Rails, gallinules, and coots are also found worldwide.

HABITAT

The Gruiformes as a group occupy diverse habitats. Sungrebes are aquatic, and generally live in marshes, lakes, and streams. Sunbitterns live in rainforests and swamps. Limpkins live in marshes or swamps. Cranes live in freshwater and marine wetlands. Rails live near swamps, marshes, and lakes. Trumpeters live in tropical rainforests. Kagus inhabit forestlands. Mesites live in a wide variety of habitats, including rainforest, deciduous forest, and dry scrubland. Seriemas occupy grassland habitats. Bustards live in brush and scrub habitats as well as open grassland.

DIET

As a group, the Gruiformes eat a wide variety of plant and animal matter. Sungrebes eat small insects and other aquatic animals, as well as seeds and leaves. Sunbitterns eat insects, small fish, and crustaceans. The limpkin's primary prey is apple snails, but they also eat insects and seeds. Cranes have a diverse diet, eating seeds and other vegetable and animal matter. Rails also eat a diverse diet of animal and plant matter. Trumpeters eat fruits, berries, seeds, and other plant matter. The kagu eats insects, worms, small frogs, and mollusks.

Mesites eat fruit, seeds, and insects. Seriemas eat insects, small reptiles, mammals, and some plant matter. Bustards eat seeds, insects, and other small animals.

BEHAVIOR AND REPRODUCTION

Sunbitterns, limpkins, sungrebes, kagus, and rails tend to be solitary, living alone. Some species are territorial, that is, individuals defend a territory against other members of the same species. Other Gruiformes, however, such as seriemas and mesites, are frequently found in male-female pairs. Finally, some species of bustards, trumpeters, and cranes occur in flocks and can be highly social.

Gruiforms vary from highly able fliers to flightless species. Many cranes, for example, carry out long migrations between their breeding grounds and wintering grounds. Other Gruiformes are reluctant to fly, and flightlessness has in fact evolved many times in the group, particularly among the rails.

Reproductive behavior also varies within the Gruiformes. Cranes are monogamous (muh-NAH-guh-mus)—that is, each male mates with a single female and both parents are involved in building the nest, incubating the eggs, and caring for the chicks once they hatch. In order to strengthen the bond between the pair, cranes engage in elaborate "dances" in which they leap, extend their wings, and bob their heads. Mated crane pairs also sing, or trumpet, together. Crane pairs typically stay together all year round, rather than just during the breeding season, and some mate for life. At the other extreme in reproductive behavior, bustard males mate with as many females as they can. Females build nests, incubate eggs, and raise young on their own, without assistance from the male.

CRANES, RAILS, RELATIVES, AND PEOPLE

Gruiforms have been important to humans for a variety of reasons. Many species currently or traditionally have been hunted for food. Mesites are hunted for food in their habitats in Madagascar. Many species of buttonquails are also hunted for food, although this became illegal in many countries in 2001. Several species of buttonquails are now farmed as domestic livestock. In addition, some buttonquails play a role in the religious ceremonies of the Australian aborigines, and one species, the barred buttonquail, is used as a fighting bird. Cranes are symbols of good luck in many parts of the world, appearing in some

FLIGHTLESSNESS

Flightlessness has evolved in many bird groups, but is particularly common among gruiforms. Rails that occupy island habitats appear to be especially likely to lose the ability to fly, in part because there are no natural predators on many island habitats. Flightless species have the advantage of no longer having to maintain the large avian flight muscles.

cases as national symbols or on coins. The whooping crane is frequently used as a symbol of conservation because of the extensive effort devoted to saving it from extinction. Limpkins were once hunted for meat. Today their calls represent a significant part of the culture of some aboriginal peoples. Kagus have always been hunted for meat, their feathers have been used for decoration by indigenous cultures, and kagu songs were imitated in war dances. In addition, kagus were once kept as pets by Europeans. They now frequently appear as a symbol of New Caledonia. Rails have been hunted for food and sport throughout the world, and rail eggs are often eaten as well. Some species have also served as fighting birds, incubators of chicken eggs, or as pets. Sunbitterns have been kept as pets. Trumpeters have also been kept as pets or used to guard chicken coops from snakes. They have also been hunted for food. Seriemas are sometimes used to guard chicken coops, again because they kill large numbers of snakes. Bustards make an important contribution to human agriculture by eating large numbers of insect pests. Some bustards are also hunted, particularly in North Africa and Cambodia, in some cases with the use of trained falcons. Finally, many species of Gruiformes attract birdwatchers and ecotourists throughout the world.

CONSERVATION STATUS

In 2000 the World Conservation Union (IUCN) reported that, of the ninety-three species of Gruiformes examined, twenty-two species were already Extinct. In addition, one species, the Guam rail, exists only in captivity and is considered Extinct in the Wild. Four rail species are listed as Critically Endangered, facing an extremely high risk of extinction, while an additional eleven are listed as Endangered, facing a very high risk of extinction. Most endangered rails are threatened by introduced species of non-native mammals such as rats, cats, dogs, mongooses, pigs, snakes, and humans, as well as habitat destruction. The kagu is listed as Endangered, primarily because of the introduction of dogs onto the island of New Caledonia. Habitat destruction due to logging also plays a role. Three species of bustards are listed as Endangered: the great Indian bustard,

Bengal florican bustard, and lesser florican bustard. Bustard populations have been harmed by human hunting, habitat loss to agricultural and grazing land, and cattle and crows, which harm nests. Six additional bustard species are listed as Vulnerable. The cranes as a group are highly threatened, with one Critically Endangered species (the Siberian crane), two Endangered Species (the whooping crane and the Japanese crane), and six Vulnerable species, facing a high risk of extinction (Sarus crane, wattled crane, hooded crane, black-necked crane, blue crane, and white-naped crane).

FOR MORE INFORMATION

Books:

del Hoyo, J., A. Elliott, and J. Sargatal, eds. *Handbook of the Birds of the World*. Vol. 3, *Hoatzin to Auks*. Barcelona: Lynx Edicions, 1996.

Matthiessen, Peter. *The Birds of Heaven: Travels with Cranes*. New York: North Point Press, 2001.

Perrins, Christopher, ed. *Firefly Encyclopedia of Birds*. Buffalo, NY: Firefly Books, 2003.

Taylor, P. B., B. Taylor, and B. van Perlo. *Rails: A Guide to the Rails, Crakes, Gallinules, and Coots of the World*. New Haven, CT: Yale University Press, 1998.

Web sites:

"Birds of the World." Bird Families of the World, Cornell University. http://www.es.cornell.edu/winkler/botw/families.htm (accessed on March 25, 2004).

The Internet Bird Collection. http://www.hbw.com/ibc/phtml/families.phtml (accessed on March 25, 2004).

"Order Gruiformes (Cranes, Coots, and Rails)." Animal Diversity Web. http://animaldiversity.ummz.umich.edu/site/accounts/classification/gruiformes.html (accessed on March 25, 2004).

MESITES AND ROATELOS
Mesitornithidae

Class: Aves
Order: Gruiformes
Family: Mesitornithidae
Number of species: 3 species

PHYSICAL CHARACTERISTICS

The three species of mesites and roatelos are approximately 12 inches (30 centimeters) in length. Mesites and roatelos are characterized by short, rounded wings, long, wide tails, and sturdy legs. Their bills curve downward, making it easier for them to forage, or hunt for food, on the forest floor.

GEOGRAPHIC RANGE

Mesites and roatelos are found exclusively on the large island of Madagascar, off the eastern coast of Africa. The brown mesite (also known as the brown roatelo) occupies forested areas in the eastern part of the island. The white-breasted mesite (or white-breasted roatelo) is found in forests in the western and northern parts of the island. The subdesert mesite occupies a small area between the coast and hills in the southwestern potion of the island.

HABITAT

Mesites and roatelos are found in distinct habitats on Madagascar. The brown mesite inhabits humid rainforests. The white-breasted mesite inhabits deciduous (leafy) forests. The subdesert mesite occupies open, spiny thicket habitats.

DIET

The brown mesite and white-breasted mesite eat insects and other invertebrates, seeds, and small fruits from the leaf litter on the forest floor. The brown mesite and white-breasted mesite have bills that are adapted to lifting leaves without disturbing prey that may be hiding underneath. The subdesert mesite has a longer, more extensively curved bill that allows it to find invertebrates on the ground. Like the other mesite species, however, the subdesert mesite will sometimes feed in the leaf litter.

BEHAVIOR AND REPRODUCTION

Mesites are diurnal, that is, they are active during the day. Mesites spend most of their time on the ground. Although they are able to fly, they generally do so only when threatened. Mesites are social species, that is, individuals congregate with other members of the same species. In the brown mesite and the white-breasted mesite, birds can often be found in groups of three. This is frequently a male and female pair with their most recent young. The subdesert mesite is generally found in larger groups, of anywhere from six to ten individuals. Both white-breasted mesites and subdesert mesites are territorial, that is, they will defend their territory from other individuals of the same species.

Mesite songs can be fairly complex. In both brown mesites and white-breasted mesites, the male and female of a pair will sometimes sing together.

The brown mesite and white-breasted mesite are monogamous (muh-NAH-guh-mus), with each male bird mating with only a single female. The subdesert mesite is polygamous (puh-LIH-guh-mus), with each male mating with multiple females. Mesites build nests of sticks in low bushes. Usually the female lays one to three eggs at a time sometime during the rainy season from October to April. It is not known how long the eggs take to hatch. Mesite chicks are precocial (pree-KOH-shul), meaning that they are fairly well developed when they hatch. For example, they have feathers and are able to move around. Mesite chicks tend to stay with their parents for quite some time. In the case of the white-breasted mesite, chicks may remain with the parents for up to a year.

MESITES, ROATELOS, AND PEOPLE

All three species of mesites are well known to local humans and are hunted for food. However, in certain portions of

PRECOCIAL CHICKS

Some species of birds, including mesites, many wading birds, and species like chickens and ducks, have precocial chicks. Precocial chicks are developmentally advanced by the time they hatch. They are born with down feathers and are also able to move around and fend for themselves to some degree. Precocial chicks are contrasted with the altricial (al-TRISH-uhl) young of other bird species, including most songbirds. Altricial chicks are featherless and helpless when they hatch.

Madagascar, the brown mesite is not hunted because it is protected by a taboo, one so strictly observed that it is forbidden to mention the bird's name.

CONSERVATION STATUS

The three species of mesites are considered Vulnerable, facing a high risk of extinction, by the World Conservation Union (IUCN). This is due primarily to habitat loss, especially the destruction of forest habitats for agricultural use, logging, or the production of charcoal. Species associated with humans, such as dogs and rats, also negatively affect some populations.

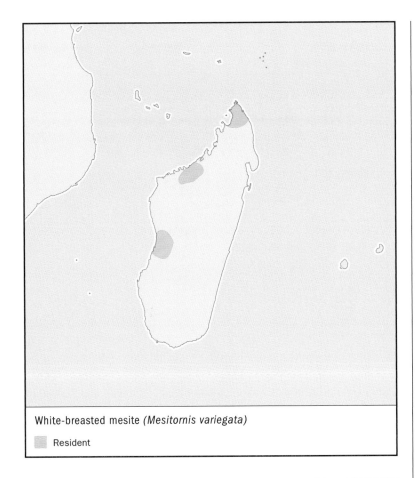

White-breasted mesite *(Mesitornis variegata)*

☐ Resident

WHITE-BREASTED MESITE
Mesitornis variegata

Physical characteristics: The white-breasted mesite, also known as the white-breasted roatelo, is about 12 inches (30 centimeters) in length. Males weigh approximately 3.5 to 4 ounces (99 to 113 grams) while females are somewhat lighter. White-breasted mesites have reddish brown backs. The throat, eyebrows, and breast are a pale cream color. The neck area is sometimes gray. White-breasted mesites also have black crescent-shaped markings scattered on the sides of the breast and upper belly.

Geographic range: White-breasted mesites are found only on the large island of Madagascar.

White-breasted mesites are usually found on the ground, in groups of three—a male, female, and their chick. (Illustration by Amanda Humphrey. Reproduced by permission.)

Habitat: Where it occurs in western and northern Madagascar, the white-breasted mesite occupies dry, deciduous forests with sandy soils. The eastern portion of its range is characterized by more humid rainforest.

Diet: White-breasted mesites primarily eat invertebrates and plant seeds. It searches for these food items in the leaf litter and low bushes.

Behavior and reproduction: The white-breasted mesite is a secretive species that is most commonly found on the ground. The species does not migrate, but remains near its breeding grounds all year. White-breasted mesites are often found in groups of approximately three individuals, frequently a male and female pair and their most recent young. White-breasted mesites are territorial, meaning individuals defend their territory from others of the same species.

The white-breasted mesite is believed to be a monogamous species. White-breasted mesites build nests 3 to 9 feet (0.9 to 2.7 meters) off the ground. Their nests are generally simple platforms of sticks. The female lays one to three eggs during the breeding period between October and April. White-breasted mesite chicks are precocial, and young remain with their parents for up to a year.

White-breasted mesites and people: White-breasted mesites are sometimes hunted for meat. Because of their small size, however, hunting occurs only irregularly.

Conservation status: The white-breasted mesite is considered Vulnerable by the World Conservation Union (IUCN). Its status is primarily due to a loss of forest habitat to logging and agricultural use. ■

FOR MORE INFORMATION

Books:

Langrand, O. *Guide to the Birds of Madagascar.* New Haven, CT: Yale University Press, 1990.

Morris, P., and F. Hawkins. *Birds of Madagascar: A Photographic Guide.* East Sussex, U.K.: Pica Press, 1998.

Perrins, Christopher, ed. *Firefly Encyclopedia of Birds.* Buffalo, NY: Firefly Books, 2003.

Web sites:

"Family Mesitornithidae (Mesites)." Animal Diversity Web. http://animaldiversity.ummz.umich.edu/site/accounts/classification/Mesitornithidae.html#Mesitornithidae (accessed on March 29, 2004).

"Mesites, Roatelos." Bird Families of the World, Cornell University. http://www.es.cornell.edu/winkler/botw/mesoenatidae.html (accessed on March 29, 2004).

"Mesitornithidae (Mesites)." The Internet Bird Collection. http://www.hbw.com/ibc/phtml/familia.phtml?idFamilia=41 (accessed on March 29, 2004).

BUTTONQUAILS
Turnicidae

Class: Aves

Order: Gruiformes

Family: Turnicidae

Number of species: 17 species

PHYSICAL CHARACTERISTICS

Buttonquails are small birds that are short and thick in build. They have small heads, short necks, short legs, and almost no tail. Unlike most birds, buttonquails have only three toes; the hind toe is absent. Buttonquails have short bills that vary between slender (in species that eat mostly insects) and stout (in species that eat mostly seeds). Buttonquails vary in size from 4 to 9 inches (10 to 23 centimeters) in length and 0.7 to 5.3 ounces (20 to 150 grams) in weight.

Buttonquails tend to be brownish, grayish, or dullish red in color. Their backs are often mottled, that is, covered with spots or splotches, or irregularly striped, helping them to blend in against their habitat. The breast, however, is often red or black and white. Buttonquail females are larger and more brightly colored than the males.

GEOGRAPHIC RANGE

Buttonquails are found in southern Europe, Africa, south and Southeast Asia, Australia, and the Solomon Islands.

HABITAT

Buttonquails live in grassland, brush, and some forest habitats. Although they can fly, they live almost exclusively on the ground, often in grasses or amid crops or weeds.

DIET

Buttonquails are primarily seed-eaters. However, they may also eat plant material, insects, and snails. In order to help grind up their food, buttonquails also swallow a small amount of sand. They find their food on the ground, in litter (the layer of leaves and other material covering the ground), and in low vegetation. In many species, individuals have a distinctive foraging (food hunting) behavior of standing on one foot while scratching the ground with the other, turning in a circle.

BEHAVIOR AND REPRODUCTION

The buttonquail breeding period is generally spring and summer, although tropical species breed all year round. In dry areas, buttonquails tend to breed only during the rainy season.

Buttonquails have an elaborate courtship routine. Females puff up, call with booming notes, stamp their feet, and scratch at the ground. In some species the wings are also spread. Then the male and female rock together, huddle together, dust bathe together, and preen each other's feathers. The female also offers the male a bit of food. In the "scrape ceremony," the female and male act out the motions of building a nest. The actual nest site tends to be in grass, frequently next to a tree. Either the male or female will throw bits of vegetation to the site, while the other partner builds it into a bowl shape, sometimes with a roof. The female does most of the work of nest-building.

Some species of buttonquails are monogamous (muh-NAH-guh-mus), meaning a female mates with a single male. In other species, however, there is a mating system known as sequential polyandry (PAH-lee-an-dree), in which a female courts a male, lays a set of eggs, and then leaves the male to incubate the eggs and raise the chicks while she courts another male. This mating system is fairly unusual among birds.

The number of eggs per clutch varies by species, but is generally between two and seven. Eggs hatch after twelve or thirteen days. Chicks are precocial, meaning they hatch at a developmentally advanced stage, covered with feathers and able to move. They follow the father, who feeds them termites and seeds.

SEQUENTIAL POLYANDRY, AN UNUSUAL BREEDING SYSTEM

Sequential polyandry, found in some buttonquails, is a mating system in which females mate with multiple males over the course of one breeding season. It is rare among birds. Both monogamy, in which a single female mates with a single male, and polygamy, in which a single male mates with multiple females, are more common. Sequential polyandry accounts for buttonquail females being more brightly colored than males, since it is the females who have to convince the males to mate with them.

BUTTONQUAILS AND PEOPLE

Many buttonquail species were once hunted for food, although this is no longer legal in most western countries. Some species, including the common buttonquail and some Australian species, are bred for food. Buttonquails have also been important in some of the rituals of the Australian Aborigines.

CONSERVATION STATUS

Of the seventeen species of buttonquails, two are listed as Endangered, facing a very high risk of extinction, or dying out, in the wild, by the World Conservation Union (IUCN), the black-breasted buttonquail and buff-breasted buttonquail. There are approximately 500 black-breasted buttonquails in existence, and 5,000 buff-breasted buttonquails. Four additional species are listed as Vulnerable, facing a high risk of extinction in the wild: the Worcester's buttonquail, Sumba buttonquail, Australian chestnut-backed buttonquail, and plains-wanderer. The spotted buttonquail is listed as Near Threatened, not in immediate danger of extinction. Most species of buttonquails are declining due to habitat destruction for agriculture.

Small buttonquail (*Turnix sylvatica*)

▮ Resident

SMALL BUTTONQUAIL
Turnix sylvatica

Physical characteristics: The small buttonquail is 5.9 to 6.3 inches (15 to 16 centimeters) in length and 1.4 to 1.9 ounces (39 to 54 grams) in weight. It is chestnut in color with a reddish breast and shoulders and a slender blue-gray bill. The female is somewhat larger and more brightly colored than the male.

Geographic range: The small buttonquail is found in southwestern Spain and northern Africa, in sub-Saharan Africa, in southern and Southeast Asia, in the Philippines, and in Indonesia.

Habitat: The small buttonquail inhabits grassland, farmland, and scrub areas.

Diet: The small buttonquail tends to be primarily insectivorous, that is, eating insects and other invertebrates. It also eats seeds.

Behavior and reproduction: The small buttonquail is primarily diurnal, or active during the day, although it is also partly nocturnal,

or active at night. The small buttonquail breeds year-round during the rainy season in all parts of its range except Europe, where breeding occurs only in spring and summer. Females are sequentially polyandrous (the female mates with one male, leaves him a clutch of eggs to tend, and then mates with another male, repeating the process throughout the breeding season). Usually four eggs are laid at a time by the female and hatch after twelve to fifteen days. Chicks can fly by seven to eleven days old and become independent at eighteen to twenty days.

Small buttonquails and people: The small buttonquail is hunted for food throughout its range except in Europe, where it used to be hunted. The small buttonquail is also raised for food.

Conservation status: The small buttonquail is not threatened, although its European populations have been declining, and it is now only rarely found there. ■

Painted buttonquail (*Turnix varia*)

■ Resident   ■ Breeding

PAINTED BUTTONQUAIL
Turnix varia

Physical characteristics: The painted buttonquail is a large species 6.7 to 9.1 inches (17 to 23 centimeters) in length and 1.9 to 4.7 ounces (53 to 134 grams) in weight, with the female significantly larger than the male. The painted buttonquail is generally red in color with a gray breast and red eyes.

Geographic range: The painted buttonquail is found in eastern, southeastern, and southwestern Australia, on islands off the coast of southwestern Australia, and in New Caledonia.

Painted buttonquails scratch on the ground to find seeds, insects and other invertebrates, and green plant shoots to eat. (Illustration by John Megahan. Reproduced by permission.)

Habitat: The painted buttonquail is found in diverse habitats from grassland to grassy or open forest, and in grassy clearings within dense forests.

Diet: The painted buttonquail eats seeds, insects and other invertebrates, and green plant shoots. Food is found by scratching on the ground.

Behavior and reproduction: Reproduction occurs in late winter to autumn in southern and eastern habitats, and all year round in tropical regions. Female painted buttonquails are sequentially polyandrous. Generally three or four eggs are laid at a time; these hatch after thirteen to fourteen days. The male feeds the chick for seven to ten days. At ten days chicks can fly, and by twenty-three days they are the same size as adults.

Painted buttonquails and people: Painted buttonquails are bred for food.

Conservation status: Painted buttonquails are not threatened. ■

FOR MORE INFORMATION

Books:

del Hoyo, J., A. Elliott, and J. Sargatal, eds. *Handbook of the Birds of the World.* Vol. 3, *Hoatzin to Auks.* Barcelona: Lynx Edicions, 1996.

Johnsgard, P. A. *Bustards, Hemipodes, and Sandgrouse.* New York: Oxford University Press, 1991.

Perrins, Christopher, ed. *Firefly Encyclopedia of Birds.* Buffalo, NY: Firefly Books, 2003.

Web sites:

"Button-quails, quail-plover." Bird Families of the World, Cornell University. http://www.es.cornell.edu/winkler/botw/turnicidae.html (accessed on April 1, 2004).

"Turnicidae (Buttonquails)." The Internet Bird Collection. http://www.hbw.com/ibc/phtml/familia.phtml?idFamilia=42 (accessed on April 1, 2004).

CRANES

Gruidae

Class: Aves

Order: Gruiformes

Family: Gruidae

Number of species: 15 species

family

C H A P T E R

PHYSICAL CHARACTERISTICS

Cranes are tall birds with large wings, long legs, and long, graceful necks. Most species are black and white or gray in color. Often there are bright patches of bare red skin that are shown in threat and dance displays.

GEOGRAPHIC RANGE

Cranes are found on all continents except for Antarctica and South America.

HABITAT

Most cranes live in wetland habitats. Breeding generally occurs during the summer in freshwater wetlands. Some cranes spend the winter in coastal saltwater marshes. A small number of crane species live primarily in grassland habitats.

DIET

Grassland crane species primarily eat insects and seeds and have relatively short bills. Cranes with medium length bills eat insects and seeds from grain fields, in addition to a wide variety of plant and animal matter from wetland areas. Cranes with long bills use one of two feeding strategies. "Diggers" dig holes in wet mud to look for tubers, root vegetables like potatoes. The holes are sometimes 1.6 feet (0.5 meters) deep. "Catchers" look for live animals on the ground.

BEHAVIOR AND REPRODUCTION

Many cranes are migratory, meaning they travel from breeding (summer) areas to wintering areas each year. Some species

phylum

class

subclass

order

monotypic order

suborder

▲ **family**

travel thousands of miles during their migration. In many species, breeding occurs during the wet season. During the non-breeding dry season, cranes may gather in large flocks, or groups of birds. This flocking behavior is believed to allow individuals to find mates.

Cranes have loud, trumpeting calls. These calls are used to communicate a wide variety of messages to individuals of the same species. A contact call is given between individuals that know each other, such as a crane and its mate or a parent and its chicks. Other calls used by cranes signal aggression, an intention to fly, pain, or a warning of danger. The unison call is made simultaneously by a male and female pair and is intended to warn other cranes away from their territory.

In addition to calls, cranes also have elaborate displays, characteristic motions used in communicating with others of the same species. These displays can involve raising feathers around the head, unique motions of the bills, and exposing and/or changing the size of red skin patches on the heads that are normally covered by gray feathers. Displays are often used to threaten other cranes or to express submission to a more dominant crane. Conflicts that are not resolved by a threat display proceed to a ritualized fight that will not seriously injure either crane. The ritualized fight involves leaping up with the legs folded, and then using the legs to push at the other bird's breast. Conflicts between cranes are particularly common during flocking, when large numbers of birds are gathered together.

Cranes are monogamous (muh-NAH-guh-mus), a single male breeds with a single female. Cranes often mate for life. They are also territorial; a pair of cranes will defend their area of land, or territory, against other cranes of the same species. Nests are built within the wetland or grassland habitat. Females generally lay two eggs at a time and both parents incubate, sit on and warm the eggs for chick development. Eggs hatch after about a month, and offspring are able to fly after about two or three months. However, young cranes usually remain with the parents until about nine months of age. If both eggs hatch, one of the crane offspring is generally dominant to the other, that is, it has higher rank and receives more food from the parents. In the majority of cases, only the dominant offspring survives from each nest.

CRANES AND PEOPLE

Cranes symbolize good luck in many places throughout the world. The whooping crane is used as a symbol of conservation in the North American because it nearly became extinct before intense efforts by the United States and Canada helped populations increase in number.

CONSERVATION STATUS

Of the fifteen crane species, one is listed as Critically Endangered, facing an extremely high risk of extinction, or dying out, in the wild. Two are listed as Endangered, facing a very high risk of extinction in the wild, and six are listed as Vulnerable, facing a high risk of extinction in the wild, by the World Conservation Union (IUCN).

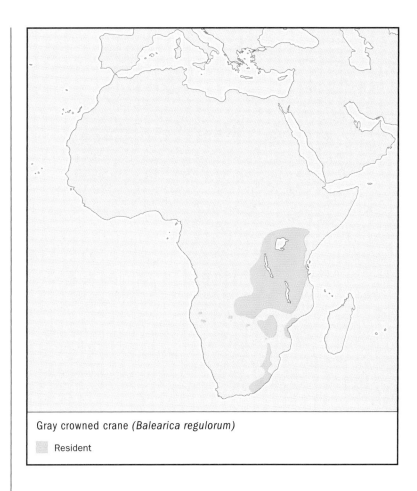

Gray crowned crane (*Balearica regulorum*)

Resident

GRAY CROWNED CRANE
Balearica regulorum

Physical characteristics: Gray crowned cranes are named for their characteristic crown of gold feathers. They have a pale gray neck and red throat wattles. The rest of their bodies are black, white, and gold in color. Gray crowned cranes are 39 to 43.3 inches tall (100 to 110 centimeters) and weigh anywhere from 6.6 to 8.8 pounds (3 to 4 kilograms). They have a wingspan of between 71 and 79 inches (180 to 200 centimeters).

Geographic range: Gray crowned cranes are found in portions of eastern Africa.

Habitat: Gray crowned cranes occupy both wetland and grassland habitats.

Diet: Gray crowned cranes eat a wide variety of food items, but focus primarily on seeds and insects.

Behavior and reproduction: Gray crowned cranes are frequently found in trees. Individuals nest in wetland or grassland areas. Instead of building their own nests, gray crowned cranes frequently use ground nests that have been abandoned by other large bird species. In general two eggs are laid. Both the male and female incubate, or sit on, the eggs. These hatch after about a month and the young are able to fly after two or three months. However, they may remain with their parents for as long as nine months.

Gray crowned cranes and people: The gray crowned crane is the national bird of Uganda. It is also regarded as an important symbol in other parts of its range, including Kenya, Namibia, South Africa, and Zambia.

Conservation status: Although gray crowned cranes are not currently considered threatened, many populations have declined due to the drainage of its wetland habitats. ∎

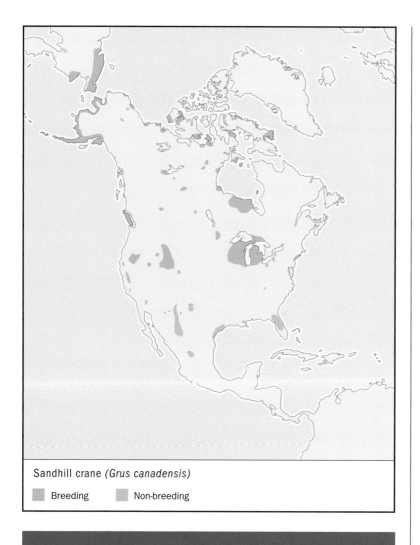

Sandhill crane (*Grus canadensis*)

◼ Breeding   ◼ Non-breeding

SANDHILL CRANE
Grus canadensis

Physical characteristics: Sandhill cranes have gray bodies, necks, and heads, and a bare patch of red skin on the top of the head. Individuals can achieve heights up to 47.2 inches (120 centimeters) and generally weigh between 7.3 and 12 pounds (3.3 to 5.4 kilograms). Sandhill cranes have a wingspan of between 63 and 82.6 inches (160 to 210 centimeters).

Geographic range: Sandhill cranes are found across North America from Quebec to British Columbia, and north to Alaska and

Sandhill cranes live in groups in wetland areas. (© C.K. Lorenz/ Photo Researchers, Inc. Reproduced by permission.)

eastern Siberia. Some populations also occur in portions of the United States and Cuba.

Habitat: Sandhill cranes inhabit wetland areas. In the winter it is sometimes found in grassland areas or agricultural fields as well.

Diet: Sandhill cranes have a varied diet including grains, berries, insects, and rodents.

Behavior and reproduction: Some sandhill cranes are migratory while others remain in their breeding areas all year round. During the breeding season, female sandhill cranes generally lay two eggs. Both parents incubate and feed chicks after they hatch. Chicks hatch after twenty-nine to thirty-two days and are able to fly by fifty to ninety days after hatching.

Sandhill cranes and people: Sandhill cranes are an important part of Native American culture. Elements of the cranes' mating dance appear in some Native American dances.

Conservation status: Of the six subspecies, population groups within a species, of sandhill crane, four are not considered threatened, but two subspecies, the Mississippi and the Cuban, are listed as endangered by the U.S. Fish and Wildlife Service. ∎

Red-crowned crane (Grus japonensis)

Resident　　Breeding　　Nonbreeding

RED-CROWNED CRANE
Grus japonensis

Physical characteristics: Red-crowned cranes, or Japanese cranes, have white bodies and bare red skin on the top of the head. This crane is about 59 inches (150 centimeters) in height, 15.4 to 22 pounds (7 to 10 kilograms) in weight, and has a wingspan of between 86.6 and 98.4 inches (220 to 250 centimeters).

Geographic range: The red-crowned cranes are found in parts of China, Russia, Korea, and Japan.

Habitat: The red-crowned crane is a rather aquatic species among cranes. It inhabits both freshwater and saltwater wetlands and marshes as well as some rivers.

Diet: Red-crowned cranes eat a wide variety of items, including insects, fish, rodents, and plants.

Behavior and reproduction: Red-crowned cranes are well-known for their elaborate courtship dances. Generally, the female lays two eggs during the breeding season. Both parents incubate and feed the chicks after they hatch. Eggs hatch after twenty-nine to thirty-four days. The young are able to fly after approximately ninety-five days.

Red-crowned cranes and people: Red-crowned cranes are considered sacred in many parts of its range in East Asia. They are associated with happy marriages, love, long life, and good luck. Red-crowned cranes have frequently appeared in East Asian poetry and art.

Conservation status: Red-crowned cranes are listed as Endangered by the IUCN. ■

FOR MORE INFORMATION

Books:

del Hoyo, J., A. Elliott, and J. Sargatal, eds. *Handbook of the Birds of the World.* Vol. 3, *Hoatzin to Auks.* Barcelona: Lynx Edicions, 1996.

Matthiessen, Peter. *The Birds of Heaven: Travels with Cranes.* New York: North Point Press, 2001.

Perrins, Christopher, ed. *Firefly Encyclopedia of Birds.* Buffalo, NY: Firefly Books, 2003.

Web sites:

"Cranes." Bird Families of the World, Cornell University. http://www.es.cornell.edu/winkler/botw/gruidae.html (accessed on April 5, 2004).

"Family Gruidae (Cranes)." Animal Diversity Web. http://animaldiversity.ummz.umich.edu/site/accounts/classification/Gruidae.html#Gruidae (accessed on April 24, 2004).

"Gruidae (Cranes)." The Internet Bird Collection. http://www.hbw.com/ibc/phtml/familia.phtml?idFamilia=43 (accessed on April 24, 2004).

International Crane Foundation. http://www.savingcranes.org/ (accessed on July 12, 2004).

LIMPKIN

Aramidae

Class: Aves

Order: Gruiformes

Family: Aramidae

One species: Limpkin (*Aramus guarauna*)

family

phylum

class

subclass

order

monotypic order

suborder

▲ **family**

PHYSICAL CHARACTERISTICS

Limpkins are medium-sized gruiform (member of the order Gruiformes) species that have long legs with spread toes, a long, downward-curving bills, and rounded wings and tails. Limpkin bills curve slightly to the right at the tip, a feature that helps them extract its primary prey item, the apple snail, from its shell. There is also an unusual, small gap in the bill which appears to help limpkins carry and manipulate apple snails. Finally, the tip of the upper bill is sharpened and used to cut snails from their shells. Limpkins are primarily dark brown in color although there are white spots on the neck, breast, and the outside surface of the wings. Limpkins are about 26 inches (66 centimeters) in length and can weigh up to 2.4 pounds (1.1 kilograms). They have a wingspan of approximately 40 inches (102 centimeters). Male and female limpkins are generally similar in size and coloration.

GEOGRAPHIC RANGE

Limpkins are found only in the Western Hemisphere, from Florida through most of Mexico, the West Indies, and Central America. They are also in South America east of the Andes mountain range and as far south as central Argentina.

HABITAT

Limpkins generally occur in wetland habitats, including shallow-water areas near ponds, lakes, and slow-moving rivers.

DIET

Limpkins are highly specialized feeders, meaning they focus on very few food items and have special adaptations which help them deal with their diet. The limpkin's primary prey is the apple snail, a large freshwater mollusk which occurs throughout the range of limpkins. Limpkins search for apple snails in the muddy bottoms of shallow bodies of water, trying to find them either visually, or by prodding the mud with their long bills. They search for food in the open, as the cranes do. Once a limpkin finds a snail, it carries it to shallow water to cut it from its shell and eat it. Although adult limpkins never swallow snails whole, young limpkins do. Young limpkins are brought small snails by their parents and swallow them entire. Although apple snails form the bulk of their diet, limpkins may also eat mussels, insects, crayfish, small reptiles or frogs, and the seeds of some plants.

BEHAVIOR AND REPRODUCTION

Most limpkins are solitary, they live alone. In some cases, limpkins may be found in pairs, usually male and female breeding partners, or in small groups. Limpkins are good swimmers and slow but strong fliers. The name limpkin comes from the slightly awkward walk of the species. However, limpkins are in fact strong runners. At night, limpkins tend to roost either in shrubs or in the tops of dead trees. Most limpkins are not migratory, spending the entire year in one location. However, some South American limpkin populations move between a wet season habitat and a dry season habitat.

The limpkin is the only species in the family Aramidae and has no close relatives. However, within the Gruiformes, similarities to both cranes and rails have long been noted. In particular, the general physical appearance and hunting behavior of limpkins resemble that of cranes, but other aspects of behavior, including a more secretive nature, resemble that of rails and their relatives.

The call of a limpkin is extremely distinctive. It is a loud, wild-sounding scream or wail that is frequently described as a

SNAIL EATERS

The apple snail is important to the limpkin's diet. Limpkins have several physical adaptations that help it deal with this prey. Since the apple snail's shell curves to the right, limpkins adapted a bill that also curves to the right, making it possible to insert the bill into the snail shell. The tip of the upper beak is sharpened to allow limpkins to cut the snail out of the shell. Finally, limpkins have a small gap in the bill which helps them carry and handle snails.

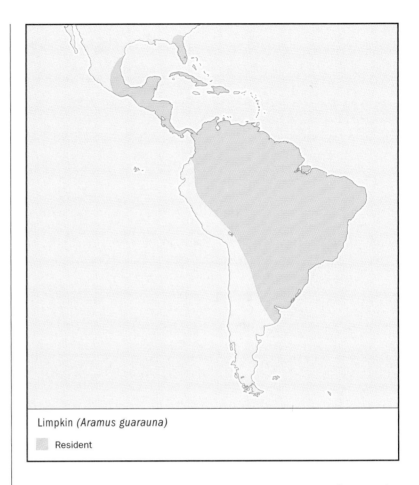

Limpkin (*Aramus guarauna*)

Resident

"kree-ow kree-ow" sound. The call is given most often in the early morning or at night, as well as on cloudy days. This loud, distinctive cry accounts for some of the nicknames the limpkin has picked up in parts of its range. These include wailing bird, crying bird, and crazy widow. Limpkins also make a quieter clicking noise.

Limpkins build their nests near water. Most often, nests are built either on the ground, hidden in dense vegetation, or up in a tree. In some cases, nests may be 20 feet (6 meters) off the ground or even higher. Nests are built from reeds and grass and lined with softer plant material. In general, four to eight eggs are laid at a time by the female. The eggs range from white to pale brown in color, and may or may not be lightly spotted. Both male and female limpkins participate in all phases of reproductive activity, including nest-building, incubating the eggs, and feeding and caring for the young once they hatch. Limpkin young are

precocial (pree-KOH-shul), meaning they are fairly developmentally advanced when they hatch, being covered with down (rather than featherless) and able to move. Limpkin chicks are able to leave the nest about one day after hatching, and follow one of the parents around until they become independent.

LIMPKINS AND PEOPLE

Limpkins were once hunted for meat, but hunting is no longer common. Now they are important in the tourist industry, attracting birdwatchers in many parts of their range. Limpkins are also important to many local cultures, and are particularly well-known for their powerful wailing cries.

CONSERVATION STATUS

Limpkins are not considered threatened at the present, although they have been designated a "species of special concern" in Florida, the only place in the United States where they occur. However, at the beginning of the twentieth century, limpkins were almost hunted to extinction in the U.S. for their meat. Protection since then has allowed many populations to recover. At present, many limpkin populations are again declining due to damage and destruction of the wetland habitats they require.

FOR MORE INFORMATION

Books:

del Hoyo, J., A. Elliott, and J. Sargatal, eds. *Handbook of the Birds of the World.* Vol. 3, *Hoatzin to Auks.* Barcelona: Lynx Edicions, 1996.

Eckert, A. W. *The Wading Birds of North America (North of Mexico).* New York: Weathervane, 1981.

Perrins, Christopher, ed. *Firefly Encyclopedia of Birds.* Buffalo, NY: Firefly Books, 2003

Web sites:

"Aramidae (Limpkin)." The Internet Bird Collection. http://www.hbw.com/ibc/phtml/familia.phtml?idFamilia=44 (accessed on April 25, 2004)

"Family Aramidae (Limpkin)." Animal Diversity Web. http://animaldiversity.ummz.umich.edu/site/accounts/classification/Aramidae.html#Aramidae (accessed on April 25, 2004)

"Limpkin." Bird Families of the World, Cornell University. http://www.es.cornell.edu/winkler/botw/aramidae.html (accessed on April 25, 2004)

family

CHAPTER

PHYSICAL CHARACTERISTICS

An adult kagu is about the size of a domestic chicken, with a head-and-body length of about 22 inches (55 centimeters), and a weight of 1.5 to 2.5 pounds (24 to 40 ounces). A kagu resembles a small crane with a coat of very light gray feathers, a short tail, and reddish-orange beak, eyes, legs, and feet. A crest of feathers crowns the kagu's head. When not raised for display, the crest lays down towards the back of the head.

The beak is long and slender. The edges of the nostrils are raised into ringlike flanges, making the nostrils look like short tubes. The flanges keep soil from getting into the nostrils as the bird forages in leaf litter and soil for food. The scientific name of the bird, *Rhynochetos jubatus*, from the Latin, translates as "tube-nosed, head-crested."

The wings are light gray with black, dark, lighter gray, and brownish spots arranged in rows or bars along the outer sides of the open wings. The dark spots are covered when the wings are closed. Although the wings are large and look flightworthy, kagus cannot fly, since they have lost most of the mass of their once-powerful flight muscles. The open wingspan can reach 32 inches (80 centimeters).

Although most bird species that spend time on forest floors are camouflaged (KAM-uh-flajd), the adult kagu doesn't follow that rule, being light-colored and very obvious in a dark forest. It may be that kagus never needed camouflage before people brought dogs, cats, and other predators, animals that hunt them for food, to Grand Terre. Or, the light coats may have evolved

phylum

class

subclass

order

monotypic order

suborder

▲ **family**

for a territorial role, enabling kagus to easily spot other kagus, during mating times or for defending territories. Kagus are always ready to chase off other kagus that intrude on individual territories. Kagu chicks are brown and light brown colored, which does help them to blend into the colors of the forest floor.

GEOGRAPHIC RANGE

Grand Terre, the largest island of the New Caledonia island group, in the southwestern Pacific Ocean. Presently, the entire population of kagus is broken up into isolated groups in various forest areas on Grande Terre. The largest population lives in Blue River Territorial Park, near the southern tip of the island. The park is patrolled and dogs are kept at bay. The second largest population is legally protected in Nodela Special Reserve, but the reserve has no guards or controls on dogs. There is a third small, partly fenced park for semi-captive breeding of kagus, near Noumea, the capital of New Caledonia.

HABITAT

Kagus live in most kinds of forest on Grand Terre, although they seem to prefer tropical rainforests, from sea level up to 4,200 feet (1,400 meters). They will forage in shrubby or bushy areas and in low-growing dry forest, during the seasonal rains, when their sort of animal food becomes abundant. Kagus do not inhabit grasslands.

DIET

The kagu eats ground-living snails, insects, spiders, earthworms and lizards, which it forages for on forest floors. The most popular foods among kagus are earthworms and snails. Since the abundance and types of food creatures change with the seasons, and to keep from eating too much food in one area, kagus forage in different parts of their territories at different times of the year.

A kagu begins a feeding run in the early morning by simply standing still. With its excellent vision and hearing, the kagu is listening for the faintest noises and looking for the slightest movements that may betray the presence of food animals. After picking out certain spots that harbor food creatures, the kagu walks slowly and starts probing the layer of dead leaves on the forest floor at those spots.

When a kagu spots a prey animal, the bird approaches it carefully, then lunges at it and snags it in a quick motion. Kagus hunt not only in the layer of fallen leaves on the forest floor for spiders, beetles and snails, but pokes its beak into the soil to expose worms and larvae. It deals with snails by smashing the shell on a rock to get at the snail's body.

BEHAVIOR AND REPRODUCTION

Kagus are active during the day and sleep at night. A kagu sleeps out the night at one of several sleeping stations in its territory, rotating its overnights at the various stations over time. Most of the time, a kagu climbs a tree to perch for the night on a branch 5 to 12 feet (1.5 to 3.7 meters) above the ground. In high, mountainous territory with cool nights, a kagu prefers nighttime shelter in enclosures formed by rocks or in tree roots.

Kagu male and female pairs mate for life. Mated pairs stake out large forest floor territories, through which the birds wander daily, searching for food. Outside of the breeding season, the male and female stay in their territory but temporarily split up and wander alone.

Kagus make dog-like barkings, hissings, and rattling noises. Every morning, shortly before dawn, kagu pairs sound off with barkings, the male and female taking turns. A threatened kagu warns with a hissing sound.

The breeding season runs from June to December, the most breeding taking place in July. During those months, unmated kagus display for mates by raising the head crest into a magnificent plume and spreading their wings out as wide as possible and tipping them up and forwards so that the outer wing surface faces forward, showing the dark markings. Both sexes display. A female will answer a displaying male with a similar display. Then they perform a courtship dance, circling each other. The dance may end with mating, or the pair may lose interest and stop the dance, each bird going its separate way. Kagus of both sexes also display to defend territory.

A mated kagu pair builds a ground nest of dry leaves, eight to twelve inches in diameter, in which the female lays a single egg weighing two and a half ounces. The male and female take turns sitting on the egg for twenty-four hour stretches, one parent usually replacing the other at midday. The incubation period lasts an average of thirty-five days. The young chick has a coat of brown, downy feathers. Both parents care for the chick, and feed it with insects, spiders, and earthworms.

At only three days of age, the chick will begin walking away from the nest. At first, it doesn't wander very far, but by the end of its first week, it has hiked up to 450 feet (137 meters) from the nest. After about six weeks, the young bird begins roosting overnight on low-placed tree branches, as its parents do.

Should a chick die before it matures, the female will soon lay a second fertilized egg as a replacement. The parents stop feeding the young when they are three and a half to four months old, forcing the young to strike out on their own for feeding. Nevertheless, the young may stay with their parents indefinitely, even when mature, and assist the parents in caring for younger brothers and sisters. This is a very rare behavior among birds, but routine in some mammal species like the small, New World monkeys known as marmosets and tamarins.

Kagus in captivity can live up to thirty years. Those in the wild generally live fifteen years.

KAGUS AND PEOPLE

Like many island bird species, the ancestors of the kagus lost their powers of flight and became ground-living animals. With no predators to fear and plenty of food on the forest floors, kagus had no need of flight and the enormous amounts of energy that flying requires. So the ancestral kagus gave up flying, keeping large wings for display purposes. They were safe on the ground and must have been quite numerous, even into the hundreds of thousands, until the arrival of humans on the islands.

Kagu species, living and extinct, were hunted for food and for ornamental feathers by the native people of New Caledonia, and this most likely pushed the extinct kagu out of existence. European settlers captured kagus for keeping as pets or for use of their feathers as decorative hat plumes, which were popular in the early 1900s.

Other major, human-made threats to kagus include loss of habitat and fragmentation of populations. Forests are being cleared for agriculture and especially for mining, since Grand Terre has some of the world's most abundant supplies of nickel ore. Once free to roam all over the island, the original population of kagus is split up and isolated into small pockets throughout Grand Terre. This is not good for breeding, since there is no free exchange of genes across a large population, which is the healthy state of things in a wild species.

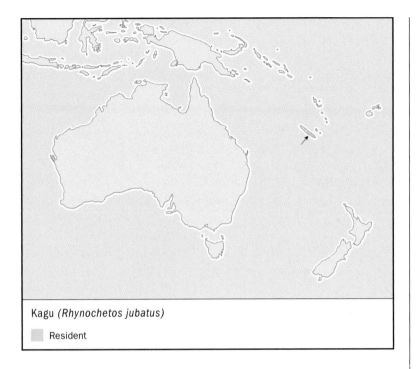

Kagu *(Rhynochetos jubatus)*

Resident

CONSERVATION STATUS

The kagu is listed as Endangered, facing a very high risk of extinction, under the U.S. Endangered Species Act and on the Red List of the World Conservation Union (IUCN).

The rehabilitation of the kagu is one of conservation's better success stories, although the birds are still listed as Endangered. That kagus still survive and have even increased their numbers since 1980 is largely due to the efforts of one man, Yves Letocart, a New Caledonian citizen, who has been working with kagus and their environment since 1980. Much of what we know about kagu behavior comes from Letocart's field work.

Today, as a result of Letocart's field work, captive breeding and release of young birds, and predator control, an estimated 300 kagus inhabit Blue River Park, which has been classified and proclaimed a territorial park by the governments of New Caledonia and France. The kagu is now the official emblem of New Caledonia.

Most important for the survival of the kagu is protecting it in areas made inaccessible to invasive animals by trapping, shooting, and the use of fencing; increasing the kagu's numbers

through captive breeding; and creating forest "corridors" that allow isolated populations to intermingle.

FOR MORE INFORMATION

Books:

Balouet, Jean Christophe, and Storrs L. Olson. *Fossil Birds from Late Quaternary Deposits in New Caledonia.* Smithsonian Contributions to Zoology Series. Washington, DC: Smithsonian Institution Press, 1989.

Logan, Leanne, and Geert Cole. *Lonely Planet New Caledonia,* 4th ed. Oakland, CA: Lonely Planet Publishing, 2001.

Wheatley, Nigel. *Where to Watch Birds in Australasia and Oceania.* Princeton, NJ: Princeton University Press, 1998.

Periodicals:

Clements, James F. "Kagu!" *WildBird* (October 1998): 46–49.

Cook, S. "The Kagu." *Birding World* 11 (1998): 440–441.

Salas, Michel, and Yves Letocart. "Spatial Organisation and Breeding of Kagu, *Rhynochetos jubatus,* in Rivière Bleue Park, New Caledonia." *Emu* 97, no. 2 (1997).

Storer, Robert W. "Avian Exotica: The Kagu." *Birder's World* (August 1993): 64–65.

family

phylum

class

subclass

order

monotypic order

suborder

family

PHYSICAL CHARACTERISTICS

Rails are usually colored to blend into their environments. Browns, blacks, grays, and blue-gray shades are particularly common in the group. One group of gallinules, however, tends to have brighter colors such as purples, blues, and greens. Rails often have spotted, barred, or streaked patterns. The underside of the tail is frequently differently colored from the rest of the animal. Generally, females and males are similarly colored, with a few exceptions such as the flufftails and some of the New Guinea forest rails.

Rails vary in size from 4.7 inches (12 centimeters) and 0.7 ounces (20 grams) for the black rail, the smallest member of the family, to 24.8 inches (63 centimeters) and 9.2 pounds (4.2 kilograms) for the takahe, a large, flightless rail species. In most rails, males and females are similar in size. However, males are much larger than females in a few species.

The bodies of rails are often laterally compressed, flattened on the sides, a trait which allows them to move easily through dense vegetation. Many species have long necks. The wings of most rails are short, broad, and rounded. An unusually large number of rails are flightless, unable to fly. These are generally species found on islands that have no natural predators, animals that hunt them for food. Even some rails that are able to fly sometimes escape danger by running away instead of flying. Some rails also have a sharp claw on the wing that helps individuals, particularly young rails, climb. Rails generally have short tails. Bills vary a lot among the rails, and may be long or short, straight or downwardly curved, and thick or thin. Bill shape depends primarily on diet. Rails have strong legs and feet. In some species the legs are rather long.

GEOGRAPHIC RANGE

Rails are found worldwide except in the Arctic and Antarctica, and in very dry deserts. They are particularly common on oceanic islands. In part, this is because of their weak flying abilities, which causes them to be easily thrown off course.

HABITAT

Rails live in a wide variety of habitats, including wetland, grassland, scrub, and forest. Wetlands have the largest number of rail species, although many species are also found in rainforests. Both freshwater and coastal saltwater wetlands are used by rails. Coots are the most aquatic rails and live in freshwater habitats such as lakes and ponds. Rails that live in forested areas can inhabit diverse forest types with almost any type of ground cover, either clear, with leaf litter, with mud, or covered with dense vegetation.

DIET

Rails are omnivorous, meaning they eat both plant and animal matter. The more aquatic rails, such as coots and gallinules, tend to eat primarily plant matter, whereas wetland and terrestrial rails tend to have a diet consisting mostly of animal matter. Animal matter eaten by rails can include insects, spiders, worms, mollusks, crustaceans, and sometimes small fish, frogs, tadpoles, lizards, snakes, or turtle hatchlings. Rails will also eat the eggs or chicks of other birds. Some rails even eat carrion, dead animal matter. Plant matter eaten by rails can include fruits, seeds, stems, leaves, tubers, roots, and, in some species, cultivated crops. Most rails are generalists, that is, they eat a wide variety of foods, concentrating on whatever food is most abundant at the time. However, there are a few specialists. The chestnut rail and rufous-necked wood-rail, for example, inhabit mangrove forests and eat mostly crabs.

BEHAVIOR AND REPRODUCTION

Most rails are solitary, meaning they live alone, although some can be found in pairs, usually male and female breeding partners, or in small groups. Some species, however, including most coots and some gallinules and moorhens, sometimes

FLIGHTLESSNESS IN RAILS

Flightlessness is unusually common in rails, with 24 of the 134 rail species having lost the ability to fly. All flightless species occur on islands, particularly those where there are no natural predators. Flightlessness may be common in rails because they are weak fliers with a tendency to avoid predators by running rather than flying away. Flightless species usually have smaller wings and stronger legs than species that fly.

gather in large flocks during the nonbreeding season. The black-tailed native-hen, an Australian rail, can form flocks of as many as 20,000 individuals.

Breeding strategies vary across the rails. Many species are monogamous (muh-NAH-guh-mus), with one male mating with one female. Some species are polygamous (puh-LIH-guh-mus), meaning single males mate with multiple females. Other species are polyandrous (pah-lee-AN-drus), where a single female mates with multiple males. In some species, older siblings help their parents feed and care for younger siblings. Intraspecific brood parasitism is also common among the rails. This describes a strategy in which a female lays eggs in the nests of other females so that other individuals will feed and raise her young.

Many rails are territorial and will defend their territories from other individuals of the same species. To prevent serious injuries from actual fighting, territorial disputes between rails are decided using displays, characteristic postures or behaviors that help determine which individual would win in an actual fight.

Rails are shy, and generally stay in areas of dense vegetation. At night, they roost on the ground, hidden in dense vegetation, or, less commonly, in trees.

RAILS AND PEOPLE

Many species of rails have been and continue to be hunted either for food or for sport. Rail eggs are also sometimes collected and eaten. Some species of rails are considered pests because they damage crops. The purple swamphen appears in Egyptian wall paintings and was also considered sacred by the Greeks and Romans.

CONSERVATION STATUS

Of the 134 rail species in existence, thirty-three are considered threatened by the World Conservation Union (IUCN). Of these, four are Critically Endangered, facing an extremely high risk of extinction in the wild. Twelve are Endangered, facing a very high risk of extinction, and sixteen are Vulnerable, facing a high risk of extinction. One, the Guam rail, is Extinct in the Wild. No fewer than twenty rail species have become extinct since 1600, the majority of them flightless species on islands. Threatened species have suffered population declines due primarily to habitat destruction. Some island species have also been severely affected by the introduction of animals such as cats, dogs, pigs, mongooses, and snakes.

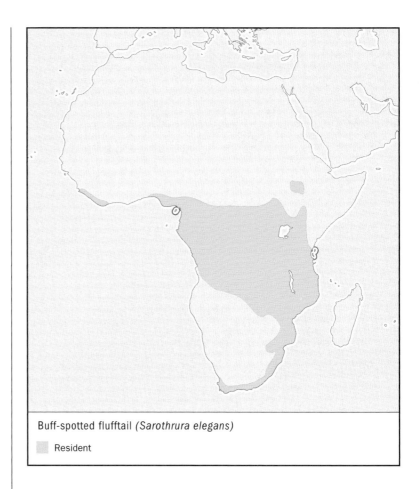

Buff-spotted flufftail (*Sarothrura elegans*)

Resident

BUFF-SPOTTED FLUFFTAIL
Sarothrura elegans

Physical characteristics: The male buff-spotted flufftail has an orange-chestnut head and neck and spotted body. The female is golden brown in color with a spotted back and barred belly. Buff-spotted flufftails range from 6 to 6.7 inches (15 to 17 centimeters) in length and 1.4 to 2 ounces (39 to 61 grams) in weight.

Geographic range: Buff-spotted flufftails are found in Africa from Guinea east to the Democratic Republic of the Congo and Uganda and south to northern Angola, as well as from southern Sudan and Ethiopia to South Africa.

During the breeding season, male buff-spotted flufftails sing at night to attract females, sometimes for as long as twelve hours continuously. (Illustration by Wendy Baker. Reproduced by permission.)

Habitat: Buff-spotted flufftails are found in forests, but may also inhabit abandoned agricultural lands.

Diet: Buff-spotted flufftails eat primarily invertebrates, animals without backbones, such as insects and spiders. They forage on the ground.

Behavior and reproduction: Buff-spotted flufftails are highly territorial during the breeding season. Individuals are active during the day, although males sing to attract females at night, sometimes for as long as twelve hours continuously. Some buff-spotted flufftail populations migrate while others do not.

Buff-spotted flufftails are monogamous, and nests are built on the ground. Nests are dome-shaped and built from dead leaves or grass. The female lays three to five eggs at a time. Eggs hatch after fifteen to sixteen days, and the young are independent after nineteen to twenty-one days.

Buff-spotted flufftails and people: The buff-spotted flufftail's loud, hooting calls, which can last all night, are the source of local legends.

Conservation status: Buff-spotted flufftails are not threatened. ■

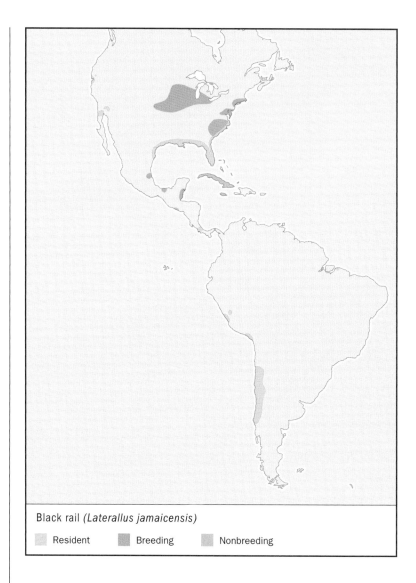

Black rail *(Laterallus jamaicensis)*

Resident   Breeding   Nonbreeding

BLACK RAIL
Laterallus jamaicensis

Physical characteristics: Black rails are small, dark birds with a slightly reddish brown upper back and spots or bars on the lower parts of their backs and bellies. Females are slightly paler in color. Black rails range from 4.7 to 6 inches in length (12 to 15 centimeters) and from 0.7 to 1.6 ounces (20.5 to 46 grams) in weight.

Geographic range: Black rails have a scattered distribution, with populations in California, the eastern United States, portions of Central America, and western South America.

Habitat: Black rails lives in marshes and moist grassland areas.

Diet: Black rails eat primarily small invertebrates such as insects and spiders. They will sometimes eat larger animals such as fish or tadpoles, as well as plant seeds.

Behavior and reproduction: Black rails are territorial during the breeding season. Some populations migrate while others remain in the same place throughout the year. Most black rails are monogamous, although in rare instances a male may breed with multiple females (polygamy). In the United States black rails breed in the summer. In other parts of its range breeding occurs during the rainy season. Black rails nest in low vegetation, where they build a bowl-shaped nest out of grass. The nest is covered with a woven canopy. Females lay anywhere from two to thirteen eggs at a time. Eggs hatch after seventeen to twenty days.

Black rail populations in the United States have decreased because their habitats, marshes and grasslands, have been lost to development and farming. (Illustration by Wendy Baker. Reproduced by permission.)

Black rails and people: No significant interactions between black rails and humans are known.

Conservation status: One black rail subspecies, found in the Peruvian Andes, is considered Endangered, while the others are considered Near Threatened. In the United States, black rail populations declined greatly during the twentieth century, due largely to habitat loss.

Corncrake (*Crex crex*)

■ Breeding ■ Nonbreeding

CORNCRAKE
Crex crex

Physical characteristics: Corncrakes are a blue-gray color on the face, neck, and breast. The backs are a streaked brownish color. They range from 10.6 to 12 inches in length (27 to 30 centimeters) and from 4.6 to 7.4 ounces (129 to 210 grams) in weight.

Geographic range: Corncrakes breed in Europe and central Asia, then migrate to northern and eastern Africa for the winter.

Habitat: Corncrakes inhabit grasslands during both the breeding season and the winter.

Diet: Corncrakes eat insects, spiders, and other invertebrates as well as seeds and grass. They look for food under the cover of vegetation, rather than foraging in the open.

Behavior and reproduction: Corncrakes are particularly active in the morning and at dusk, although males may call all night. Corncrakes are serially polygamous, meaning males mate with multiple females, but have only one breeding partner at a time. Nests are cup-shaped and built on the ground, usually hidden in dense vegetation. Six to fourteen eggs are laid at a time, and hatch after sixteen to twenty days. Only females incubate eggs. Chicks become independent at ten to twenty days.

Corncrakes and people: Corncrakes are hunted for food. They are particularly vulnerable during their migration.

Conservation status: Corncrakes are considered Vulnerable due to the loss of much of their grassland habitat areas. ■

Corncrakes eat insects, spiders, other invertebrates, seeds, and grass, which they find in their grassland habitat. (© D. Tipling/VIREO. Reproduced by permission.)

FOR MORE INFORMATION

Books:

del Hoyo, J., A. Elliott, and J. Sargatal, eds. *Handbook of the Birds of the World.* Vol. 3, *Hoatzin to Auks.* Barcelona: Lynx Edicions, 1996.

Perrins, Christopher, ed. *Firefly Encyclopedia of Birds.* Buffalo, NY: Firefly Books, 2003

Taylor, P. B., B. Taylor, and B. van Perlo. *Rails: A Guide to the Rails, Crakes, Gallinules, and Coots of the World.* New Haven, CT: Yale University Press, 1998.

Web sites:

"Rallidae (Rails and Coots)." The Internet Bird Collection. http://www.hbw.com/ibc/phtml/familia.phtml?idFamilia=46 (accessed on April 25, 2004)

"Family Rallidae (Coots and Rails)." Animal Diversity Web. http://animaldiversity.ummz.umich.edu/site/accounts/classification/Rallidae.html#Rallidae (accessed on April 25, 2004)

"Crakes, rails, coots, gallinules." Bird Families of the World, Cornell University. http://www.es.cornell.edu/winkler/botw/rallidae.html (accessed on April 25, 2004)

SUNGREBES
Heliornithidae

Class: Aves

Order: Gruiformes

Family: Heliornithidae

Number of species: 3 species

phylum

class

subclass

order

monotypic order

suborder

▲ **family**

PHYSICAL CHARACTERISTICS

Sungrebes have long necks and slender bodies. They have brown backs and a long white stripe that extends down the side of the neck. Male and female sungrebes tend to have slightly different coloration on the heads and necks. The brightly colored bills of sungrebes are sharp and pointed, and the tail is long and broad. In one species, the African finfoot, the tail feathers are stiffened, and the tail is spread out on the water during swimming. All three species of sungrebes have brightly colored feet. These are orange in the African finfoot, green in the masked finfoot, and yellow with black stripes in the sungrebe.

GEOGRAPHIC RANGE

The African finfoot occurs in Africa, where it is found through most of sub-Saharan Africa. The sungrebe is a New World species found in parts of Mexico and through most of Central and South America. The masked finfoot is found in Asia, including portions of Bangladesh, India, Sumatra, and the Malay Peninsula.

HABITAT

All sungrebe species require overhanging trees or other forms of dense cover over aquatic bodies. They are found in swamps and other wetland habitats, as well as ponds, lakes, dams, and a wide variety of rivers and streams, from coastal creeks to mountain streams as high as 6,600 feet (2,000 meters) in elevation. Although sungrebes and finfoots are sometimes found in fast-flowing streams, most prefer slow-moving currents or still water. Some populations inhabit flooded rainforests.

DIET

Sungrebes feed primarily on insects, particularly midgets, mayflies, and dragonflies. They may also eat beetles, grasshoppers, and flies, as well as some mollusks, crustaceans, worms, millipedes, and spiders. Occasionally they can eat larger animals such as frogs, tadpoles, or small fish. Sungrebes are also known to eat a small amount of plant material, such as seeds and leaves. Most of their food is found on the water surface, but sungrebes also forage in overhanging vegetation or along banks.

BEHAVIOR AND REPRODUCTION

Sungrebes may be solitary, that is, may live by themselves, or are found in pairs, generally male and female breeding partners, or family groups. Sungrebes are permanently territorial, meaning they defend their territories from other individuals of the same species during the breeding season as well as the nonbreeding season. Sungrebes are shy birds rarely seen by people. They usually swim close to cover and may hide either in vegetation or in the water, with their bodies underwater and their heads lowered, when they are disturbed. They are good swimmers but also capable walkers and climbers. Sungrebes tend to roost, or spend the night, in trees or bushes.

Although all three subgrebe species have distinctive calls, these are not often heard. The African finfoot makes a loud booming sound during breeding. The masked finfoot has a bubbling call. The sungrebe has a "eeyoo" call that it makes to warn other sungrebes away from its territory.

Sungrebes breed when water levels are high. All three species are monogamous (muh-NAH-guh-mus), meaning a single male breeds with a single female. Courtship rituals, which are characteristic behaviors individuals perform before mating, vary among the species. In the African finfoot, one individual raises and opens its wings while the other individual remains under cover and responds with a snapping noise. In sungrebes, potential mates swim

RIDING UNDER THE WING

In monogamous birds, where each male mates with only one female during the breeding season, it is common for males to help with nest building, incubating the eggs, and caring for hatched chicks. Sungrebe males do one additional thing for their chicks—after the chicks hatch, the male carries one under each wing, secured in a pocket of skin. Males can even carry them while flying.

in circles towards each other, raising their wings and lowering their heads in a characteristic manner. Both males and females participate in building the nest, which is generally a shallow bowl of sticks lined with dead leaves. Nests are generally built in areas of thick vegetation about 3 feet (1 meter) over water, often on top of debris that remains caught in branches. Usually, two to three eggs are laid at a time, and both parents incubate, or sit on, the eggs. Eggs hatch after ten to eleven days.

In the sungrebe, chicks are altricial (al-TRISH-uhl), that is, they hatch naked, without feathers, blind, and unable to move. Males carry the chicks in pockets of skin under the wings until they are better able to fend for themselves. In the African finfoot and the masked finfoot, the chicks are semi-precocial (semi-pree-KOH-shul), a state between altricial and precocial, fully developed. Although they cannot leave the nest immediately, as fully precocial chicks can, they generally leave the nest after a few days.

SUNGREBES AND PEOPLE

Masked finfoots are hunted for food. Their eggs and chicks may also be collected for food.

CONSERVATION STATUS

Masked finfoots are considered Vulnerable, facing a high risk of extinction in the wild. There are probably somewhere between 2,500 and 10,000 individuals left in the wild. Populations have suffered due to the loss of wetland habitats to agricultural or other human use, as well as hunting. The African finfoot is considered Vulnerable in South Africa, but may be in decline in other parts of its range as well. Because all three sungrebe species rarely come into contact with humans, population declines are often unlikely to be noticed.

Sungrebe *(Heliornis fulica)*

Resident

SUNGREBE
Heliornis fulica

Physical characteristics: Sungrebes are black on top of the head and on the back of the neck. The throat is white, the back is brown, and the belly is pale in color. The males has a dark upper bill, whereas the female's upper bill is red. The lower bill is pale in both sexes. Sungrebes have yellow and black striped feet. Sungrebes vary from 10.2 to 13 inches (26 to 33 centimeters) in length and 4.2 to 5.3 ounces (120 to 150 grams) in weight.

Geographic range: Sungrebes are found in the New World, from southeastern Mexico through most of Central America and South America as far as Bolivia and northeastern Argentina.

Habitat: Sungrebes occupy river, stream, pond, and lake habitats in forested areas, usually with dense, overhanging vegetation.

Diet: Sungrebes eat primarily aquatic insects. They catch their food on the water surface, or, less frequently, on land.

Behavior and reproduction: Sungrebes are territorial throughout the year, with males defending a length of shoreline usually about 590 feet (180 meters) long. In the northern part of its range, sungrebes breed in the spring. Elsewhere, they breed during the rainy season. Females lay two to three eggs which hatch after ten or eleven days. Both parents help incubate the eggs. The male carries the chicks in pouches under the wings.

Sungrebes and people: No significant interactions between humans and sungrebes are known.

Conservation status: The sungrebe is not considered threatened. However, due to the extreme shyness of the species, it is uncertain how populations are doing. ■

FOR MORE INFORMATION

Books:

Ali, S., and S. D. Ripley. *Handbook of the Birds of India and Pakistan.* New York: Oxford University Press, 1983.

del Hoyo, J., A. Elliott, and J. Sargatal, eds. *Handbook of the Birds of the World.* Vol. 3, *Hoatzin to Auks.* Barcelona: Lynx Edicions, 1996.

Perrins, Christopher, ed. *Firefly Encyclopedia of Birds.* Buffalo, NY: Firefly Books, 2003.

Web sites:

"Family Heliornithidae (Finfoots)." Animal Diversity Web. http://animal diversity.ummz.umich.edu/site/accounts/classification/Heliornithidae. html#Heliornithidae (accessed on April 28, 2004).

"Heliornithidae (Finfoots)." The Internet Bird Collection. http://www. hbw.com/ibc/phtml/familia.phtml?idFamilia=47 (accessed on April 28, 2004).

"Sun-Grebes, Finfoots." Bird Families of the World, Cornell University. http://www.es.cornell.edu/winkler/botw/heliornithidae.html (accessed on April 28, 2004).

SUNBITTERN
Eurypygidae

Class: Aves

Order: Gruiformes

Family: Eurypygidae

One species: Sunbittern (*Eurypyga helias*)

PHYSICAL CHARACTERISTICS

Sunbitterns range from 18 to 21 inches (46 to 53 centimeters) in length and 6.3 to 7.8 ounces (180 to 220 grams) in weight. They have long, slender necks and black heads with two extended white stripes above and below the eyes. The eyes are red in color. Their bills are long and straight. The upper part of the bill is black in color, while the lower bill is bright orange. Sunbitterns have orange legs. When they have their wings open, a bright sunburst-like pattern of black, yellow, and red markings appears. These are actually intended to frighten away potential predators. Sunbitterns also have long, broad fan-shaped tails marked with striking chestnut and black stripes. When the wings and tail are folded, the bright colors are concealed and the sunbittern blends in well with its environment, being either brown or chestnut-colored with black bars on the back, and paler on the neck and belly. Male and female sunbitterns tend to be fairly similar in appearance, though males are sometimes more brightly colored.

GEOGRAPHIC RANGE

Sunbitterns are found in the New World tropics in Central America and South America. They occupy most of the southern part of Central America south to western Ecuador, and South America east of the Andes Mountains through the Amazonian portions of Colombia, Venezuela, and Guineas, as well as portions of Brazil, Ecuador, and Peru.

HABITAT

Sunbitterns prefer forested habitats near permanent water sources. These include fast-flowing mountain streams, slow-flowing rivers, pond areas, and swamps. Sunbitterns are generally found at altitudes between 300 and 4,000 feet (100 to 1,200 meters) although they have been seen at higher elevations as well.

DIET

Sunbitterns have a diverse diet including vertebrates, animals with backbones, such as small fish, tadpoles, eels, and frogs, as well as smaller animals such as spiders, flies, water beetles, cockroaches, katydids, dragonfly larvae, shrimp, crabs, earthworms, and moths. Sunbitterns hunt by walking slowly, looking for and following prey carefully with their necks pulled back, then quickly jabbing and spearing with their long bills. Much of the hunting is done in shallow water, although sunbitterns also forage along the forest floor. Sunbitterns have the unusual habit of washing their food before eating, particularly when they are feeding their young.

WELL-HIDDEN

When their bright wings and tails are folded, sunbitterns blend right into their environment. The barred black and brown feathers on the bird's back melt into the background of dappled sunlight under trees, which is where sunbitterns spend most of their time. They also walk slowly while they hunt for food along streams, bringing little attention to themselves.

BEHAVIOR AND REPRODUCTION

Sunbitterns are often solitary, that is, they frequently live alone. However, they are sometimes found in pairs, usually male and female breeding partners. Sunbitterns are not particularly shy, but will fly to the low branches of trees if they are disturbed. Sunbitterns do not migrate, but stay generally in the same place throughout the year. However, individuals who live in dry areas may move short distances in order to find appropriate habitat.

Sunbitterns are known for their defensive posture, which they use to frighten away potential predators. The defensive posture involves opening the wings and rotating them forward to reveal the sunburst pattern, and raising and fanning the tail at the same time. This causes the sunbittern to appear to be a large and alarmingly colored bird. In order to protect a nest and chicks, adult sunbitterns will also perform a "broken-wing" display in which one wing is dragged along the ground as if broken. By drawing attention to what appears to be a helpless adult, sunbitterns are able to distract attention from the more vulnerable nest.

The sunbittern song is a high, ringing whistle and is sung most often in the morning. Sunbitterns also have an alarm call that is used to warn others of danger.

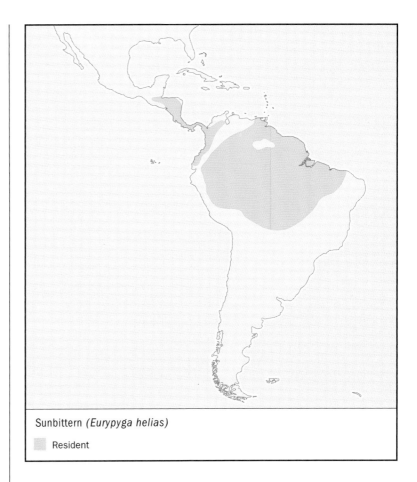

Sunbittern *(Eurypyga helias)*

Resident

Breeding in sunbitterns occurs during the rainy season. Courtship involves calls and singing duets as well as flight displays, head bobbing displays, preening, and begging displays. Both males and females participate in nest-building. The nest is usually built on a horizontal branch 3 to 23 feet (1 to 7 meters) above the ground and consists of a large bowl of decaying leaves, mud, and other plant material. More rarely, nests are built directly on the ground. The nest is usually placed under the cover of vegetation and close to water. The female lays two or three eggs at a time. These are pink in color, often with purplish-brown spots, and hatch after twenty-seven to thirty days. Chicks hatch already covered with down, fine fluffy feathers, and with their eyes open. One chick often hatches one or two days before the other. Both males and females incubate, or sit on, the eggs, and both help feed and take care of the chicks once they hatch. Chicks are able to stand and flap their wings a week after birth, and leave the nest after approximately thirty days.

SUNBITTERNS AND PEOPLE

Because sunbitterns are exceptionally good at catching flies and spiders, sunbittern chicks are sometimes taken from their nests and raised as pets. The birds are also hunted occasionally.

CONSERVATION STATUS

The sunbittern is not considered threatened at this time. However, their populations are declining in many parts of their range due to habitat damage and destruction.

FOR MORE INFORMATION

Books:

del Hoyo, J., A. Elliott, and J. Sargatal, eds. *Handbook of the Birds of the World.* Vol. 3, *Hoatzin to Auks.* Barcelona: Lynx Edicions, 1996.

Perrins, Christopher, ed. *Firefly Encyclopedia of Birds.* Buffalo, NY: Firefly Books, 2003.

Web sites:

"Eurypygidae (Sunbittern)." The Internet Bird Collection. http://www.hbw.com/ibc/phtml/familia.phtml?idFamilia=49 (accessed on April 28, 2004).

"Family Eurypygidae (Sunbittern)." Animal Diversity Web. http://animaldiversity.ummz.umich.edu/site/accounts/classification/Eurypygidae.html#Eurypygidae (accessed on April 28, 2004).

"Sun-bittern." Bird Families of the World, Cornell University. http://www.es.cornell.edu/winkler/botw/eurypygidae.html (accessed on April 28, 2004).

The sunbittern's defensive posture, rotating the wings forward, causes the sunbittern to appear to be a large and alarmingly colored bird. (© François Gohier/Photo Researchers, Inc. Reproduced by permission.)

family

phylum

class

subclass

order

monotypic order

suborder

▲ **family**

PHYSICAL CHARACTERISTICS

Trumpeters range from 17 to 21 inches (43 to 53 centimeters) in length, and are approximately 2.2 pounds (1 kilogram) in weight. They have black feathers and, depending on the species, a paler patch of gray, green, or white on the back from the folded inner wing feathers. Trumpeter chicks, which are colored to blend into their environments, have brown and black stripes. Trumpeters have hunched backs, long necks which are usually held close to the body, small heads, long legs, and short tails. The bill is short and sharp. Males and females are similar in appearance, although males tend to be larger in size.

GEOGRAPHIC RANGE

Trumpeters are found in northern South America, including portions of Venezuela, Colombia, Ecuador, the Guianas, Peru, Bolivia, and Brazil.

HABITAT

Trumpeters live in areas of tropical rainforests where there are many trees and little ground cover. Because they are primarily fruit eaters, their habitats generally have many fruit trees.

DIET

Trumpeters eat primarily fruit, with their favorites being soft fruits with thin skins. Trumpeters rely largely on monkeys to knock fruit onto the ground, since they are not able to fly up to high trees themselves. They also take advantage of fruits that grow on low bushes. Trumpeters also eat large numbers of insects off the forest floor, particularly beetles, ants, and termites. On occasion they will also eat larger animals, such as small snakes.

BEHAVIOR AND REPRODUCTION

Trumpeters are found in large groups which include a single dominant female and several males whom she breeds with, as well as their young. All adult trumpeters participate in feeding and caring for the young. This reproductive system, which is rare among birds, is known as cooperative polyandry (PAH-lee-an-dree). As with many species where many individuals live together, dominance relations, a system where some individuals have higher rank and others have lower rank, are well established among individual trumpeters. Subordinate individuals in the group, those with lower rank, often crouch and spread their wings in front of the dominant individuals. Trumpeters also preen each other, or clean each other's feathers, feed each other, and engage in mock fights. All these behaviors help to strengthen bonds between individuals in the group.

FOOD, SOCIABILITY, AND TERRITORIALITY

Trumpeters are social birds, found in close-knit groups of as many as a dozen individuals. These usually consist of a single dominant female, up to three dominant males, and their young. It is believed that trumpeters form large groups to defend their large territories from other groups of trumpeters. The large territories, in turn, are necessary for trumpeters to find as much food as they need.

Groups of trumpeters are highly territorial, defending their territories against other trumpeters. In order to find enough food during the dry season, trumpeter groups require large territories. When a group of trumpeters finds other trumpeters in their territory, they sneak up on the intruders, then scream the loud, distinctive calls which give trumpeters their name. Fights involve kicking and pecking, and continue until the intruders leave the territory. At night, trumpeters roost in trees, sometimes in branches as high as 30 feet (9 meters) off the ground. Even at night, trumpeters make their loud territorial calls every few hours.

A single dominant female in the trumpeter group mates with as many as three dominant males. All adults help to feed and care for the young. Trumpeters like to build their nests in tree cavities, holes in trees which have been dug and abandoned by other birds. The nest is built from sticks. Before the act of mating takes place, the male feeds the female. The female then walks in a circle showing her back end while the male follows. Generally, the female lays three white eggs at a time. All the adults help incubate, or sit on, the eggs until they hatch, although the majority of the incubation is performed by the female and the dominant male. Chicks depend on adults to feed them for several weeks. They are unable to fly at first, so roost, or spend the night, close to the ground rather than high in trees like adult trumpeters. Because of this, many are eaten by snakes, predatory birds, and other species. Only about half the trumpeter chicks that hatch survive to become adults.

TRUMPETERS AND PEOPLE

Trumpeters interact with humans in a variety of ways. They are kept as pets in some parts of their range. Some people use trumpeters in chicken coops to alert humans when there are snakes. Trumpeters are also hunted for food in some areas. Because trumpeters tend to stay with their group, even in the face of danger, they often make easy targets for hunters.

CONSERVATION STATUS

Trumpeters are not considered threatened. However, because their rainforest habitats are being destroyed in many parts of their range, and because trumpeters require large territories in order to find enough food, many populations are declining. In addition, some of the monkey species which trumpeters depend on to obtain fruit are in trouble because of habitat loss and hunting. This is harming trumpeter populations as well.

Common trumpeter *(Psophia crepitans)*

Resident

COMMON TRUMPETER
Psophia crepitans

Physical characteristics: Common trumpeters are 18 to 20 inches (42 to 52 centimeters) in length and 2 to 3 pounds (1 to 1.5 kilograms) in weight. They are dark in color with a patch of light gray on the back. They have long legs and a long neck. Young common trumpeters are dark gray with reddish stripes.

The common trumpeter lives in dense tropical rainforests, and is generally found in groups of three to twelve individuals. (© J. Alvarez A./VIREO. Reproduced by permission.)

Geographic range: Common trumpeters are found in northwestern Brazil as well as portions of Colombia, Ecuador, Peru, Venezuela, and the Guianas.

Habitat: Common trumpeters are found in dense areas of tropical rainforest.

Diet: Common trumpeters eat fruit, mostly that which has been knocked to the ground by monkeys. They also eat some insects, particularly beetles, ants, and termites.

Behavior and reproduction: The common trumpeter is generally found in groups of three to twelve individuals. A single dominant female mates with as many as three dominant males. Three eggs are laid at a time, usually in a hole in a tree. Eggs hatch after approximately twenty-eight days. All adults in the group help in feeding and caring for the offspring.

Common trumpeters and people: Common trumpeters are sometimes hunted for food.

Conservation status: The common trumpeter is not considered threatened. However, populations have been declining due to the loss of tropical rainforest habitat as well as hunting. ■

FOR MORE INFORMATION

Books:

del Hoyo, J., A. Elliott, and J. Sargatal, eds. *Handbook of the Birds of the World.* Vol. 3, *Hoatzin to Auks.* Barcelona: Lynx Edicions, 1996.

Perrins, Christopher, ed. *Firefly Encyclopedia of Birds.* Buffalo, NY: Firefly Books, 2003.

Web sites:

"Family Psophiidae (Trumpeters)." Animal Diversity Web. http://animaldiversity.ummz.umich.edu/site/accounts/classification/Psophiidae.html#Psophiidae (accessed on April 28, 2004).

"Psophiidae (Trumpeters)." The Internet Bird Collection. http://www.hbw.com/ibc/phtml/familia.phtml?idFamilia=45 (accessed on April 28, 2004).

"Trumpeters." Bird Families of the World, Cornell University. http://www.es.cornell.edu/winkler/botw/psophiidae.html (accessed on April 28, 2004).

SERIEMAS
Cariamidae

Class: Aves

Order: Gruiformes

Family: Cariamidae

Number of species: 2 species

phylum

class

subclass

order

monotypic order

suborder

▲ family

PHYSICAL CHARACTERISTICS

Seriemas range in size from about 28 to 35 inches (70 to 90 centimeters) in length and 2.6 to 3.3 pounds (1.2 to 1.5 kilograms) in weight. They have long legs, long tails, long necks, and short, rounded wings. Seriemas have sturdy, hooked bills that resemble those of hawks. Their backs and necks are light brown in color, whereas the belly is pale or white. Male and female seriemas are similar in size and general appearance.

GEOGRAPHIC RANGE

Seriemas are found in central and eastern South America, from portions of Brazil to as far south as Argentina.

HABITAT

Seriemas are found in grassland habitats as well as areas of open forest or brushland.

DIET

Seriemas are omnivorous, meaning that they eat both plant and animal matter. They hunt a wide variety of prey, including small animals such as insects, snails, and worms, as well as larger animals such as rodents, snakes, and lizards. These birds frequently smash medium-sized prey, such as rodents, against rocks to make them easier to swallow whole. They tear larger prey into smaller pieces using their strong, sharp bills. Seriemas hunt during the day by stalking, or quietly following, potential prey. They will also eat some fruit and other plant matter.

BEHAVIOR AND REPRODUCTION

Seriemas are often found either alone or in pairs, made up of male and female mates. Sometimes larger groups, consisting of parents with their offspring, are also seen. They spend most of the day on the ground hunting for food. They spend the night in trees. Seriemas tend to run away rather than fly away when threatened. Among birds, they are very fast runners and can achieve speeds as high as 37 miles per hour (60 kilometers per hour). Their call has been described as a yelping noise. Seriemas often stand in trees or on top of termite mounds to call, which helps the call travel further.

Seriemas are territorial, that is, they defend areas of land from other members of the same species. Disputes over territories are decided by intense calling as well as kicking. Offspring often help their parents defend territories by calling.

DANGEROUS FOOD

Snakes are part of the diet of both species of seriemas. Unlike many snake-eaters, however, the black-legged seriema appears to be unable to tell the difference between poisonous snakes and non-poisonous snakes. They are not immune to snake venom and are therefore sometimes killed by their intended prey. Farmers sometimes keep them in chicken coops to kill snakes, as well as to give warning when predators approach.

Seriemas breed during the rainy season, generally between September and May each year. To convince females to mate, male seriemas perform struts and leaps and also show the normally hidden feathers of their wings and tails. Both the male and female help in building the nest, which is made from sticks and twigs and lined with either clay or cattle dung. Nests are usually built in trees and may be anywhere from 3 to 30 feet (1 to 9 meters) above the ground. The female lays two or three eggs at a time, and these hatch after anywhere from twenty-four to thirty days. Offspring are able to leave the nest after two weeks, and reach adult size at five months of age.

SERIEMAS AND PEOPLE

Seriemas are sometimes hunted for their meat. They are also used by humans to guard chicken coops, since they will make loud warning calls if predators approach. Seriemas are also believed to benefit humans by killing a large number of venomous snakes.

CONSERVATION STATUS

The two species of seriemas are not currently considered threatened. However, their populations are declining in some areas due to hunting and habitat destruction.

Red-legged seriema (*Cariama cristata*)

[shaded box] Resident

RED-LEGGED SERIEMA
Cariama cristata

Physical characteristics: The red-legged seriema has, as its name suggests, red legs. It also has a red bill. The eyes are yellow and surrounded by a patch of featherless blue skin. The tip of the tail is white in color. The feathers are generally brownish on the back and pale on the belly. The red-legged seriema also has a 3- to 4-inch (7- to 10-centimeter) crest of stiffened feathers on top of its head. Males and females are generally similar in appearance, although the males are slightly larger than the females. Juvenile seriemas have black bills rather than red ones.

Geographic range: The red-legged seriema is found in central and eastern Brazil as well as portions of Paraguay, Bolivia, Uruguay, and northeastern Argentina.

Habitat: The red-legged seriema inhabits grassland habitats, as well as open scrub or brushland areas and the edges of wooded forests.

Diet: Red-legged seriemas forage, or hunt for food, in pairs or small groups. They have a diverse diet including animals such as insects, worms, small mammals, frogs, snakes, and lizards, as well as fruit and other plant material. Red-legged seriemas will also eat either the eggs or chicks of other bird species. Some prey are smashed against rocks to make them easier to swallow whole.

Behavior and reproduction: The red-legged seriema spends much of its time on the ground. It rarely flies but prefers to run away from danger. However, they do roost, or spend the night, in trees. Red-legged seriemas sunbathe—they lie on the ground on their sides and appear, sometimes, to be dead. Red-legged seriemas have very loud calls that can be heard as far as a mile away. The call is described as sounding like the yelp of a dog. Calling generally occurs in the morning, as a male and female pair cry out to each other. The purpose of the calling is to defend their territory from other members of the same species.

Red-legged seriemas are monogamous, that is, a single male mates with a single female. They build their nests as high as 10 feet (3 meters) off the ground, usually in a tree. Nest building is a long process for this species, taking up to a month. Both the male and female participate in nest building. Before mating, males show off their feathers by extending their wings. They also strut, walking around with their heads down and their crest of feathers up. The female red-legged seriema lays two eggs at a time. Both parents help incubate, or sit on, the eggs, which hatch after twenty-five to twenty-eight days. Chicks are able to fly after approximately one month.

Red-legged seriemas and people: Humans sometimes use red-legged seriemas in their chicken coops, because they will give an alarm cry if predators approach. Red-legged seriemas are also hunted for their meat.

Conservation status: The red-legged seriema is not currently considered threatened. However, it is declining or disappearing from parts of its range. It is now extremely rare in Uruguay. Argentine populations of red-legged seriemas appear to be declining due to hunting and habitat destruction. ■

FOR MORE INFORMATION

Books:

del Hoyo, J., A. Elliott, and J. Sargatal, eds. *Handbook of the Birds of the World.* Vol. 3, *Hoatzin to Auks.* Barcelona: Lynx Edicions, 1996.

Perrins, Christopher, ed. *Firefly Encyclopedia of Birds.* Buffalo, NY: Firefly Books, 2003.

Web sites:

"Cariamidae (Seriemas)." The Internet Bird Collection. http://www.hbw.com/ibc/phtml/familia.phtml?idFamilia=50 (accessed on April 12, 2004).

"Family Cariamidae (Seriema)." Animal Diversity Web. http://animaldiversity.ummz.umich.edu/site/accounts/classification/Cariamidae.html#Cariamidae (accessed on April 12, 2004).

"Seriemas." Bird Families of the World, Cornell University. http://www.es.cornell.edu/winkler/botw/cariamidae.html (accessed on April 12, 2004).

BUSTARDS
Otididae

Class: Aves
Order: Gruiformes
Family: Otididae
Number of species: 26 species

phylum

class

subclass

order

monotypic order

suborder

▲ **family**

PHYSICAL CHARACTERISTICS

Bustards vary in size from 15 to 47 inches (40 to 120 centimeters) in length. They are among the heaviest flying birds, weighing 1 to 42.2 pounds (0.45 to 19 kilograms). Male bustards are generally larger than females, although there is less difference between the sexes in smaller bustard species. Bustards have stout bodies with long legs and long necks. The bills tend to be short and straight. Bustards have large wings and small feet with no hind toe. Since Bustards do not perch on tree branches, preferring instead to remain on the ground, hind toes are not needed. The large wings are helpful when flying away from potential predators.

Bustards are generally colored to blend in with their environments. The back is brownish, with either white or dark bellies. Some bustard species have white or black patches on the wings, which are hidden when the wings are folded and only revealed during flight. In some species of bustards males and females are similarly patterned, while males are brighter in other species. In a number of bustards, males also have long feathers on the head, neck, or chest that are used to attract females.

GEOGRAPHIC RANGE

Bustards are found across much of the Old World, including Africa, Europe, and Asia, as well as in Australia.

HABITAT

Bustards are found primarily in grassland habitats with low vegetation where they are able to look out over long distances.

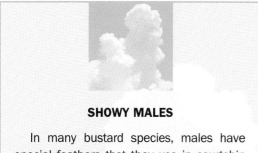
Some bustards occupy taller grasslands or even slightly wooded areas. Bustards are also frequently found in cultivated fields.

DIET

Bustards are omnivores, consuming both plant and animal matter. They are opportunistic feeders who are often able to take advantage of any food. In most species, the diet consists mostly of plant matter, including leaves, shoots, flowers, roots and bulbs, fruit, and seeds. Individuals that occupy cultivated areas frequently eat crops as well. Bustards eat insects such as beetles and grasshoppers. Insects are a particularly important part of the diet during the breeding season, while chicks are being fed. Bustards sometimes eat larger animals as well, such as reptiles and rodents. In most cases, however, these animals are killed during fires or by traffic, rather than hunted by the bustards themselves.

Bustards are often seen foraging, or searching for food, near large herds of grazing mammals. This is probably because there is less danger from predators near other individuals. In addition, bustards may eat the insects which have been disturbed by the mammals.

BEHAVIOR AND REPRODUCTION

Bustards range from solitary, or, living alone, to highly social, forming groups of as many as thousands in the case of the little bustard. Bustards that occupy semi-desert habitats generally tend to be more solitary. Many species of bustards migrate, moving from a breeding habitat to a wintering habitat. Asian bustard species, in particular, frequently migrate to avoid harsh winter conditions.

Bustards often breed during the rainy season in their habitat. Males perform elaborate courtship displays to attract females. These can involve booming calls, showing off long feathers that only the males possess, fanning out the tail, and performing leaps. Males generally do not participate in either nest building, incubating (warming) the eggs, or raising chicks. The female lays anywhere from one to six eggs at a time. These hatch after twenty to twenty-five days. Bustard young are precocial (pree-KOH-shul), meaning that they hatch at a fairly advanced stage of development. They are covered with down and are able to move, usually walking within a few hours of hatching.

BUSTARDS AND PEOPLE

Bustards play an important role in agriculture in some parts of their range by eating large numbers of insect pests. On the other hand, they are hunted in some parts of the world for food or sport. (In Asia, hunting has caused population declines in several species.) Some hunters use trained falcons to hunt bustards.

CONSERVATION STATUS

Of the twenty-six species of bustards in existence, four are considered Threatened with extinction and six are considered Near Threatened, in danger of becoming threatened. Most other species are also declining. Bustards are threatened primarily due to hunting (particularly in India and Indochina), habitat destruction, and pesticide use.

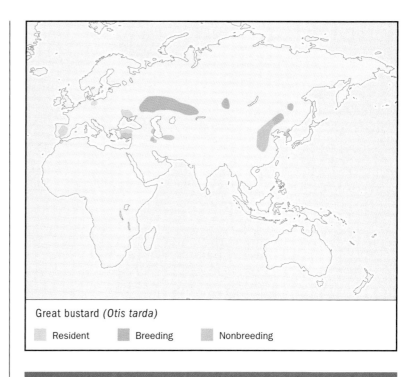

Great bustard (*Otis tarda*)

Resident   Breeding   Nonbreeding

GREAT BUSTARD
Otis tarda

Physical characteristics: Male great bustards reach lengths of 41 inches (105 centimeters) and can weigh between 13 and 40 pounds (5.8 to 18 kilograms). Females are smaller, at 30 inches in length (75 centimeters) and 7 to 12 pounds (3.3 to 5.3 kilograms) in weight. Great bustards have black and gold barred backs and tails and white bellies. The head is pale blue-gray in color in females and nonbreeding males. Breeding males have white and rust colored feathers on the neck and long white barbs on the chin.

Geographic range: The great bustard has a scattered distribution and is found in portions of Morocco, Spain, Portugal, Germany, Hungary, Ukraine, Turkey, Iran, Russia, Syria, Uzbekistan, Tajikistan, Mongolia, and China.

Habitat: The great bustard occupies short-grass plains.

Diet: Great bustards eat plant material and insects. Sometimes they will eat larger animals such as reptiles, amphibians, and the chicks of other species.

Behavior and reproduction: Great bustards live in large groups, with the males found in separate groups from the females. Some great bustards are migratory, while others remain in the same place year-round. During the breeding season, males perform elaborate courtship displays, characteristic behaviors intended to attract female mates. Females lay two or three eggs at a time. These hatch after about twenty-five days. Chicks are able to fly after between thirty and thirty-five days.

Great bustards and people: In Europe, great bustards sometimes appeared on family insignias. The great bustard is also currently the symbol of a grassland conservation program.

Conservation status: The great bustard is considered vulnerable. Declines are primarily due to habitat destruction, pesticide use, and hunting. ■

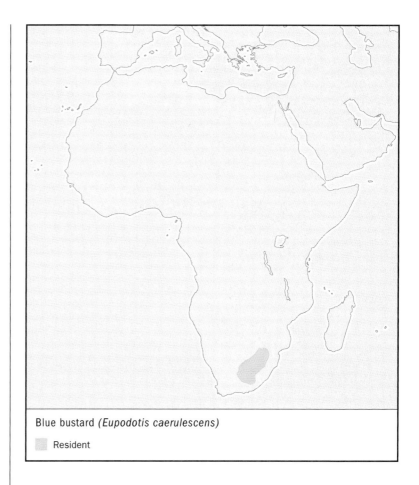

Blue bustard *(Eupodotis caerulescens)*

▨ Resident

BLUE BUSTARD
Eupodotis caerulescens

Physical characteristics: The blue bustard has a brown back and blue-gray neck and belly. It is about 21.5 inches (55 centimeters) in length and 2.5 to 3.5 pounds (1.1 to 1.6 kilograms) in weight.

Geographic range: Blue bustards are found in eastern and central South Africa and in Lesotho.

Habitat: Blue bustards are found in grasslands as well as in cultivated fields. They are a high altitude species that is generally found above 4,900 feet (1,500 meters).

Blue bustards live in grasslands and cultivated fields, where they eat plant matter as well as insects and larger animals such as small reptiles. (© W. Tarboton/VIREO. Reproduced by permission.)

Diet: Blue bustards eat plant matter as well as insects and larger animals such as small reptiles.

Behavior and reproduction: Blue bustards are found in small groups of between two and six individuals. Blue bustard groups are territorial and defend their territories against other members of the same species. Blue bustards do not migrate but remain in the same place year-round. Breeding generally occurs in October and November. One to three eggs are laid by the female, and hatch after a period of twenty-four to twenty-eight days. Young remain with their parents for as long as two years.

Blue bustards and people: No significant interactions between blue bustards and people are known.

Conservation status:　The blue bustard is currently considered Near Threatened. Population declines are generally due to habitat loss as grasslands are converted for use in agriculture.　■

FOR MORE INFORMATION

Books:

del Hoyo, J., A. Elliott, and J. Sargatal, eds. *Handbook of the Birds of the World.* Volume 3, *Hoatzin to Auks.* Barcelona: Lynx Edicions, 1996.

Johnsgard, P. A. *Bustards, Hemipodes and Sandgrouse: Birds of Dry Places.* Oxford, U.K.: Oxford University Press, 1991.

Perrins, Christopher, ed. *Firefly Encyclopedia of Birds.* Buffalo, NY: Firefly Books, 2003.

Web sites:

"Otodidae (Bustards)." The Internet Bird Collection. http://www.hbw.com/ibc/phtml/familia.phtml?idFamilia=51 (accessed on April 13, 2004).

"Family Otididae (bustards)." Animal Diversity Web. http://animaldiversity.ummz.umich.edu/site/accounts/classification/Otididae.html#Otididae (accessed on April 13, 2004).

"Bustards." Bird Families of the World, Cornell University. http://www.es.cornell.edu/winkler/botw/otididae.html (accessed on April 13, 2004).

order
CHAPTER

PHYSICAL CHARACTERISTICS

Birds of the order Charadriiformes range in size from 0.06 to 4.4 pounds (25 grams to 2 kilograms). They vary greatly in body length, body shape, leg length, and bill shape, making generalizations about their physical characteristics difficult.

GEOGRAPHIC RANGE

Charadriiforms are found worldwide, including all seven continents.

HABITAT

Species in the order Charadriiformes occupy diverse habitats. They are generally found near water, whether coastal, inland, or on the ocean. Many charadriiforms inhabit wetland areas, both marine and freshwater. Others spend large amounts of time in or near the ocean.

DIET

As a group, charadriiforms range greatly in their diet and feeding strategies. Because of their use of aquatic habitats, many Charadriiformes species eat primarily fish. Among the fish-eaters, there are various methods for pursuing prey. The terns, for example, dive from the air into water to catch fish near the surface of the ocean. Alcids (auks, puffins, and murres) are good swimmers and swim underwater after their prey. Skimmers fly low over the water and scoop up fish from near the surface.

Other Charadriiformes have a diet formed primarily of insects and other invertebrates. Plovers search for insects and

phylum

class

subclass

● **order**

monotypic order

suborder

family

COLONIAL NESTERS

Colonial nesters are species in which large numbers of individuals build their nests and raise their young in a single location. Among the Charadriiformes, the gulls, terns, and alcids are particularly known for their colonial nesting habits. During the breeding season, colonies can range in size from several hundred individuals to as many as hundreds of thousands of birds. Charadriiformes are able to gather in such large numbers because the habitats they prefer tend to be extremely rich with food resources.

other prey using their eyes, and then pick them from the ground with their short bills. Most sandpipers, on the other hand, rely largely on the sense of touch, using their long, sensitive bills to locate prey hidden in mud.

Plants and other vegetable matter form an important part of the diet of some Charadriiformes species as well. Sheathbills, for example, eat large amounts of algae (AL-jee). Plains-wanderers eat primarily seeds. Seed-snipes, despite their name, eat primarily buds, leaf tips, and small green leaves.

BEHAVIOR AND REPRODUCTION

Some species of Charadriiformes do not migrate, remaining instead in the same area throughout the year. Other charadriiforms, however, do migrate, traveling from one area to another and back during the course of the year. Migrations generally occur between breeding grounds in the spring or summer and wintering grounds. Among the charadriiforms, shorebirds and terns are particularly well-known for their long, difficult migrations. The Arctic tern travels more than 18,000 miles each year (28,960 kilometers) between its breeding areas in the Arctic and its wintering areas in the Southern Hemisphere. The Pacific golden plover migrates between Alaska and Hawaii, a distance of 2,200 miles (3,540 kilometers), in less than two days.

Many species of charadriiforms can be found in large flocks, either during the breeding or winter season. Gulls, terns, and alcids are regularly found in groups as large as a hundred thousand individuals during the breeding season. Even larger collections of charadriiforms are found during migrations, or during the winter. In the Copper River Delta in Alaska, as many as five million shorebirds may be seen during their spring migration.

The majority of Charadriiformes species are monogamous (muh-NAH-guh-mus), meaning that a single male mates with a single female during the breeding season. In some species, individuals keep the same mate from one breeding season to the next. In monogamous Charadriiformes, both male and female help defend the nest and take care of young chicks once they hatch. Other charadriiforms have more unusual breeding systems. The jacanas are polyandrous (pah-lee-AN-drus), with a single female mating with multiple males. Still other charadriiforms, such as many species of sandpipers, are polygamous (puh-LIH-guh-mus), with a single male mating with multiple females.

Charadriiformes tend to build fairly simple nests, often just a hollow in the ground lined with a few pebbles or pieces of vegetation. Some charadriiform seabirds nest in rocky cliff areas, and lay their eggs directly on rock ledges without building any nest at all. The other end of the spectrum, some murrelets and sandpipers build nests in trees or use nests that have been built and abandoned by other bird species. Generally, females lay between one and four eggs at a time. Eggs hatch after a period of three weeks or longer. Some Charadriiformes, including most shorebirds species, have precocial chicks. These hatch at a fairly advanced stage of development, covered with down and able to move. Precocial chicks are usually able to leave the nest soon after they hatch. Others, such as most seabirds, have altricial chicks, which hatch at a less developed state. These hatch blind and without feathers, and usually stay in the nest for a longer period of time.

GULLS, TERNS, PLOVERS, OTHER SHOREBIRDS, AND PEOPLE

Humans have hunted many species of charadriiform birds for meat, feathers, oil, and eggs. Because Charadriiformes are often found in large flocks during breeding, migration, or the winter season, they have frequently made easy targets for hunters. For example, between 1988 and 1989 alone, some 300,000 to 400,000 thick-billed murres were killed in Greenland.

CONSERVATION STATUS

Of the 343 species of Charadriiformes, thirty-four are currently considered Threatened, in danger of extinction, by the World Conservation Union (IUCN). Threatened species have been affected by habitat destruction and damage (particularly

HUNTERS AND CHARADRIIFORMES

Because different species of Charadriiformes gather in large numbers during breeding, migration, or wintering seasons, they are frequently attractive targets for hunters. Many species have been hunted for their meat, feathers, oil, and eggs. Hunting by humans is believed to have resulted in the extinction of at least two Charadriiformes, the Eskimo curlew and the great auk. Hunting continues to contribute to the threatened state of many other charadriiform species.

in wetland areas as well as rivers and streams), pollution, hunting, and other factors. Some species have declined as over-fishing by humans eliminates important seabird prey populations. Finally, certain Charadriiformes species are periodically devastated by large oil spills.

FOR MORE INFORMATION

Books:

del Hoyo, J., A. Elliott, and J. Sargatal, eds. *Handbook of the Birds of the World.* Vol. 3, *Hoatzin to Auks.* Barcelona: Lynx Edicions, 1996.

Perrins, Christopher, ed. *Firefly Encyclopedia of Birds.* Buffalo, NY: Firefly Books, 2003.

Web sites:

The Internet Bird Collection. http://www.hbw.com/ibc/phtml/families. phtml (accessed on April 15, 2004).

"Order Charadriiformes (Shorebirds and Relatives)." Animal Diversity Web. http://animaldiversity.ummz.umich.edu/site/accounts/classification/ Charadriiformes.html (accessed on April 15, 2004).

"Birds of the World." Bird Families of the World, Cornell University. http://www.es.cornell.edu/winkler/botw/families.htm (accessed on April 15, 2004).

JACANAS

Jacanidae

Class: Aves
Order: Charadriiformes
Family: Jacanidae
Number of species: 8 species

family

CHAPTER

PHYSICAL CHARACTERISTICS

Jacanas (juh-KAH-nuhz) vary from about 6 to 23 inches (15 to 58 centimeters) in length and from 1.4 to 9.7 ounces (40 to 275 grams) in weight. Jacanas have long, slender necks and extremely long toes and claws, as long as 4 inches (10.2 centimeters) in certain species. Their large feet allow them to balance on and move over lily pads and other floating vegetation, a practice that has given the jacana nicknames such as "lily trotters" and "Jesus birds." Jacanas also have bony spurs that jut out from their wings. These are used in battles with other jacanas, as well as to defend individuals from potential predators, animals that hunt them for food. Jacanas are unusual among birds in that the females are larger than the males, weighing, in some cases, as much as 60 percent more.

Jacanas are generally black or reddish brown in color. Most species have very bright wings and will sometimes spread their wings suddenly to frighten off potential predators. Jacanas also have bright patches of feathers on their foreheads. Male and female jacanas have similar coloration. Young jacanas, however, generally have brown backs and pale bellies, colors that allow them to blend into their environments well. Chicks develop adult coloration after about a year.

GEOGRAPHIC RANGE

Jacanas are found in the Old World and New World tropics, including parts of Central America, South America, Africa, Asia, Australia, and Madagascar.

phylum

class

subclass

order

monotypic order

suborder

▲ **family**

DOMINANT FEMALES

Jacana females are much larger than the males and are dominant over them. A single female breeds with up to four males during the breeding season, defending a large territory against other jacana females. Males are responsible for building the nest, sitting on the eggs, and caring for the chicks once they hatch. Females show their dominance to males by pecking at their necks and backs. To show his submission, the male crouches and lowers his head.

HABITAT

Jacanas inhabit aquatic environments such as marshes or ponds in open (rather than forested) areas. They prefer water bodies that are covered in vegetation, since they use floating vegetation for both feeding and shelter. Jacanas have also been found in flooded pastures or rice fields.

DIET

Jacanas eat primarily insects. They forage, or search for food, by floating on water lilies or other vegetation and turning over the large leaves with their long toes. They then eat the insects or seeds caught in the water lily's roots. Jacanas also forage for seeds among the blades of marsh grasses. Rarely, they will eat larger prey such as small fish.

BEHAVIOR AND REPRODUCTION

Most jacanas do not migrate, but remain in the same place year-round. During the breeding season, they are generally found in pairs or small groups. During the non-breeding season, jacanas congregate in flocks of as many as several hundred individuals.

Jacanas are good swimmers and divers and frequently move into water to escape potential predators. In several species, jacana chicks have breathing holes at the ends of their bills that allow them to hide with most of their bodies underwater. The jacanas' swimming skills are particularly important during the molting season, when jacanas lose their flight feathers and are temporarily flightless.

A single female jacana mates with multiples males, usually between one and four. This breeding system, which is not very common in birds, is known as polyandry (PAH-lee-an-dree). The female jacana is significantly larger than the males and is responsible for defending the territories of her mates. When another female approaches, males call to their mate. Disputes between female jacanas are usually resolved using displays in which the wings are spread, showing off the sharp wing spurs, followed by physical fights if necessary. Physical fights involve jabbing with either the bill or the wing spurs. If the intruder succeeds in chasing off the original female, she will generally kill any chicks from the previous matings so that the male jacanas will be free to tend new sets of eggs. The new female will also peck at the male's neck and back to show her dominance. Males crouch and lower their heads in response. Jacana territories are usually about the size of half a football field.

Jacanas generally breed during the rainy season. Males begin by building several potential nest sites. The female decides which to lay eggs in, or chooses a new site within the territory for a nest. Jacana nests typically consist of water lily leaves or other plant material on top of a mat of floating vegetation. The male and female flash their wings at each other before mating. Males are responsible for incubating, or sitting on and warming, the eggs. Generally, four eggs are laid at a time, and chicks hatch after twenty-two to twenty-eight days. Males are responsible for feeding the chicks and for protecting them. Males call to the chicks when there is danger and settle them under the wings. Males will also sometimes fake a broken wing in order to attract the attention of predators and allow the chicks to escape. Numerous predators prey on young jacanas, including the purple gallinule (a rail of the family Rallidae), snakes, otters, and turtles. Fewer than half of all jacana chicks make it out of the nest, and another half die before reaching adulthood.

JACANAS AND PEOPLE

Jacanas live close to humans in many parts of their range and are therefore well-known to them.

CONSERVATION STATUS

No jacana species are currently considered threatened. However, wetland habitats are being drained for agricultural or other human uses in many parts of the world. Other populations have suffered due to pollution from pesticides.

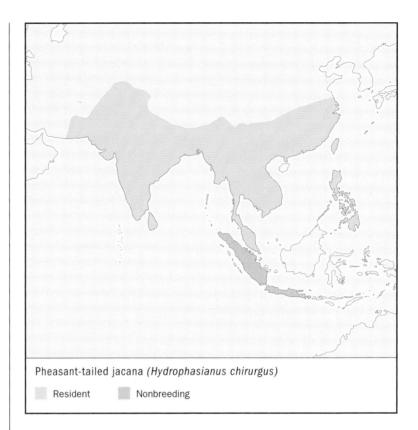

Pheasant-tailed jacana *(Hydrophasianus chirurgus)*

☐ Resident ☐ Nonbreeding

PHEASANT-TAILED JACANA
Hydrophasianus chirurgus

Physical characteristics: The pheasant-tailed jacana is the largest species in the group, measuring from 11 to 12.2 inches (28 o 31 centimeters) in length and weighing in at 4.8 to 8 ounces (126 to 231 grams). It has dark feathers with a yellow band around the neck and white wingtips. Males have long, brightly colored tail feathers during the breeding season.

Geographic range: The pheasant-tailed jacana is found in Asia, including portions of Pakistan, India, Nepal, Sri Lanka, Myanmar, China, Java, and the Philippines.

Habitat: The pheasant-tailed jacana inhabits marshes, ponds, and lakes with patches of floating vegetation.

Diet: The pheasant-tailed jacana eats primarily insects and other invertebrates, animals without a backbone.

Behavior and reproduction: Pheasant-tailed jacanas walk across floating vegetation with their large feet, only rarely taking to the air. They are polyandrous, with females having up to four mates at one time. Four eggs are laid by the female in each nest and hatch after twenty-two to twenty-eight days. Males are responsible for sitting on eggs and caring for chicks after they hatch. Fewer than half of all chicks survive to adulthood.

Pheasant-tailed jacanas and people: No significant interactions between pheasant-tailed jacanas and people are known.

Conservation status: This species is not considered threatened, although some populations in China and Taiwan have declined dramatically due to loss of wetland habitats. ■

Pheasant-tailed jacana females have up to four mates at one time. Males are responsible for sitting on eggs and caring for chicks after they hatch. (© T. D. Singh/VIREO. Reproduced by permission.)

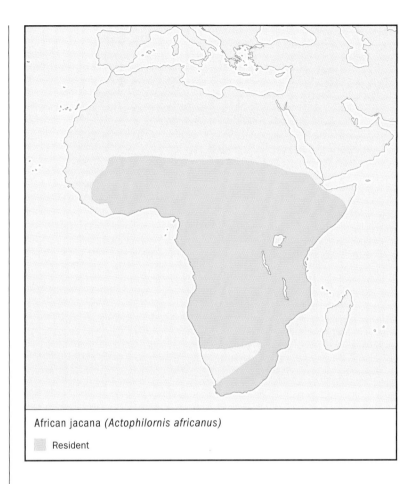

African jacana *(Actophilornis africanus)*

☐ Resident

AFRICAN JACANA
Actophilornis africanus

Physical characteristics: The African jacana ranges in length from 9 to 12.2 inches (23 to 31 centimeters) and in weight from 4 to 9 ounces (137 to 261 grams). African jacanas have brown, black, and white feathers and a blue patch on the forehead.

Geographic range: African jacanas are found in Africa south of the Sahara desert.

Habitat: African jacanas inhabit marshes, ponds, and lakes with mats of floating vegetation.

Diet: African jacanas eat primarily insects, other invertebrates, and the seeds of aquatic plants.

Behavior and reproduction: African jacanas breed during the rainy season. Females defend territories and mate with as many as four different males. Four eggs are laid at a time and hatch after twenty-two to twenty-eight days.

African jacanas and people: No significant interactions between African jacanas and people are known.

Conservation status: The African jacana is not currently considered threatened. ■

African jacanas walk across the floating vegetation in marshes, ponds, and lakes with their large feet, only rarely taking to the air. (© Nigel Dennis/Photo Researchers, Inc. Reproduced by permission.)

FOR MORE INFORMATION

Books:

del Hoyo, J., A. Elliott, and J. Sargatal, eds. *Handbook of the Birds of the World.* Vol. 3, *Hoatzin to Auks.* Barcelona: Lynx Edicions, 1996.

Perrins, Christopher, ed. *Firefly Encyclopedia of Birds.* Buffalo, NY: Firefly Books, 2003.

Web sites:

"Jacanidae (Jacanas)." The Internet Bird Collection. http://www.hbw.com/ibc/phtml/familia.phtml?idFamilia=52 (accessed on April 16, 2004).

"Family Jacanidae (Jacanas)." Animal Diversity Web. http://animaldiversity.ummz.umich.edu/site/accounts/classification/Jacanidae.html#Jacanidae (accessed on April 16, 2004).

"Jacanas." Bird Families of the World, Cornell University. http://www.es.cornell.edu/winkler/botw/jacanidae.html (accessed on April 16, 2004).

PAINTED SNIPES
Rostratulidae

Class: Aves
Order: Charadriiformes
Family: Rostratulidae
Number of species: 2 species

family
CHAPTER

PHYSICAL CHARACTERISTICS

Painted snipes range in size from 7.4 to 10.9 inches (19 to 28 centimeters) in length and from 2.3 to 7 ounces (65 to 200 grams) in weight. They have strong legs and long toes. Painted snipes have bills that curve downward at the tip and spread slightly to take on a spatula-like shape. The South American painted snipe is black-brown on the back and white on the belly. The head and neck are reddish brown in color with a contrasting cream-colored stripe. Males and females are generally similar in appearance, but females are slightly brighter in color and also slightly larger in size. The other species in the family is the greater painted snipe. In greater painted snipes, females have brown heads and necks, bronze-green wings, and black-barred backs. Males are duller in color, with spotted heads and gray-gold backs. Both male and female greater snipes have a striking pale streak around the eye, as well as a pale stripe on top of the head.

GEOGRAPHIC RANGE

Greater painted snipes are found in Africa, south Asia, Southeast Asia, the Philippines, Indonesia, and Australia. The South American painted snipe is found only in South America.

HABITAT

Painted snipes occur primarily in wetland habitats such as marshes. They can also be found in moist grasslands and along streams and rivers with vegetation along the banks. Some populations inhabit human-made environments, including rice

fields. Both painted snipe species regularly move short distances to find appropriate wet habitats.

DIET

Painted snipes are omnivorous, taking in both plant and animal matter. Animals they eat include invertebrates, animals without a backbone, such as insects, snails, earthworms, and crustaceans. Plant matter includes items such as grass seeds and cultivated grains. Painted snipes forage, or search for food, by standing in mud or shallow water and sifting through water and soil with their spatula-shaped bills. Greater painted snipes forage primarily at dusk and at night.

BEHAVIOR AND REPRODUCTION

Painted snipes are usually either solitary and living alone, or are found in pairs. In some instances, however, groups of as many as one hundred individuals have been observed, probably because dry weather reduces the amount of appropriate habitat.

The South American painted snipe is monogamous (muh-NAH-guh-mus), meaning that a single male mates with a single female during the breeding season. Males call to court females. South American painted snipes nest in small colonies, with five or six nests per 2.5 to 3.7 acres (1.0 to 1.5 hectares). The female lays two, or, on rare occasions, three eggs at a time. It is not known how long the eggs take to hatch or whether both parents are involved in taking care of the chicks. It is also not known how soon after hatching chicks leave the nest.

In the greater painted snipe, the more brightly colored females court the males. Courtship involves calling at dusk with what is described as a series of hiccup-like hoots made either from the ground or while in flight. Greater painted snipes are usually polyandrous (pah-lee-AN-drus), with a single female mating with multiple males, often as many as four. Sometimes, however, they are monogamous, with a female mating with only one male. Males are responsible for building the nests, incubating, or sitting on the eggs, and feeding and protecting the young once they hatch.

The female generally lays between two and five eggs at a time. Greater painted snipe chicks are precocial (pree-KOH-shul), hatching at an advanced stage of development, covered with feathers and being able to move. Male greater painted snipe males breed at one year of age, and females breed at age two.

Both painted snipe species build nests that are shallow bowls of reeds and grass. Painted snipes usually choose nest sites that are hidden in dense vegetation, although sometimes they will use more open areas.

PAINTED SNIPES AND PEOPLE

Both painted snipe species have long been hunted for food and sport. Greater painted snipes fly slowly, however, and are often considered too easy a target.

CONSERVATION STATUS

Neither species of painted snipe is considered threatened at present. However, the Australian form of the greater painted snipe should, in the opinion of some biologists, be considered a separate species. If it were recognized as a separate species, it would most likely be designated either Vulnerable, facing a high risk of extinction, dying out, or Endangered, facing a very high risk of extinction, by the World Conservation Union (IUCN). Australian greater painted snipes have declined due to the loss of wetland and grassland habitats, as well as long periods of drought.

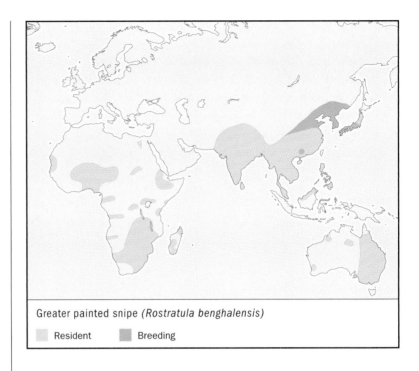

Greater painted snipe (*Rostratula benghalensis*)

Resident   Breeding

GREATER PAINTED SNIPE
Rostratula benghalensis

Physical characteristics: The greater painted snipe measures 9 to 10.9 inches (23 to 28 centimeters) in length and 3.2 to 6.7 ounces (90 to 190 grams) in weight. The female greater painted snipe has a reddish brown head and neck with a bronze-green back and wings. The male has a gray head and back spotted with gold. Both males and females have white eye patches and a white stripe on the top of the head. Young greater painted snipes resemble adult males.

Geographic range: The greater painted snipe is found in Madagascar, sub-Saharan Africa, south Asia, Southeast Asia, Japan, southeast Russia, the Philippines, Indonesia, and Australia. The Australian populations are distinct from other greater painted snipes and may be a separate species.

Habitat: Greater painted snipes occupy wetland habitats. They sometimes inhabit human-made areas such as rice fields.

Diet: Greater painted snipes are omnivorous, eating both plant and animal matter. Their diet includes small invertebrates, including insects, worms, and crustaceans, as well as seeds and grains.

Behavior and reproduction: Greater painted snipes are usually found either alone or in small groups. They forage, or search for food, around dusk as well as at night.

Greater painted snipes are either polyandrous, with each female mating with multiple males, or monogamous, with each female mating with only one male. The greater painted snipe may breed at any time during the year, but most frequently breeds after rainfalls. Females usually lay four eggs at a time in a shallow grass bowl-shaped nest. Nests are usually hidden in moist vegetation. Males are responsible for incubating, or sitting on, the eggs. Chicks hatch after fifteen to twenty-one days. Greater painted snipe chicks are precocial, and are usually able to leave the nest fairly quickly after hatching. Chicks are cared for exclusively by the male.

Greater painted snipes and people: Greater painted snipes have long been hunted for sport.

Conservation status: The greater painted snipe is not considered threatened at the present time. However, some populations have declined due to the large-scale loss of wetland habitats. The Australian greater painted snipes may represent a distinct species, and if so, would likely be considered either Vulnerable or Endangered. ■

FOR MORE INFORMATION

Books:

del Hoyo, J., A. Elliott, and J. Sargatal, eds. *Handbook of the Birds of the World.* Vol. 3, *Hoatzin to Auks.* Barcelona: Lynx Edicions, 1996.

Perrins, Christopher, ed. *Firefly Encyclopedia of Birds.* Buffalo, NY: Firefly Books, 2003.

Web sites:

"Painted Snipes." Bird Families of the World, Cornell University. http://www.es.cornell.edu/winkler/botw/rostratulidae.html (accessed on April 20, 2004).

"Rostratulidae (Painted-Snipes)." The Internet Bird Collection. http://www.hbw.com/ibc/phtml/familia.phtml?idFamilia=53 (accessed on April 20, 2004).

family

C H A P T E R

PHYSICAL CHARACTERISTICS

Crab plovers range in size from 13 to 16 inches (33 to 41 centimeters) in height and 8 to 11.2 ounces (230 to 325 grams) in weight. They are mostly white in color, but have a black patch on the back and some black on the wings. The wings of crab plovers are long and pointed, and the wingspan, or the distance from wingtip to wingtip when the wings are open, ranges from 29 to 30.7 inches (74 to 78 centimeters). The tail is short and gray and the legs are long and blue-gray in color. Crab plovers have webbed feet and a strong first toe, which is used for digging nest burrows. Crab plovers have bills that are designed for eating crabs. These are large, heavy, black in color, and shaped liked daggers. Male and female crab plovers are generally similar in size and appearance, but males have larger, heavier bills. Young crab plovers differ slightly in coloration from adults, with gray on top of the neck, behind the neck, and on the wings.

GEOGRAPHIC RANGE

Crab plovers are found in coastal habitats along the Indian Ocean. Populations are found in portions of Africa, Madagascar, the Middle East, and India.

HABITAT

Crab plovers occupy desert and semi-desert habitats, generally within 0.6 miles (1 kilometer) of the ocean. They require sand dunes for nesting.

phylum

class

subclass

order

monotypic order

suborder

▲ **family**

NEST BURROWERS

Crab plovers are the only species in the order Charadriiformes (gulls, terns, plovers, and other shorebirds) that nest in underground burrows. Their burrows help provide a cool environment for adults, eggs, and chicks. Breeding in crab plovers generally occurs during the hottest months of the year, when outside temperatures can reach 104°F (40°C). Burrows also help protect young from potential predators.

DIET

Crab plovers are specialized feeders, that is, their diet includes only a few items. Crab plovers eat crabs almost exclusively. They hunt their prey by running after them in mudflats or shallow water and then stabbing them with their sharp, powerful bills. Small crabs are generally swallowed whole, while larger crabs are torn to pieces and then eaten. Both adult and young crab plovers eat crabs. Adults give young chicks bits of prey, and older chicks entire prey items. Other foods that crab plovers eat occasionally include other crustaceans, small fish, marine worms, and other invertebrates.

BEHAVIOR AND REPRODUCTION

Crab plovers are found in large groups throughout the year. They gather in large flocks of as many as hundreds of individuals to forage, or hunt for food. Crab plovers also breed in large colonies, digging their nest burrows close together in sand dunes. Roost sites, where birds rest, can include as many as a thousand crab plovers. The calls from these sites, described as a barking "crow-ow-ow" are sometimes heard as far as a mile (1.6 kilometers) away.

Some populations of crab plovers migrate during the year, traveling from one living area to another and back. Other populations remain in the same place throughout the year. All crab plovers are most active at dawn and dusk as well as at night, because their habitats tend to be extremely hot during the day.

Unlike many other birds, crab plovers nest during the hottest, driest times of year, generally between the months of April and June. Crab plovers time their reproduction so that there will be plenty of crabs available as prey when the chicks hatch. Because of the extreme heat, however, crab plovers build their nests underground, using their bills and feet to dig large burrows in sand dunes. Burrows measure approximately 47.2 to 74 inches (120 to 188 centimeters) long. Crab plovers are the only species in the order Charadriiformes (which includes gulls, terns, plovers, and other shorebirds) to nest in burrows. Burrows not only provide a cool environment for adults, eggs, and chicks, but help provide protection from potential predators.

Crab plover *(Dromas ardeola)*

Resident

Crab plovers are believed to be monogamous, with a single male breeding with a single female during the breeding season. However, as many as ten adult birds are sometimes seen at a single nest burrow, suggesting that some individuals may nest together, or that adult siblings may help their parents raise younger siblings. Females lay only one egg at a time. The crab plover egg is extremely large compared to the bird's body size. It is not known how long eggs take to hatch. It is also not known for certain whether both parents help raise chicks, but it is likely that only females are responsible for this task. Although crab plover young are precocial (pree-KOH-shul), hatching at an advanced stage of development, feathered and able to move, they remain in the burrow for a considerable length of time, being fed by adults.

CRAB PLOVERS AND PEOPLE

Crab plovers have little contact with humans because of the harsh climates they live in. However, in the past both crab plovers and their eggs have been eaten by humans.

Crab plovers hunt crabs by running after them in mudflats or shallow water and then stabbing them with their sharp, powerful bills. (© H. and J. Eriksen/VIREO. Reproduced by permission.)

CONSERVATION STATUS

Crab plovers are not considered threatened at this time, with surveys suggesting that there are as many as 50,000 individuals in existence. However, some populations have been affected by oil production activity, habitat destruction, pollution, and other factors.

FOR MORE INFORMATION

Books:

del Hoyo, J., A. Elliott, and J. Sargatal, eds. *Handbook of the Birds of the World.* Vol. 3, *Hoatzin to Auks.* Barcelona: Lynx Edicions, 1996.

Perrins, Christopher, ed. *Firefly Encyclopedia of Birds.* Buffalo, NY: Firefly Books, 2003.

Web sites:

"Crabplover." Bird Families of the World, Cornell University. http://www.es.cornell.edu/winkler/botw/dromadidae.html (accessed on April 20, 2004).

"Dromadidae (Crab Plover)." The Internet Bird Collection. http://www.hbw.com/ibc/phtml/familia.phtml?idFamilia=54 (accessed on April 20, 2004).

OYSTERCATCHERS

Haematopodidae

Class: Aves
Order: Charadriiformes
Family: Haematopodidae
Number of species: 7 species

family

CHAPTER

PHYSICAL CHARACTERISTICS

Oystercatchers vary in length from 15.8 to 19.8 inches (40 to 49 centimeters) and in weight from 0.9 to 1.5 pounds (400 to 700 grams). Some oystercatcher species have dark feathers throughout the body while others are dark with white feathers on the lower breast, belly, and parts of the wings and tail. All-dark oystercatcher species tend to be somewhat larger than black-and-white oystercatchers. One species, the variable oystercatcher, has individuals with both coloration patterns as well as individuals that are somewhere between the two. Oystercatchers have bright red or orange bills with a blade-like or dagger-like shape. The eye and a narrow ring around the eye are red in Old World oystercatcher species. In New World species, the eyes are yellow while the eye rings are either yellow or orange-red. The legs are pink and the feet are stout, with toes that are partially webbed. Oystercatchers have short necks, long, pointed wings, and short tails. Females are larger than males in oyster-catchers, and also have longer wings and bills.

GEOGRAPHIC RANGE

Oystercatchers are found in coastal habitats worldwide, including North America, Europe, Africa, east Asia, Australia, and New Zealand. They also inhabit lakeshore areas in New Zealand, temperate (mild) Europe and Asia, and northern Africa.

HABITAT

Oystercatchers occupy diverse types of shoreline habitat. These include beaches of rock, sand, pebble, and shell. Some

HELPING CHICKS SURVIVE

Oystercatchers have a difficult time successfully raising young. Many eggs are washed away by storms before they even hatch, and chicks, when they do hatch, are often taken by predators. Because of the danger of predators, oystercatcher chicks become fully mobile within a day of hatching, and are able to run and hide from danger. Parents also feed chicks for a long period of time, helping them grow quickly in order to better escape predators.

species can be found in marshes or coastal lagoons. A small number of species live on agricultural land or pastures.

DIET

Oystercatchers eat many different types of marine invertebrates, including mollusks, crabs, chitons (KYE-tunz; a type of mollusk), sea urchins, and snails. They also occasionally eat fish. Inland oystercatcher populations focus on arthropods such as insects and spiders. Oystercatchers use their sensitive bills to search for food in shallow water or soft mud. They are effective hunters that are able to defeat their prey using a variety of techniques. With mollusks, oystercatchers sometimes stab their narrow bills into a slightly open shell. They may also pound mollusks against sharp rocks to crack them open.

BEHAVIOR AND REPRODUCTION

Most species of oystercatchers are migratory, moving from breeding areas during the breeding season to nonbreeding grounds in the winter. Many individuals return to the same locations from one year to the next. All species defend territories from other members of the species during the breeding season, and some defend territories year-round. In oystercatchers that are not territorial during the winter, such as the African black oystercatcher, individuals gather in large numbers for better protection against predators, animals that hunt them for food. This behavior also helps individuals stay warm in cold climates. Oystercatchers sometimes also gather in flocks to forage, or search for food. Foraging flocks in coastal species tend to have no more than fifty individuals, but in inland oystercatchers, groups of as many as a thousand individuals are sometimes observed. The oystercatcher call is commonly described as a trill followed by a loud peep.

Oystercatchers breed during the summer in most parts of the world. All species are monogamous (muh-NAH-guh-mus), that is, a single male breeds with a single female during the breeding season. In many cases, individuals also keep the same mate from year to year. Courtship in oystercatchers is sometimes called "piping" because it involves a male and female singing a single "piped" note together while walking, running, or flying next to each other, making frequent synchronized turns. Nearby pairs often perform the piping routine at the same time. The piping routine is also used to alert other members of the species to the boundaries of a pair's territory.

Females lay between one and four eggs at a time, usually two or three. Nests are simple hollows on the ground, either unlined or lined. Both parents help incubate, or sit on, the eggs. Eggs hatch after between twenty-four and thirty-nine days. Chicks are colored gray-brown to blend into their environments. They are able to leave the nest within a day of hatching. However, parents continue to feed the chicks for at least sixty days after hatching. Most oystercatcher pairs are only able to raise one offspring successfully during each breeding season. Storms can wash away eggs, and chicks are frequently lost to predators.

OYSTERCATCHERS AND PEOPLE

It is sometimes claimed that oystercatchers help deplete oyster beds used by humans, but there is no evidence to back up these claims.

CONSERVATION STATUS

Of the seven species of oystercatchers in existence, one is considered Endangered, facing a very high risk of extinction, and one is considered Near Threatened, in danger of becoming threatened. Chatham Island oystercatchers are Endangered. There are only 100 to 150 individuals left in their natural habitat on four small islands in New Zealand. Chatham Island oystercatcher populations did increase in number during the 1990s as a result of predator removal from critical habitat areas and artificial incubation of eggs. African black oystercatchers are considered Near Threatened. Populations number about 4,800 total. African black oystercatchers have been affected primarily by human disturbance, particularly off-road vehicles and other coastal human recreation.

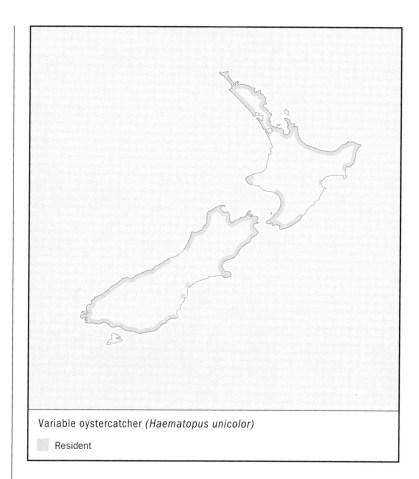

Variable oystercatcher *(Haematopus unicolor)*

▨ Resident

VARIABLE OYSTERCATCHER
Haematopus unicolor

Physical characteristics: The variable oystercatcher is about 18.5 to 19.3 inches (47 to 49 centimeters) in length. Males weigh about 1.5 pounds (678 grams) while females are a little heavier at 1.6 pounds (724 grams). The variable oystercatcher is the only species that includes all black individuals as well as black-and-white colored individuals. Some individuals have a coloration that is intermediate between the two primary types. They are known as "smudgies." The eye, eye ring, and bill are all red in this species.

Geographic range: The variable oystercatcher is found exclusively on the coasts and islands of New Zealand.

Habitat: Variable oystercatchers occupy rocky and sandy seashore areas.

Diet: Variable oystercatchers eat primarily marine invertebrates such as bivalves, crabs, snails, and polychaetes (PAHL-ee-keets; marine worms).

Behavior and reproduction: Variable oystercatchers are territorial, but occasionally form flocks. There is frequent breeding between differently colored variable oystercatchers. The breeding season occurs in December and January. Nests are built on beaches and sand dunes. Females typically lay three eggs which hatch after twenty-five to thirty-two days.

Variable oystercatchers and people: No significant interactions between variable oystercatchers and people are known.

Conservation status: Variable oystercatchers are not officially considered threatened at this time. However, the total population is only about 3,900 individuals. Variable oystercatchers have been affected by human disturbance and predation by introduced mammals. ■

FOR MORE INFORMATION

Books:

BirdLife International. *Threatened Birds of the World.* Barcelona: Lynx Edicions, 2000.

del Hoyo, J., A. Elliott, and J. Sargatal, eds. *Handbook of the Birds of the World.* Vol. 3, *Hoatzin to Auks.* Barcelona: Lynx Edicions, 1996.

Perrins, Christopher, ed. *Firefly Encyclopedia of Birds.* Buffalo, NY: Firefly Books, 2003.

Web sites:

"Family Haematopodidae (Oystercatchers)." Animal Diversity Web. http://animaldiversity.ummz.umich.edu/site/accounts/classification/Haematopodidae.html#Haematopodidae (accessed on April 22, 2004).

"Haematopodidae (Oystercatchers)." The Internet Bird Collection. http://www.hbw.com/ibc/phtml/familia.phtml?idFamilia=55 (accessed on April 22, 2004).

"Oystercatchers." Bird Families of the World, Cornell University. http://www.es.cornell.edu/winkler/botw/haematopodidae.html (accessed on April 22, 2004).

Class: Aves
Order: Charadriiformes
Family: Recurvirostridae
Number of species: 8 species

family
CHAPTER

PHYSICAL CHARACTERISTICS

Stilts and avocets range from 14 to 20 inches (35 to 51 centimeters) in height and from 5.8 to 16.2 ounces (166 to 461 grams) in weight. All species have striking bill shapes. In avocets, the bills curve upward, particularly in females. The ibisbill has a bill that curves downward. In stilts, the bills are generally straight or slightly curved. Stilts and avocets have the longest legs (in proportion to body size) of any shorebirds. These may be red, blue, or gray in color. Most stilts and avocets are black and white in color, sometimes with reddish-brown areas.

GEOGRAPHIC RANGE

Stilts and avocets are found worldwide, on all continents except Antarctica. The largest number of species occupy areas near Australia.

HABITAT

Most stilts and avocets occupy large wetland areas. The ibisbill, however, prefers rocky habitats along slow-moving streams. Avocets, as well as the banded stilt, generally live in saltwater wetlands. Other stilt species use both saltwater and freshwater wetlands. The Andean stilt occurs only close to high altitude saline lakes. Many stilt and avocet species also use man-made areas as habitat, including dams, irrigation sites, and sewer ponds.

DIET

Stilts and avocets eat aquatic invertebrates such as crustaceans, insect larvae, worms, and mollusks. They also eat small

phylum

class

subclass

order

monotypic order

suborder

▲ **family**

CROSS-BREEDING IN AN ENDANGERED STILT

The black stilt, which is found exclusively in New Zealand, is endangered for a variety of reasons. Wetland habitats have been destroyed by humans, and mammals not originally found on New Zealand eat black stilt eggs. Black stilts also cross-breed, that is, mate with individuals of other species. In the case of black stilts, cross-breeding occurs with black-winged stilts, which are also found on New Zealand. There are now fewer than one hundred black stilts left in existence.

fish and, sometimes, plant material. Stilts and avocets generally obtain food by pecking at items. In addition, some avocets swing their bills through water or soft mud and filter out small food items. Some stilts and avocets also stick their entire heads underwater to look for food. The ibisbill uses its bill to rake through pebbles in the rocky stream habitats it prefers. It then snatches whatever small aquatic animals it disturbs. Finally, some stilts and avocets have been known to snap at flying insects.

BEHAVIOR AND REPRODUCTION

A few species of stilts and avocets, such as black-winged stilts, pied avocets, and American avocets, migrate from breeding grounds to wintering grounds over the course of the year. Ibisbills migrate altitudinally, moving from higher to lower elevations and back. In addition, most species move short distances to find suitable wetland areas.

Most species of stilts and avocets form large flocks while feeding. Flocks can include several thousand individuals. In most cases, feeding occurs during the daytime. However, some stilts also feed at night. Stilts and avocets generally roost, or spend the night, standing in water. They may also rest during the day, either sitting on the ground or standing on one foot with the head tucked under the wing. Unlike other members of the group, ibisbills are usually found alone, in pairs, or in much smaller groups that rarely exceed seven or eight individuals.

Except for the ibisbill, stilt and avocet species also nest in large colonies, groups, which may include multiple shorebird species. Breeding colonies tend to be very noisy. Stilts and avocets use a variety of calls to communicate with mates or offspring, or to signal danger.

Most stilts and avocets are monogamous (muh-NAH-guh-mus), with a single male breeding with a single female at one time. Birds may change mates over the course of a breeding season, however. To attract females, males perform a display that involves dipping their heads, shaking, and then preening, or smoothing their feathers. After mating, the male and female cross bills and walk together, the male holding one wing over the back of the female. Generally, the female lays three or four eggs at a time. Both the male and the female participate in incubating, or sitting on the eggs, and feeding and protecting the chicks once they hatch. Adults dive-bomb potential predators and may also fake a broken wing in order to distract intruders and draw them away from the nest.

STILTS, AVOCETS, AND PEOPLE

There are no significant interactions between most species of stilts and avocets and people. However, humans have appreciated these birds for a long time and are generally enthusiastic about conservation measures to help protect populations.

CONSERVATION STATUS

The black stilt, which is restricted to New Zealand, is considered Critically Endangered, facing an extremely high risk of extinction. It has suffered primarily from habitat destruction and non-native predators introduced by humans, which eat large numbers of black stilt eggs. There are currently fewer than 100 black stilts in existence. The Hawaiian subspecies of the black-winged stilt is also considered Endangered, facing a very high risk of extinction. There are approximately 1,800 individuals left in the wild. Populations have declined due to habitat destruction and predators introduced by humans.

Black-winged stilt *(Himantopus himantopus)*

☐ Resident ☐ Breeding ☐ Nonbreeding

SPECIES ACCOUNTS

BLACK-WINGED STILT
Himantopus himantopus

Physical characteristics: The black-winged stilt has long pink legs and a straight or upwardly curved black bill. In the male, the back and wings are black, the belly is white, and the tail is marked with gray bands. Females have dullish brown backs. The color of the head and neck varies in black-winged stilts from white to black.

Geographic range: The black-winged stilt is widely distributed and occurs on all continents except Antarctica.

Habitat: Black-winged stilts occupy wetland habitats including marshes, swamps, lakeshores, river-edges, and flooded fields.

Diet: Black-winged stilts eat aquatic insects, mollusks, crustaceans, worms, small fish, and tadpoles. They sometimes forage, or search for food, at night, particularly when there is no moon and therefore little light.

Behavior and reproduction: Black-winged stilts can be found in large flocks of as many as several thousand individuals. They have a display where they leap up and then float down, but it is not known what the purpose of the display is. Their call is described as a sharp "yep" sound.

Black-winged stilts and people: No significant interactions between black-winged stilts and people are known.

Conservation status: The black-winged stilt is not considered threatened globally, but the Hawaiian subspecies is considered Endangered. There are about 1,800 individuals left in the wild. ■

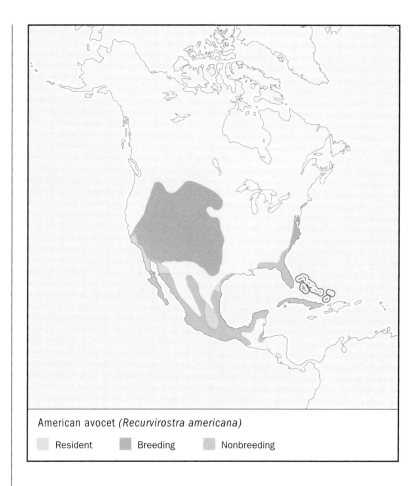

American avocet *(Recurvirostra americana)*

| | Resident | | Breeding | | Nonbreeding |

AMERICAN AVOCET
Recurvirostra americana

Physical characteristics: American avocets have blue legs and upwardly curved black bills. The wings and the back are black. The head, neck, and breast are gray during the nonbreeding season but change to orange during the breeding season. Males and females are similar in color but males are often larger. Females have shorter bills with a more pronounced upward curve.

Geographic range: American avocets occupy the western United States, Baja California and much of Mexico, Florida, the eastern coast of the United States, and the Bahamas to Cuba.

Habitat: American avocets use temporary wetland areas, such as areas that flood for part of the year, in the western United States, as well as more permanent wetland habitats.

Diet: American avocets eat aquatic insects, crustaceans, worms, and small fish. They also eat seeds. American avocets often forage, or look for food, in large flocks. They swing their bills through the water to find food, but are also known to peck at food or plunge underwater for it.

Behavior and reproduction: American avocets are found in large flocks during the nonbreeding season. During the breeding season, male-female breeding pairs form and defend territories from other individuals. American avocets threaten an intruder by facing the other bird and extending their necks. Females generally lay four eggs at a time in a grass-lined nest on the ground. Eggs hatch after twenty-two to twenty-nine days. Both the male and female help incubate, or sit on, the eggs, and both feed the chicks once they hatch. Chicks leave the nest after four or five weeks.

Both the male and female American avocet help incubate the eggs, and both feed the chicks once they hatch. Chicks leave the nest after four or five weeks. (© David Weintraub/Photo Researchers, Inc. Reproduced by permission.)

American avocets and people: The American avocet was hunted in its habitats in California during the early 1900s, but this practice has stopped.

Conservation status: The American avocet is not considered threatened at this time. However, pollution and destruction of wetland habitats have led to population declines in many parts of its range. ■

FOR MORE INFORMATION

Books:

del Hoyo, J., A. Elliott, and J. Sargatal, eds. *Handbook of the Birds of the World.* Vol. 3, *Hoatzin to Auks.* Barcelona: Lynx Edicions, 1996.

Perrins, Christopher, ed. *Firefly Encyclopedia of Birds.* Buffalo, NY: Firefly Books, 2003.

Web sites:

"Avocets, Stilts." Bird Families of the World, Cornell University. http://www.es.cornell.edu/winkler/botw/recurvirostridae.html (accessed on May 1, 2004).

"Family Recurvirostridae (Avocets and Stilts)." Animal Diversity Web. http://animaldiversity.ummz.umich.edu/site/accounts/classification/Recurvirostridae.html#Recurvirostridae (accessed on May 1, 2004).

"Recurvirostridae (Stilts and Avocets)." The Internet Bird Collection. http://www.hbw.com/ibc/phtml/familia.phtml?idFamilia=57 (accessed on May 1, 2004).

THICK-KNEES
Burhinidae

Class: Aves
Order: Charadriiformes
Family: Burhinidae
Number of species: 9 species

family

CHAPTER

PHYSICAL CHARACTERISTICS

Thick-knees vary in size from 12.5 to 23 inches (32 to 59 centimeters) in length and 0.7 to 2.4 pounds (0.3 to 1.1 kilograms) in weight. Their heads are round, their necks are slender, and their bodies are large. Thick-knees have long legs, long tails, and a pointed bill. All thick-knees have large yellow or amber colored eyes and stripes either above the eyes, through the eyes, or below the eyes. Most species are a light sandy brown on top and pale on the belly. The wings are either solid-colored, striped, or spotted while folded. When thick-knees are flying, however, striking black and white patterns on the wings and tail are revealed. Males and females tend to be similar in both size and color. Young thick-knees are colored to blend into their stony or sandy habitats.

GEOGRAPHIC RANGE

Thick-knees are found primarily in the Old World, including portions of Asia, Europe, the Middle East, and Africa. Two species occupy parts of Central America and South America, and several species occur in Australia.

HABITAT

Many species of thick-knees are found in either grassland or brush habitats. Others occupy dry desert areas, usually adjacent to a river or stream. The beach thick-knee is found in seashore areas. One species, the Senegal thick-knee, lives in large cities such as Cairo, Egypt, where it finds appropriate nesting areas on the flat roofs of houses and other buildings.

phylum

class

subclass

order

monotypic order

suborder

▲ **family**

NOCTURNAL BIRDS

Many thick-knee species are crepuscular (kri-PUS-kyuh-lur; active at dusk) or nocturnal (active at night). The bold, black-and-white wing and tail markings that characterize thick-knees are easy to see in fading light. Because they are nocturnal, thick-knees also defend their territories using loud calls, rather than the visual postures and displays used by other bird species. Their calls are loud and carry a long distance, and thick-knees have become an important part of the folklore in parts of their range.

Several species of thick-knees are occasionally found in agricultural lands and pastures.

DIET

Thick-knees have a diet that consists primarily of invertebrates, animals without a backbone, such as beetles, crickets, grasshoppers, crustaceans, mollusks, snails, slugs, and worms, as well as larger vertebrate prey, animals with backbones, such as frogs, lizards, and rodents. Some thick-knees will also eat plant material, including seeds and the shoots of plants. The beach thick-knee eats large numbers of crabs. Thick-knees forage, or search for food, by walking slowly while looking for prey on the ground. Food items are picked up using their strong bills. Larger prey are broken into pieces if necessary before swallowing.

BEHAVIOR AND REPRODUCTION

Some thick-knees, such as the stone-curlew, are generally found alone. Other thick-knees are often found in small groups. All thick-knees spend the majority of their time on the ground, usually perching no higher than a few feet off the ground. However, thick-knees are strong fliers and will fly away if disturbed by intruders. Many species of thick-knees are nocturnal, quiet by day and active at night, when they call loudly.

Breeding in thick-knees occurs in the spring, except in the tropics, when it may occur year-round. The stone-curlew is a monogamous (muh-NAH-guh-mus) species, with a single male mating with a single female. Stone-curlews keep the same mate throughout life. Many other thick-knee species are also monogamous, but the breeding system for a few species remains uncertain. Thick-knee nests are simple and formed by scraping the ground. The male and female select the site together by bowing towards a particular spot. The male chooses the final spot, and the female scrapes at the ground with her feet to clear a nest. Twigs, small stones, and leaves may be scattered around the nest site. Often, several nests are built this way by the pair before one is finally chosen.

In most thick-knee species, the female lays two or three eggs at a time. In the beach thick-knee, only one egg is laid. The eggs are usually light brown in color and either spotted or streaked to make them less visible on the ground. Both male and female incubate, or sit on, the eggs. Eggs hatch after twenty-four to twenty-seven days. The parents immediately move the eggshells away so that potential predators will have a harder time locating the chicks. Thick-knee chicks are able to leave the nest before they are a day old. However, parents continue to protect and to help feed the young. Adults scare off potential predators by fanning their wings and tail. Thick-knee young become mature and capable of breeding after two or three years.

THICK-KNEES AND PEOPLE

Thick-knees appear in Australian folklore, where they have been given names that sound like their calls, such as "weeloo" or "willaroo." One species, the double-striped thick-knee, has been kept in farms and other human settlements to reduce the number of insects.

CONSERVATION STATUS

In Europe, stone-curlew populations have declined due to habitat destruction for agricultural development. Peruvian thick-knees are also declining in their habitats due to human disturbance. Bush thick-knees in Australia have declined due to habitat loss as well as hunting, egg collection, and predation, hunting, by foxes.

Beach thick-knee (*Esacus magnirostris*)

░ Resident

BEACH THICK-KNEE
Esacus magnirostris

Physical characteristics: The beach thick-knee is the largest species of thick-knee and ranges from 21 to 22.5 inches (53 to 57 centimeters) in length. It has thick yellow legs, a long, strong, bill, and yellow eyes. The beach thick-knee is gray-brown on the back and pale on the belly. The shoulder is black above a thin white line. The head is mostly black, with a white stripe through the eye. The bill is black except for a yellow base. There is a rust-colored patch under the tail.

Geographic range: The beach thick-knee is found in the Andaman Islands, the Philippines, Indonesia, New Guinea, other Southwest Pacific islands, and the northern coast of Australia.

Habitat: The beach thick-knee is found on seashore beach habitats. These include sand, shingle, rock, and mud beaches.

Diet: The beach thick-knee eats crabs primarily, but also eats other crustaceans. Large crabs are torn into small pieces before they are swallowed. It generally follows its prey quietly, and then suddenly lunges and grabs. Sometimes, beach thick-knees also search in mud and sand for prey.

Behavior and reproduction: Beach thick-knees fly away when disturbed, usually over the water. Beach thick-knees are monogamous. The nest is usually a shallow depression that is sometimes surrounded by a ring of leaves. The female lays only one egg at a time. The egg hatches after thirty days. The chick is able to fly after twelve weeks, but may stay with its parents for as long as a year.

Beach thick-knees and people: No significant interactions between beach thick-knees and people are known.

Conservation status: The beach thick-knee is not currently considered threatened. However, habitat loss and disturbance may be a problem as beaches become more regularly used for human recreation. ■

The beach thick-knee lives on seashore beach habitats. It eats mostly crabs, but also eats other crustaceans. (© V. Sinha/VIREO. Reproduced by permission.)

FOR MORE INFORMATION

Books:

del Hoyo, J., A. Elliott, and J. Sargatal, eds. *Handbook of the Birds of the World.* Vol. 3, *Hoatzin to Auks.* Barcelona: Lynx Edicions, 1996.

Perrins, Christopher, ed. *Firefly Encyclopedia of Birds.* Buffalo, NY: Firefly Books, 2003.

Web sites:

"Burhinidae (Thick-knees)." The Internet Bird Collection. http://www.hbw.com/ibc/phtml/familia.phtml?idFamilia=58 (accessed on May 3, 2004).

"Family Burhinidae (Thick-knees)." Animal Diversity Web. http://animaldiversity.ummz.umich.edu/site/accounts/classification/Burhinidae.html#Burhinidae (accessed on May 3, 2004).

"Thick-knees, Stone-curlews." Bird Families of the World, Cornell University. http://www.es.cornell.edu/winkler/botw/burhinidae.html (accessed on May 3, 2004).

PRATINCOLES AND COURSERS
Glareolidae

Class: Aves

Order: Charadriiformes

Family: Glareolidae

Number of species: 16 species

phylum

class

subclass

order

monotypic order

suborder

▲ family

PHYSICAL CHARACTERISTICS

Pratincoles (PRAT-un-kohlz) and coursers vary in size from 6.7 to 11.4 inches (17 to 29 centimeters) in length and 1.3 to 6.1 ounces (37 to 172 grams) in weight. Pratincoles generally have slender bodies, long wings, and short legs. They also have beaks that open wide, which helps them catch insects while flying. One pratincole, the Australian pratincole, has very long legs, however. The coursers, on the other hand, tend to have stockier bodies, shorter wings, and very long legs. Coursers are also characterized by a square tail.

GEOGRAPHIC RANGE

Pratincoles and coursers are found in portions of Africa, Europe, Asia, and Australia.

HABITAT

Most pratincoles live near water, with many species preferring areas along large rivers. Pratincoles of Europe and Asia generally occur in grassland or desert habitats near water. The Egyptian plover occupies sandbars along tropical African rivers. Coursers occupy dry habitats of various types, including extreme desert.

DIET

All pratincoles and coursers eat primarily insects. Coursers will sometimes also eat other invertebrates, animals without a backbone, such as mollusks, as well as seeds. Pratincoles catch their insect prey "on the wing," that is, in the air while flying. Sometimes they search for insects on the ground as well.

Coursers, on the other hand, find food exclusively on the ground, pecking at food items with their bills. Some coursers have bills that curve downward, and use these bills to dig through soft sand or mud for insects and seeds.

BEHAVIOR AND REPRODUCTION

During the nonbreeding season, pratincoles can be found in flocks of as many as 100 individuals. They prefer to rest either on the ground or on rocks in the middle of rivers. All the members of the flock face the same direction, into the wind. Praticoles have loud, sharp calls which they use most often during migrations or when they are disturbed at their breeding sites.

Coursers are fast runners that generally prefer to run rather than fly from danger. However, they are good fliers as well. Unlike pratincoles, coursers are generally found alone, although small flocks of no more than five to ten individuals are sometimes seen. Many coursers, particularly those in dry, desert environments, move around a great deal as suitable habitat shifts. Coursers are often diurnal, that is, active during the day, but may switch to being nocturnal, active at night, in hot weather.

Pratincoles and coursers either build nests by scraping a shallow indentation on the ground, or use no nest at all. A few species bury their eggs partially in sand. Pratincoles sometimes nest in large colonies, while coursers are solitary nesters, with each pair isolated from other pairs. Pratincoles in the Northern Hemisphere lay two to four eggs at a time. Other species lay no more than two. One species, the double-banded courser, lays only one egg at a time. Eggs are generally either white or cream-colored and marked with spots of streaks to help them blend into their environments.

PRATINCOLES, COURSERS, AND PEOPLE

Pratincoles and coursers are hunted for food in parts of Africa and Southeast Asia. Collared pratincole eggs were collected for food in Hungary until that population was wiped out.

CATCHING INSECTS IN THE AIR AND ON THE GROUND

Pratincoles, which generally catch insects in the air, have long wings that help them maneuver (mah-NOO-ver) during flight. Coursers, which generally catch their insects on the ground, have long legs to help them run at prey. The one species in the pratincole and courser group that hunts insects both in the air and on the ground is the Australian pratincole. The Australian pratincole has long wings as well as long legs.

CONSERVATION STATUS

Of the sixteen species of pratincoles and coursers, one, the Jerdon's courser, is considered Endangered, facing a very high risk of extinction. Populations have declined in their habitats in east-central India due to habitat destruction and disturbance by humans.

Collared pratincole (*Glareola pratincola*)

Resident   Breeding   Nonbreeding

COLLARED PRATINCOLE
Glareola pratincola

Physical characteristics: The collared pratincole is 8.7 to 9.8 inches (22 to 25 centimeters) in length and weighs between 2.1 and 3.7 ounces (60 to 104 grams). It is a smoky gray-brown color on the back and pale on the belly. During the breeding season, there is a yellow patch on the throat surrounded by a thin black collar. The bill is red at the base and black elsewhere. Collared pratincoles have slender bodies, short legs, and long wings.

Geographic range: The collared pratincole is found in most of sub-Saharan Africa, with isolated breeding populations scattered in portions of Europe and Asia.

Both collared pratincole parents sit on the eggs and feed the chicks after hatching. (© H. and J. Eriksen/VIREO. Reproduced by permission.)

Habitat: The collared pratincole occupies habitats between short-grass grasslands and deserts. It is also found in seashore areas with semi-desert conditions.

Diet: Collared pratincoles eat primarily insects, which they catch in flight or grab from the ground. Grasshoppers and beetles make up the bulk of their diet.

Behavior and reproduction: Collared pratincoles are found in large flocks during both the breeding and nonbreeding seasons. They tend to spend time feeding in the air, and then rest on the ground for periods of time. They scrape a shallow indentation in the ground for a nest, sometimes lining it with pieces of vegetation. Females lay three eggs in the species' European and Asian breeding grounds, but only two in African habitats. Eggs are incubated, or sat upon, by both parents. Eggs hatch after seventeen to nineteen days. Both parents feed the chicks. Chicks are able to fly after about one month.

Collared pratincoles and people: The eggs of collared pratincoles were once collected in large numbers by humans for food. In the past, collared pratincoles also helped control locust plagues by eating large numbers of insects.

Conservation status: The collared pratincole is not considered threatened at this time. However, numbers have declined due to the use of pesticides and artificial fertilizers, as well as habitat destruction and disturbance by humans. ■

Australian pratincole *(Stiltia isabella)*

■ Resident   ■ Breeding   ■ Nonbreeding

AUSTRALIAN PRATINCOLE
Stiltia isabella

Physical characteristics: The Australian pratincole varies between 7.5 and 8.7 inches (19 to 22 centimeters) in length and weighs about 2.3 ounces (65 grams). It is light brown in color across most of its body, but has a dark brown upper belly and white lower belly. The bill has a bright red base and black tip. The Australian pratincole has a slender body, long legs, and extremely long wings.

Geographic range: The Australian pratincole is found in most of inland and northern Australia, as well as portions of New Guinea and eastern Indonesia.

Habitat: The Australian pratincole is found on short-grass plains, usually near water.

Diet: The Australian pratincole primarily eats insects. It catches these either while flying or on the ground. When pursuing prey on the ground, it may use a wing to keep insects from escaping. Australian pratincoles may also eat seeds.

Behavior and reproduction: The Australian pratincole is sometimes found alone, but is more frequently seen in flocks. Individuals are able to run quickly. They are usually silent in breeding colonies, but make considerable noise while migrating.

Australian pratincoles and people: The Australian pratincole is sometimes hunted for food in Indonesia.

Conservation status: The Australian pratincole is fairly common across its range and is not considered threatened. ■

The Australian pratincole is sometimes found alone, but is usually seen in flocks. (© B. Chudleigh/VIREO. Reproduced by permission.)

FOR MORE INFORMATION

Books:

del Hoyo, J., A. Elliott, and J. Sargatal, eds. *Handbook of the Birds of the World.* Vol. 3, *Hoatzin to Auks.* Barcelona: Lynx Edicions, 1996.

Hockey, Phil. *Waders of Southern Africa.* Cape Town, South Africa: Struik Winchester, 1995.

Perrins, Christopher, ed. *Firefly Encyclopedia of Birds.* Buffalo, NY: Firefly Books, 2003.

Web sites:

"Family Glareolidae (Coursers and Pratincoles)." Animal Diversity Web. http://animaldiversity.ummz.umich.edu/site/accounts/classification/Glareolidae.html#Glareolidae (accessed on May 4, 2004).

"Glareolidae (Coursers and Pratincoles)." The Internet Bird Collection. http://www.hbw.com/ibc/phtml/familia.phtml?idFamilia=59 (accessed on May 4, 2004).

"Pratincoles, Coursers." Bird Families of the World, Cornell University. http://www.es.cornell.edu/winkler/botw/glareolidae.html (accessed on May 4, 2004).

family

CHAPTER

PHYSICAL CHARACTERISTICS

Plovers (PLUH-verz or PLOH-verz) and lapwings vary in size from about 5.5 to 16 inches in length (14 to 40 centimeters) and from 1.25 to 10.5 ounces (35 to 298 grams) in weight. Members of the family tend to have chunky bodies, legs that are either short or of medium length, and short bills. Most species are black and white in color with some areas of brown or gray. Some species have bold markings on the face, dark rings around the neck, or black and white wing markings. Lapwing species sometimes have bright wattles, folds of skin that hang from the neck. Lapwings also have spurs on their wings that they use to fight with members of the same species or to defend their nests from intruders.

GEOGRAPHIC RANGE

Plovers and lapwings are found worldwide, on all continents except Antarctica.

HABITAT

Plovers and lapwings occupy a wide range of habitats including seashores, the banks of freshwater lakes and ponds, grasslands, and even flooded tundra areas. Many species occupy human-associated habitats such as agricultural fields, sewage ponds, airports, golf courses, roads, and rooftops.

DIET

Plovers and lapwings eat a diverse diet of aquatic and terrestrial invertebrates, animals without a backbone, small vertebrates, animals with a backbone, such as fish or lizards, and plant materials such as berries and seeds. Berries are a particularly important part of the diet of tundra species, since there are lengthy periods where few or no insects are available. Most members of this family catch food by running after prey and pecking at it with their bills. Some species use their feet to pat at or scratch the ground to reveal prey. One species, the Magellanic plover, is known for turning over stones to find prey. More aquatic plovers and lapwings, such as the red-kneed dotterel or white-tailed plover, search for food in the water, often sticking their heads underwater to snatch prey. One species, the wrybill, has a special curved bill that it uses to grab mayfly larvae or fish eggs from the bottoms of rocks.

BEHAVIOR AND REPRODUCTION

Some plovers and lapwings remain in the same area throughout the year, while others migrate between breeding habitats and wintering habitats. Most species form flocks during migration and the nonbreeding season. However, one species, Mitchell's plover, is usually found in groups of no more than six individuals. Plovers and lapwings spend a significant amount of time running on the ground, but are good fliers as well. They are active both during the day and at night. Many species are quite noisy.

Most plovers and lapwings build "nests" that are scraped indentations on the ground. One species, however, the shore plover, builds a nest at the end of a tunnel it makes through vegetation. Some species prefer to build their nests in areas that have recently been burned, in part because these areas are usually full of new plant growth, which attracts large numbers of insects. Most plovers and lapwings are monogamous (muh-NAH-guh-mus), with a single male breeding with a single female. However, there are also instances of polygyny (puh-LIH-juh-nee), in which a single male mates with multiple females; polyandry (PAH-lee-an-dree), in which a single female mates with multiple males; and cooperative breeding, in which adults other than the parents (usually the older siblings of the new chicks) help care for chicks. Females generally lay between two and six eggs at a time, with four

PROTECTING CHICKS

Plovers and lapwings have developed a wide variety of techniques to defend their young from potential predators. They will make loud warning calls, perform what are known as distraction displays, and, in some cases, even attack predators. Distraction displays are behaviors designed to distract predators from chicks. Plover and lapwing adults may pretend to have a broken wing to draw predators away from the nest, or may pretend to be incubating eggs at "fake" nest sites to mislead predators.

being most common. Eggs hatch after between eighteen and thirty-eight days. The chicks are precocial (pree-KOH-shul), meaning they are covered with down at birth and able to move. Chicks generally leave the nest soon after hatching. In most species, adults do not feed the chicks. The single exception is the Magellanic plover, which is usually able to raise only one chick per breeding season. Magellanic plover adults feed chicks by regurgitating (re-GER-jih-tate-ing; throwing up) food.

PLOVERS, LAPWINGS, AND PEOPLE

Two plover species, the black-bellied plover and golden-plover, were hunted for food in North America during the 1800s. Conservation efforts for the snowy plover and piping plover, which breed on sandy beaches, often conflict with people interested in hunting.

CONSERVATION STATUS

Among the sixty-six species of plovers and lapwings, one is considered Critically Endangered, facing an extremely high risk of extinction; two are Endangered, facing a very high risk of extinction; five are Vulnerable, facing a high risk of extinction; and six are Near Threatened, in danger of becoming threatened. The Javanese lapwing is listed as Critically Endangered and is, in fact, likely extinct—it has not been seen since 1940. The St. Helena plover is Endangered, with only about three hundred individuals remaining. The St. Helena plover declined primarily because of habitat loss, human disturbance, and predation of chicks by cats and the common myna. The shore plover is Endangered due largely to loss of habitat and predation by cats, rats, and the brown skua. There are only about 150 individuals left in the wild. Vulnerable species include the New Zealand dotterel, mountain plover, piping plover, wrybill, and sociable lapwing. Near Threatened species include the Magellenic plover, Madagascar plover, Malaysian plover, Javan plover, hooded plover, and Mitchell's plover.

Killdeer (*Charadrius vociferus*)

■ Breeding ■ Nonbreeding

KILLDEER
Charadrius vociferus

Physical characteristics: The killdeer is 8 to 11 inches in length (20 to 28 centimeters) and about 3.3 ounces (95 grams) in weight. It has two black bands on the breast and a dark line between the eyes.

The back is gray-brown in color while the belly is white. The killdeer has long wings and a long tail.

Geographic range: The killdeer is found throughout North America except in Alaska and northern Canada, through Central America, and in parts of northwest South America.

Habitat: The killdeer makes use of a variety of open habitats including mudflats, pastures, agricultural fields, roads, and sometimes even paved parking lots.

Diet: Killdeer eat primarily invertebrates, small vertebrates such as frogs or fish, and seeds and other plant material.

Behavior and reproduction: Killdeer get their name from their call, which sounds like "killdee killdee." Killdeer are often found in small or medium-sized flocks that may include other species of shorebirds. Some populations are migratory while others remain in the same place year-round. Pairs defend territories from other members of the species during the breeding season, and sometimes during the winter as well. Killdeer are monogamous, with a single male breeding with a single female. Often, individuals keep the same mate from one year to the next. Nests are either scraped on the ground or built on gravel-covered

Killdeer may feign, or fake, injury to trick a predator. The predator will follow the "injured" bird away from its nest, keeping the chicks safe. (© JLM Visuals. Reproduced by permission.)

rooftops. Females lay four eggs at a time. Eggs hatch after twenty-five days. Parents may wet their feathers before sitting on eggs to help keep them cool. Parents also defend nest and chicks from predators, animals that hunt them for food, usually by distracting potential predators.

Killdeer and people: No significant interactions between people and killdeer are known.

Conservation status: Killdeer are not currently considered threatened, although populations may be in decline in eastern North America due to interference from human activity. ■

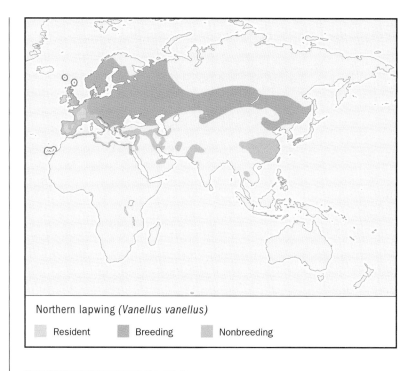

Northern lapwing *(Vanellus vanellus)*

Resident   Breeding   Nonbreeding

NORTHERN LAPWING
Vanellus vanellus

Physical characteristics: Northern lapwings have a long black crest, black neckband, green back, and white belly. The face is mostly black with a dark line extending under the eye.

Geographic range: Northern lapwings are found in Europe and Asia.

Habitat: Northern lapwings occupy diverse habitats including grasslands, fields, bogs, and deserts.

Diet: Northern lapwings eat a large number of earthworms as well as other invertebrates. In cold weather, they sometimes eat cattle dung.

Behavior and reproduction: Northern lapwings have been found in flocks of as many as 5,000 individuals, although flocks of about 100 are more common. Northern lapwings are usually monogamous, but there is some polygyny. Females usually lay four eggs at a time. These hatch after twenty-four to thirty-four days. Both parents help

Both northern lapwing parents help incubate the eggs and take care of chicks, but one of the parents, usually the female, typically deserts the nest before the young actually become independent. (Roger Wilmshurst/Bruce Coleman Inc. Reproduced by permission.)

incubate the eggs and take care of chicks, but one of the parents, usually the female, usually deserts the nest before the young actually become independent.

Northern lapwings and people: Northern lapwing eggs were once collected for food in Europe.

Conservation status: The Northern lapwing is not considered threatened. In fact, its breeding range in Europe has expanded in recent times. ■

FOR MORE INFORMATION

Books:

del Hoyo, J., A. Elliott, and J. Sargatal, eds. *Handbook of the Birds of the World.* Vol. 3, *Hoatzin to Auks.* Barcelona: Lynx Edicions, 1996.

Perrins, Christopher, ed. *Firefly Encyclopedia of Birds.* Buffalo, NY: Firefly Books, 2003.

Vaughan, R. *Plovers.* Lavenham, U.K.: Terence Dalton Limited, 1980.

Web sites:

"Charadriidae (Lapwings and Plovers)." The Internet Bird Collection. http://www.hbw.com/ibc/phtml/familia.phtml?idFamilia=60 (accessed on May 6, 2004).

"Family Charadriidae (Plovers and Lapwings)." Animal Diversity Web, The University of Michigan Museum of Zoology. http://animaldiversity. ummz.umich.edu/site/accounts/classification/Charadriidae. html#Charadriidae (accessed on May 6, 2004).

"Plovers, Lapwings." Bird Families of the World, Cornell University. http://www.es.cornell.edu/winkler/botw/charadriidae.html (accessed on May 6, 2004).

Class: Aves

Order: Charadriiformes

Family: Scolopacidae

Number of species: 86 species

family

C H A P T E R

PHYSICAL CHARACTERISTICS

Sandpipers vary a great deal in size, from 4.7 to 26 inches (12 to 66 centimeters) in length and from 0.5 to 48 ounces (14.5 to 1,360 grams) in weight. Bill size and shape also vary a lot in the group, depending largely on the type of food eaten. Different sandpiper species have long or short bills, straight bills, upwardly curved bills, or downwardly curved bills. There are also more unusual bills, such as wedge-shaped bills and spoon-shaped bills, in the family. Some sandpipers have slender bodies, while others have plump bodies. Most species have short tails, long necks, long legs, and partially webbed toes. The wings tend to be long. Many sandpipers are colored to blend into their environments, although some species develop brighter black or reddish-colored patches during the breeding season. In many sandpipers, females and males are fairly similar in appearance. However, there are exceptions. In the ruff, for example, the male is 25 percent larger than the female and also has special feathers around the head and neck during the breeding season. Young sandpipers are generally colored to blend into their habitats.

GEOGRAPHIC RANGE

Sandpipers are found worldwide on all continents except Antarctica. A large number of sandpipers breed in the Northern Hemisphere and migrate to the tropics or to the Southern Hemisphere for the winter. Only a small number of sandpipers breed in the tropics. The sandpiper family includes species which breed the farthest north of any birds, including on Franz Joseph Land, the Zemlya Islands, and the northern tip of Greenland.

HABITAT

Most sandpipers breed in inland freshwater wetlands, although a few species prefer to breed in coastal saltwater marshes. Snipes are found in marshes, swamps, and wet grassland habitats. Curlews make use of woodland, tundra, grassland, farmlands, and lakeshores. Some sandpiper species breed on gravelly or rocky tundra, treeless plains found in artic regions. Woodcocks inhabit deciduous forests, forests where there are four seasons and trees lose their leaves in the fall. Favored wintering areas for sandpipers include tropical wetlands such as river mouths, lakeshores, and marshes. The phalaropes are unusual in that they are pelagic (puh-LAJ-ik), meaning they live on the open ocean, during the winter.

DIET

Sandpipers eat primarily invertebrates, animals without backbones, such as worms, mollusks, crustaceans, insects, and spiders. They also eat some vertebrates, animals with backbones, including small fish and amphibians. Some species will also eat plant material at certain times of year, often when insect prey is unavailable. Plant material eaten may include berries, rice, seeds, and green shoots.

Sandpiper species with short bills generally obtain food by pecking at it. Snipes and woodcocks probe mud with their bills to look for food. Shanks run after fish in shallow water with their bills submerged. They sometimes work together to drive entire schools of small fish into shallow areas. Phalaropes and a few other species peck tiny prey from the water, focusing on invertebrates such as shrimp and copepods. A few members of the family have unique feeding strategies. For example, turnstones flip over stones and shells to look for prey, and the Terek sandpiper runs after small burrowing crabs.

BEHAVIOR AND REPRODUCTION

During the nonbreeding season, many sandpiper species feed and rest in large flocks. Sandpipers also migrate in large flocks of just one species. Some sandpipers migrate distances as great as several thousand miles, having built up large fat deposits to sustain them during the trip.

During the breeding season, most sandpipers are territorial, and defend areas of land from other pairs. A few species, however, including the Asian dowitcher, common redshank, and some godwits and curlews, nest close together in breeding colonies. Most sandpiper species are monogamous (muh-NAH-guh-mus), with a single male mating with a single female, during the breeding season. However, polygyny (puh-LIH-juh-nee), a single male mating with multiple females, describes the mating behavior of the Eurasian woodcock, white-rumped sandpiper, sharp-tailed sandpiper, and several other species. Polyandry (PAH-lee-an-dree), a single female mating with multiple males, is found in the spotted sandpiper and also in some phalaropes. In the phalaropes, females defend territories while males take care of the nests and chicks alone.

Courtship in sandpipers most frequently involves singing in flight and displays related to finding a site to build the pair's nest. Some species, including the ruff, buff-breasted sandpiper, and great snipe, have leks, special areas where males gather to display for females. Females go to the lek to choose a partner and mate. Species with leks are polygynous (puh-LIH-juh-nus), and males do not participate in care of eggs or young.

The sandpiper nest is most commonly a shallow indentation scraped in the ground and lined with vegetation. However, some species build more complicated nests or use old tree nests that have been abandoned by other birds. Females usually lay four eggs at a time, although some species lay only two or three. Eggs are colored to blend into the environment, and are typically pale with brown or black markings. Chicks hatch after about three weeks. Sandpiper chicks are precocial (pree-KOH-shul), meaning they hatch able to move and covered with down. Chicks usually leave the nest within a day of hatching. Woodcocks and snipes feed their young, but other species do not. However, sandpiper parents do protect their chicks from potential predators by pretending to be injured or by trying to look like rodents, fluffing up their feathers, running, and making squeaky noises. Nonetheless, in most species of sandpipers, fewer than half the chicks survive their first year.

SANDPIPERS AND PEOPLE

Many species in the family, particularly the snipe and woodcock, are widely hunted for food or sport. Some sandpipers are

THE LEMMING FACTOR

Some species of sandpipers that breed in the Northern Hemisphere share their breeding habitats with small mammals called lemmings. Biologists have observed that in these areas, the breeding success of sandpipers moves in cycles that correspond to changes in the number of lemmings. When there are fewer lemmings, lemming predators such as arctic foxes catch and eat more adult and young sandpipers.

considered pests because they eat crops, particularly rice, whereas others actually help farmers by eating large numbers of insects. Some sandpipers have also played significant roles in human folklore. One group of Australian Aborigines performs a "sandpiper dance" since the arrival of the birds marks the beginning of the rainy season. In the Russian Far East, inhabitants of the Chukchi Peninsula imitate the impressive dance of lekking male ruffs.

CONSERVATION STATUS

Two species of sandpipers are known to have gone extinct since 1600 C.E. These are the white-winged sandpiper of Tahiti and Ellis's sandpiper of Moorea. Both were probably driven to extinction by rats brought to their island habitats by humans. Of the eighty-six sandpiper species currently in existence, two are Critically Endangered, facing an extremely high risk of extinction, including the Eskimo curlew, which has not been seen since the 1980s, and the slender-billed curlew. Both species were hunted in large numbers by humans and also suffer from habitat loss. The Nordmann's greenshank is Endangered, facing a very high risk of extinction in the wild, due to hunting and habitat loss. The tuamotu sandpiper is Endangered because of habitat loss and human-introduced predators. The Vulnerable, facing a high risk of extinction, species in the family include the spoon-billed sandpiper, bristle-thighed curlew, wood snipe, Chatham snipe, Amami woodcock, and Moluccan woodcock. These species are affected by factors such as hunting, habitat destruction and disturbance, and predators introduced by humans.

African snipe *(Gallinago nigripennis)*

Resident

AFRICAN SNIPE
Gallinago nigripennis

Physical characteristics: African snipes range in size from 9.8 to 11.4 inches (25 to 29 centimeters) and weigh between 3 and 6 ounces (90 to 164 grams). Birds have dark backs and pale bellies. Females and males are generally similar in size and appearance except that females have somewhat longer bills.

Geographic range: African snipes are found in southern and eastern Africa.

Habitat: African snipes occupy wetland habitats with areas of exposed mud and short vegetation.

African snipes live in wetland areas in southern and eastern Africa. (© R. Drummond/VIREO. Reproduced by permission.)

Diet: African snipes eat primarily worms and insect larvae (LAR-vee). They forage, or search for food, at dusk and at night.

Behavior and reproduction: When disturbed, African snipes make a harsh calling noise and escape using a characteristic zigzag flight. Male African snipes attract females by making a "drumming" noise with their tail feathers. African snipes are monogamous, with a single male mating with a single female. Breeding occurs during or after the rainy season. The female lays two to three eggs at a time, generally in a hidden grassy area on moist or wet ground.

African snipes and people: No significant interactions between African snipes and people are known.

Conservation status: African snipes are not considered threatened. However, worldwide destruction of wetland habitats could endanger them in the future. ■

Long-billed curlew (*Numenius americanus*)

■ Breeding ■ Nonbreeding

LONG-BILLED CURLEW
Numenius americanus

Physical characteristics: Long-billed curlews vary between 19.7 and 25.6 inches (50 to 65 centimeters) in length and weigh from 15.5 to 33.5 ounces (445 to 951 grams). The tip of the bill is shaped like a water droplet. The back is speckled black and the belly is cinnamon-colored. Females are larger than males and have longer bills.

Geographic range: Long-billed curlews are found in portions of North America and Central America.

Habitat: Long-billed curlews occupy grassland areas during the breeding season and wetlands such as marshes and estuaries

Long-billed curlews live in grassland areas during the breeding season and wetlands during the nonbreeding season. (Gary Meszaros/Bruce Coleman Inc. Reproduced by permission.)

(EST-yoo-air-eez), where saltwater and freshwater mix, during the nonbreeding season. Long-billed curlews are sometimes found on farmland as well.

Diet: Long-billed curlews eat primarily insects, but also eat some crustaceans, mollusks, worms, frogs, and berries.

Behavior and reproduction: Long-billed curlews are monogamous, with a single male breeding with a single female. Pairs are territorial, defending their nesting area from other pairs. Females lay three to five eggs at a time, generally in short grass. Eggs hatch after twenty-seven or twenty-eight days.

Long-billed curlews and people: Long-billed curlews were once hunted in large numbers by humans, but are now protected by law.

Conservation status: Long-billed curlews are not considered threatened at this time. However, populations have declined in number due to loss of grassland habitat. ■

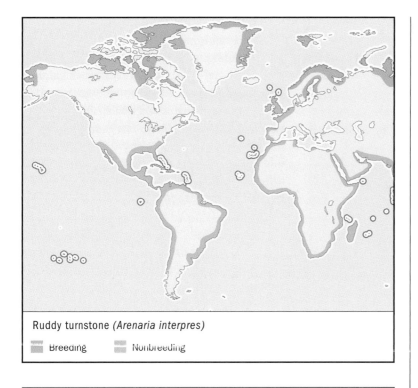

Ruddy turnstone *(Arenaria interpres)*

Breeding   Nonbreeding

RUDDY TURNSTONE
Arenaria interpres

Physical characteristics: Ruddy turnstones range in length from 8.3 to 10.2 inches (21 to 26 centimeters) and from 3 to 6.7 ounces (84 to 190 grams) in weight. The head, neck, throat, and chest have bold black and white markings. The back is chestnut and black, while the belly is pale. Females and males differ somewhat in coloration.

Geographic range: Ruddy turnstones breed in high northern latitudes worldwide, and winter further south. Either breeding or wintering populations are found on all continents except Antarctica.

Habitat: Ruddy turnstones breed in tundra habitats as well as wetlands such as marshes and stony coastal plains. They spend the winter on rocky, stony, or sandy beaches.

Diet: Ruddy turnstones flip over stones to look for food. Their diet consists largely of insects, crustaceans, mollusks, worms, fish, carrion, and bird eggs.

Ruddy turnstones flip over stones to look for food. Their diet consists largely of insects, crustaceans, mollusks, worms, fish, carrion (dead animals), and bird eggs. (© Paul J. Fusco/ Photo Researchers, Inc. Reproduced by permission.)

Behavior and reproduction: Ruddy turnstones are often found in flocks during the nonbreeding season. During the breeding season, they are found in isolated pairs. The female lays two to four eggs at a time, usually in open nests or in nests hidden in vegetation. Eggs hatch after twenty-two to twenty-four days.

Ruddy turnstones and people: No significant interactions between ruddy turnstones and people are known.

Conservation status: Ruddy turnstones are not considered threatened at this time. ■

FOR MORE INFORMATION

Books:

del Hoyo, J., A. Elliott, and J. Sargatal, eds. *Handbook of the Birds of the World.* Vol. 3, *Hoatzin to Auks.* Barcelona: Lynx Edicions, 1996.

Perrins, Christopher, ed. *Firefly Encyclopedia of Birds.* Buffalo, NY: Firefly Books, 2003.

Web sites:

"Sandpipers, Curlews, Woodcocks, Phalaropes, etc." Bird Families of the World, Cornell University. http://www.eeb.cornell.edu/winkler/botw/scolopacidae.html (accessed on June 3, 2004).

"Scolopacidae (Snipes and Sandpipers)." The Internet Bird Collection. http://www.hbw.com/ibc/phtml/familia.phtml?idFamilia=61 (accessed on June 1, 2004).

SEEDSNIPES
Thinocoridae

Class: Aves

Order: Charadriiformes

Family: Thinocoridae

Number of species: 4 species

PHYSICAL CHARACTERISTICS

Seedsnipes vary from 6 to 12 inches in length (16 to 30 centimeters) and from 1.8 to 14 ounces in weight (50 to 400 grams). They have plump bodies, short, thick bills, and short legs. The wings are long, narrow, and pointed. A membrane, thin layer of skin, covers the nostrils of seedsnipes to protect them from dust storms. Seedsnipes are generally colored to blend into their environments, and may be brown or rust-colored, and barred. Two of the four species have gray heads and necks and black markings on the throat or breast. Seedsnipes have large numbers of feathers to help protect them from cold weather.

GEOGRAPHIC RANGE

Seedsnipes are found in the New World (Western Hemisphere) tropics, occupying the Andes as well as the Patagonian and Peruvian coasts in western and southern South America.

HABITAT

Seedsnipes are found in cold, windswept areas, including rocky slopes, short grasslands, and bogs. They also occupy dry riverbeds and the shores of partly dried-up lakes.

DIET

Seedsnipes eat plant material exclusively. This includes buds, leaf tips, some seeds and succulents, plants with fleshy, water-storing stems or leaves. Despite their name, seeds are not a particularly important part of the seedsnipes' diet. Seedsnipes generally feed by biting food off with their bills and swallowing the food whole.

BEHAVIOR AND REPRODUCTION

During the nonbreeding season, seedsnipes may be found in flocks of as many as eighty individuals. During the breeding season, however, seedsnipes are usually found in pairs or in smaller groups of five or six. Seedsnipes spend a large part of their day walking slowly, looking for food. When they sense a threat, their first response is usually to turn their backs, which are colored to blend into the environment. Only if the intruder approaches will they walk away or fly away in a zigzag pattern, making loud calls.

Seedsnipes are territorial during the breeding season, with pairs defending areas from other pairs. The female typically lays three or four eggs at a time. The seedsnipe nest is usually a depression in the ground lined with bits of plant material. When neither parent is at the nest, the eggs are covered with soil or nest lining to help hide them and keep them warm. Eggs hatch after about twenty-six days in the least seedsnipe, the only species for which there is information. The chicks are able to leave the nest soon after hatching and quickly become able to feed themselves. However, both parents continue to help protect the young, often pretending to be injured to draw away potential predators and other intruders. Seedsnipes become sexually mature quickly, and are able to reproduce the same season they hatch.

QUICK MATURATION

There is evidence that chicks in some seedsnipe species become sexually mature, able to reproduce, extremely quickly. They mature so quickly, in fact, that they are able to breed the same season they hatched. This is an advantage because in some parts of the seedsnipe range, changing weather patterns means there is particularly abundant food once every four to ten years. Quick maturation enables even the newest chicks to take advantage of this.

SEEDSNIPES AND PEOPLE

Seedsnipes have little interaction with humans because of their extreme habitat. However, their loud calls sometimes enter the local folklore. Very rarely, they may be hunted.

CONSERVATION STATUS

No seedsnipes are considered threatened at this time. However, some populations have been affected by hunting and pollution.

Rufous-bellied seedsnipe *(Attagis gayi)*

Resident

RUFOUS-BELLIED SEEDSNIPE
Attagis gayi

Physical characteristics: Rufous-bellied seedsnipes are 10 to 11 inches in length (27 to 30 centimeters) and weigh between 10.6 and 14.1 ounces (300 to 400 grams). The head, neck, back, and breast are barred black, brown, and cream, a pattern that allows individuals to blend in with their environment. The belly is reddish brown or a pink cinnamon in color.

Geographic range: Rufous-bellied seedsnipes are found in the Andes of Chile, Argentina, Bolivia, Peru, and Ecuador. They generally occupy high altitudes, of at least 3,300 feet (1,000 meters) in some areas and much higher in other areas.

Habitat: Rufous-bellied seedsnipes occupy rocky slopes and alpine bogs.

Diet: Rufous-bellied seedsnipes eat the buds and leaf tips of cushion plants found in their habitat.

Behavior and reproduction: Rufous-bellied seedsnipes are usually found in pairs or small groups. They make loud calls that are described as cackles. Rufous-bellied seedsnipes are monogamous (muh-NAH-guh-mus), with a single male breeding with a single female. The female lays four eggs at a time into a nest that is usually just a scraped indentation in the ground with little or no lining. When neither parent is incubating, or sitting on, the eggs, they are covered with dirt to help keep them warm and hide them.

Rufous-bellied seedsnipes live in wetlands of the high Andes Mountains. (© Fletcher and Baylis/Photo Researchers, Inc. Reproduced by permission.)

Rufous-bellied seedsnipes and people: Rufous-bellied seedsnipes are hunted by local populations. Other than that, there is no significant interaction between rufous-bellied seedsnipes and people.

Conservation status: Rufous-bellied seedsnipes are not currently considered threatened. However, because they are hunted near mines in their range, some populations have been drastically reduced in numbers. ■

FOR MORE INFORMATION

Books:

del Hoyo, J., A. Elliott, and J. Sargatal, eds. *Handbook of the Birds of the World.* Vol. 3, *Hoatzin to Auks.* Barcelona: Lynx Edicions, 1996.

Fjeldså, Jon, and Niels Krabbe. *Birds of the High Andes.* Copenhagen: Zoological Museum, University of Copenhagen, 1990.

Perrins, Christopher, ed. *Firefly Encyclopedia of Birds.* Buffalo, NY: Firefly Books, 2003.

Web sites:

"Family Thinocoridae (Seedsnipe)." Animal Diversity Web. http://animaldiversity.ummz.umich.edu/site/accounts/classification/Thinocoridae.html#Thinocoridae (accessed on June 1, 2004).

"Seedsnipes." Birds of the World, Cornell University. http://www.eeb.cornell.edu/winkler/botw/thinocoridae.html (accessed on June 4, 2004).

"Thinocoridae (Seedsnipes)." The Internet Bird Collection. http://www.hbw.com/ibc/phtml/familia.phtml?idFamilia=63 (accessed on June 1, 2004).

	SHEATHBILLS
	Chionidae

Class: Aves

Order: Charadriiformes

Family: Chionidae

Number of species: 2 species

family
CHAPTER

PHYSICAL CHARACTERISTICS

Sheathbills vary in size from 13.4 to 16.1 inches (34 to 41 centimeters) in length and from 16 to 27 ounces (450 to 760 grams) in weight. They have plump bodies, short legs, and short conical, cone-shaped, bills with a horny sheath covering the upper bill. Sheathbills also have unusual featherless patches on the face covered with wart-like bumps called caruncles (KAR-un-kulz). The rest of the sheathbill body is covered with white feathers. Pale-faced sheathbills have a greenish sheath on the bills and pink caruncles, whereas black-faced sheathbills have black bill sheaths and black caruncles. Males are larger than females in the sheathbills, generally weighing about 15 percent more. Males also have larger bills and larger sheaths. Adult birds have more caruncles on their faces than younger birds. Older birds also have spurs on their wings which they use for defense and in fights.

GEOGRAPHIC RANGE

Sheathbills are found along the Antarctic Peninsula, on islands of the subantarctic, and in the southern parts of South America.

HABITAT

Sheathbills are found primarily on coastal plains and in coastal wetlands. They are generally found in the vicinity of large seabird colonies. During the nonbreeding season, sheathbills may be found in meadows, bogs, and ice floes, sometimes as far as 0.6 miles (1 kilometer) inland.

DIET

Sheathbills are omnivores, they eat substantial amounts of both plant and animal matter. Because they live in harsh environments where conditions often change quickly, sheathbills are opportunistic feeders that are able to take advantage of whatever food becomes available. In most areas, sheathbills feed largely on the eggs, chicks, and even excrement of penguins and other seabirds. They also try to intercept adult seabirds returning to feed their chicks and either steal the food outright, or jostle the adults enough that some of the food is spilled. Food obtained in this way is critical to sheathbill survival, but does not have a very large impact on the seabirds. Sheathbills will also eat carrion, dead and decaying flesh, usually dead seal pups, as well as seal placentas, the organ that attaches to the uterus during pregnancy. When foods derived from seabirds and seals are unavailable, sheathbills survive by eating seaweed and invertebrates.

BEHAVIOR AND REPRODUCTION

Sheathbills are monogamous (muh-NAH-guh-mus), a single male mates with a single female during the breeding season. Sheathbill pairs are territorial, and defend nesting and feeding areas within seabird colonies from other pairs of sheathbills. Territorial disputes are resolved by calling, displays, chases, and sometimes, actual battles.

The timing of the breeding season varies among populations of sheathbills, since breeding usually occurs whenever local seabirds are breeding. This strategy allows for plentiful food resources to be available when sheathbill chicks hatch. Females lay one to three eggs at a time, usually in November or December. Eggs are laid in crude nests built from feathers, bones, shells, rocks, and plant material. Nests are usually built in small caves or cracks, usually in rocky areas. However, some sheathbills will nest in the abandoned burrows of other species. Sheathbill eggs are white, flecked with brown or gray, and somewhat pear-shaped. Chicks hatch after twenty-eight to thirty-two days, and are partially covered with feathers when they hatch. Unlike the parents, chicks are brownish in color. Chicks stay near the nest for one to three weeks after hatching and are fed by their parents. The primary cause of death for chicks is starvation, although some chicks are also eaten by predators, animals that hunt them for food.

SHEATHBILLS AND PEOPLE

Because of their range, sheathbills have little contact with people. However, near Antarctic research stations, they have been known to eat food scraps and human excrement. They sometimes also nest in abandoned stations.

CONSERVATION STATUS

Neither of the two species of sheathbills is currently considered threatened. However, some predators brought by humans, including cats and mice, sometimes eat sheathbill chicks or eggs.

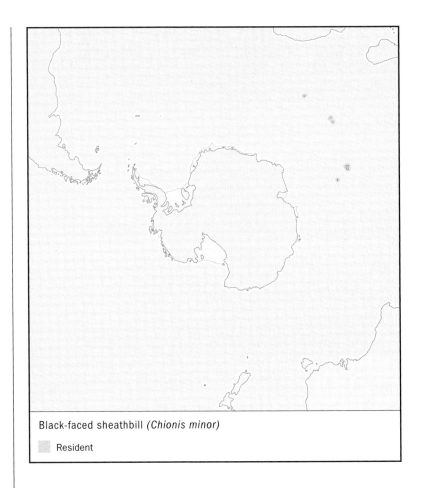

Black-faced sheathbill (*Chionis minor*)

░ Resident

BLACK-FACED SHEATHBILL
Chionis minor

Physical characteristics: Black-faced sheathbills range from 15 to 16.1 inches in length (38 to 41 centimeters) and from 19 to 32 ounces (540 to 900 grams) in weight. They have a wingspan, distance from wingtip to wingtip, of 29.1 to 31.1 inches (74 to 79 centimeters). They have black bills, black sheaths, and black carbuncles on their faces. The feathers are all white.

Geographic range: Black-faced sheathbills are found on a handful of subantarctic islands in the Indian Ocean. These include Marion, Prince Edward, Crozet, Kerguelen, Heard, and McDonald Islands.

Habitat: Black-faced sheathbills are found in the colonies of penguins and other seabirds, typically on rocky or sandy beaches. They may also occupy meadows and bogs close to shore.

Diet: Black-faced sheathbills eat the eggs, chicks, and excrement of seabirds. They also steal food that seabird parents bring back for their chicks. Black-faced sheathbills may also eat dead seal pups and seal milk. If these aren't available, they eat algae and invertebrates.

Behavior and reproduction: Black-faced sheathbills do not migrate, but remain in one place throughout the year. Pairs defend their territories from other sheathbills all year round. Black-faced sheathbills are most often associated with colonies of king penguins. Black-faced sheathbills are monogamous, with a single male breeding with a single female. The female lays two to three eggs in December or January, with breeding at the same time as that of the seabirds among which they live. Chicks hatch after twenty-seven to thirty-three days.

Black-faced sheathbills and people: Black-faced sheathbills have little interaction with people. They sometimes eat food scraps left by humans near research stations or eat human excrement.

Conservation status: Black-faced sheathbills are not considered threatened. ■

FOR MORE INFORMATION

Books:

del Hoyo, J., A. Elliott, and J. Sargatal, eds. *Handbook of the Birds of the World.* Vol. 3, *Hoatzin to Auks.* Barcelona: Lynx Edicions, 1996.

Parmalee, D. F. *Antarctic Birds: Ecological and Behavioral Approaches.* Minneapolis: University of Minnesota Press, 1992.

Perrins, Christopher, ed. *Firefly Encyclopedia of Birds.* Buffalo, NY: Firefly Books, 2003.

Web sites:

"Chionidae (Sheathbills)." The Internet Bird Collection. http://www.hbw.com/ibc/phtml/familia.phtml?idFamilia=64 (accessed on June 1, 2004).

"Family Chioniae (Sheathbill)." Animal Diversity Web. http://animaldiversity.ummz.umich.edu/site/accounts/classification/Chionididae.html#Chionididae (accessed on June 1, 2004).

"Sheathbills." Birds of the World, Cornell University. http://www.eeb.cornell.edu/winkler/botw/chionididae.html (accessed on June 4, 2004).

GULLS, TERNS, AND RELATIVES
Laridae

Class: Aves
Order: Charadriiformes
Family: Laridae
Number of species: 105 species

family
CHAPTER

PHYSICAL CHARACTERISTICS

Gulls, terns, and their relatives vary between 8 and 32 inches (20 to 81 centimeters) in length and between 1.6 and 74 ounces (46 to 2,100 grams) in weight. Gulls and terns generally have white bellies and gray or black backs. Males and females are similar in both size and coloration. Young birds, however, are usually spotted or streaked to help them blend in with their environments. During the breeding season, some gulls develop a pink or cream colored patch on the breast. Gulls have heavy bodies and long wings. Terns have narrower, longer bodies and long, slender, pointed wings. Their bills are slender and pointed. Many terns develop a black crown on top of the head during the breeding season.

Skimmers have heavy bodies and long, narrow wings. Their bills are large and laterally compressed, flattened from left to right. In skimmers, males are often significantly larger than females. Most skimmers have black backs and white bellies, although during the breeding season the legs may become cream colored.

Skuas and jaegers (YAY-gerz) have body shapes similar to that of gulls, but have heavy, hooked bills. They are exceptionally powerful fliers. Females are larger than males.

GEOGRAPHIC RANGE

Gulls and terns are found in coastal regions worldwide. Skimmers are found in temperate, not too hot or too cold, and tropical regions in North America, South America, Africa, and Asia. Skuas and jaegers are found in temperate and polar areas.

phylum

class

subclass

order

monotypic order

suborder

▲ **family**

HABITAT

Terns frequently nest on islands or in coastal areas where there are few predators. They may also avoid predators by nesting on cliffs, in trees, or even in the water on floating vegetation. Gulls nest in coastal areas as well as in wetlands or along the shores of large lakes. Gulls use beaches, marshes, river or lakeshores, sand dunes, cliffs, trees, and buildings as nest sites. One species, the gray gull, breeds in the mountainous deserts of Chile and flies over the Andes mountains each day to find food in the Pacific Ocean. During the nonbreeding season, gulls will make use of almost any habitat close to open water. Skimmers nest on coastal beaches or in salt marshes, and move to the open ocean during the nonbreeding season. Skuas breed on tundra or grassy islands. The south polar skua nests near colonies of breeding petrels and penguins.

DIET

Gulls eat a wide variety of foods. Many obtain fish and invertebrates, animals without backbones, from the seashore. Some species take advantage of human garbage or beg for handouts from people. Gulls have a wide variety of methods for obtaining food, including walking on the ground, searching in the water, and diving. They are also known to drop mollusks and other hard-shelled animals from a large height to crack the shells. Terns usually dive in the ocean for fish. Skimmers catch prey by skimming along the water with their lower bills underwater. Skimmers usually forage, search for food, either at dusk or at night. Skuas and jaegers are predatory, feeding on other bird species such as murres, gulls, and penguins.

BEHAVIOR AND REPRODUCTION

Aside from skimmers and two species of gulls, most members of the gull and tern family are diurnal, active during the day. During the breeding season, gulls and terns nest in small or large colonies. Terns in particular are found in very large groups that may include millions of individuals. Gulls and terns are territorial during the breeding season, defending a small area around the nest from other individuals of the species. Most gulls and terns will mob potential predators and intruders, with many birds attacking simultaneously. This strategy is very successful against other bird species, but does not work as well with mammalian predators.

Skimmers are nocturnal, active at night. They nest in colonies, sometimes ones that include gulls and terns. The members of a skimmer pair usually face in opposite directions while at the nest to more effectively scan for predators. Skuas and jaegers tend to be found alone, although they sometimes form foraging flocks over schools of fish.

Gulls, terns, and their relatives are monogamous (muh-NAH-guh-mus), with each male breeding with a single female. In many species, individuals keep the same mates from one year to the next. Pairs that stay together are often able to raise more young than newly mated pairs. However, in many gulls, individuals of both sexes sometimes copulate, breed, with birds other than their mates. Both male and female participate in incubating, or sitting on the eggs, defending the territory from intruders, and feeding and protecting the young once they hatch. Females lay one to three eggs at a time. The eggs are usually brown with dark markings. Eggs hatch after twenty to thirty days, and chicks are able to fly after four to six weeks. If the eggs or chicks are lost, particularly early in the breeding season, the female will often lay a new set of eggs. Chicks generally remain with their parents for some time after leaving the nest, particularly among the terns, where young have to learn the difficult art of diving for food. Some young terns will migrate with their parents and spend much of the winter with them.

GULLS, TERNS, RELATIVES, AND PEOPLE

In the 1800s, gull and tern feathers, and sometimes even whole birds, were used to decorate women's hats. The eggs of certain species have been, and continue to be, collected for food. Some eggs are considered aphrodisiacs (aff-roh-DEE-zee-acks), substances that enhance sexual desire, in parts of the world. Adult gulls and terns are also sometimes hunted for food. Gulls and terns were sometimes used as a sign that land was nearby by sailors, and terns are still used to locate schools of fish. Because of their more remote tundra habitats, skuas and jaegers have interacted less with human beings.

CONSERVATION STATUS

Chinese crested terns are Critically Endangered, facing an extremely high risk of extinction. Threats to gulls and terns include habitat destruction and disturbance, hunting, egg collection, predation by cats and other species associated with humans, pollution from oil spills and pesticides.

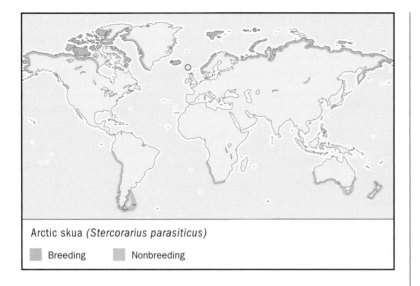

Arctic skua (*Stercorarius parasiticus*)

▨ Breeding   ▨ Nonbreeding

ARCTIC SKUA
Stercorarius parasiticus

Physical characteristics: Some Arctic skuas are entirely brown, while others have a dark gray head, white neck and belly, and dark back and wings.

Geographic range: Arctic skuas are found in far northern coastal areas, near the North Pole, during the breeding season. They spend the winter in the Southern Hemisphere in coastal areas.

Habitat: Arctic skuas breed on tundra, treeless plains found in artic regions, or grasslands. During the nonbreeding season, they occupy ocean areas close to land.

Diet: Arctic skuas eat lemmings and the eggs and chicks of other seabirds.

Behavior and reproduction: Arctic skuas are diurnal, active during the day. They are often found with other birds, particularly alcids (birds in the family Alcidae), gulls, and terns, while breeding and searching for food.

Arctic skuas live in coastal areas. They spend the breeding season near the North Pole, and travel to the Southern Hemisphere during the winter. (© A. Morris/VIREO. Reproduced by permission.)

Arctic skuas and people: Arctic skuas are sometimes shot by humans who believe they damage sheep and other livestock.

Conservation status: Arctic skuas are not considered threatened at this time. ■

Saunder's gull (*Larus saundersi*)

Resident   Nonbreeding

SAUNDER'S GULL
Larus saundersi

Physical characteristics: Saunder's gull has a black head and neck, white throat and belly, white eye crescents, and gray back. The bill is red with a dark band. Juveniles and nonbreeding adults are primarily white.

Geographic range: Saunder's gulls breed in coastal areas of eastern China and spend the winter in South Korea, southern Japan, and North Vietnam.

Habitat: Saunder's gulls live in coastal wetland areas during the breeding season. In the winter they are generally found in seashore areas.

Diet: Saunder's gulls forage, search for food, along the coast in mudflats as well as in coastal lagoons.

Saunder's gulls form breeding colonies on coastal salt marshes and spend the winters at the seashore. (Illustration by Brian Cressman. Reproduced by permission.)

Behavior and reproduction: Other than the fact that they are diurnal, little is known about the behavior of Saunder's gulls. Saunder's gulls form breeding colonies on coastal salt marshes. The female lays three eggs at a time.

Saunder's gulls and people: Local populations collect the eggs of this species for food.

Conservation status: Saunder's gulls are considered Vulnerable, facing a high risk of extinction in the wild. The total population is under 5,000 individuals. Decline has been due primarily to habitat loss for agriculture and oil exploration. ■

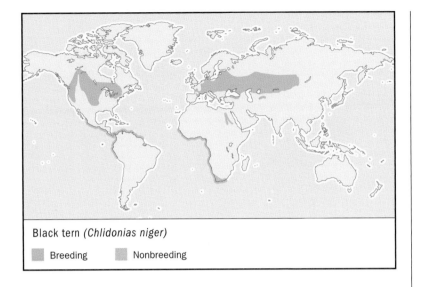

Black tern (*Chlidonias niger*)

■ Breeding   ■ Nonbreeding

BLACK TERN
Chlidonias niger

Physical characteristics: Black terns have black heads, necks, and breasts. Their backs and bellies are dark gray in color. Juveniles and nonbreeding adults are pale gray on the back and white on the belly and head, with a dark patch on the side of the breast.

Geographic range: Black terns are found in temperate North America, Europe, and Eastern Asia during the breeding season. They spend the winter in Central and South America and in Africa.

Habitat: Black terns breed in inland habitats such as ponds, lakes, and marshes. In the winter, they occupy seashore and coastal wetland habitats.

Diet: Black terns eat aquatic insects, snails, small fish, tadpoles, and frogs.

Behavior and reproduction: Black terns breed in small colonies, generally fewer than twenty individuals, although colonies of as many as a hundred birds have been seen. A single male mates with a single female, and both parents help incubate, sit on, the eggs as well as take care of young. The black tern nest is usually built on top of

The black tern nest is usually built on top of floating vegetation. Both parents help incubate, sit on, the eggs as well as take care of young. (© John Mitchell/Photo Researchers, Inc. Reproduced by permission.)

floating vegetation. The female lays two to three eggs at a time, and these hatch after twenty to twenty-three days. Chicks leave the nest after twenty-five days.

Black terns and people: The preferred nesting areas of black terns include the small lakes or marshes that are often drained by humans.

Conservation status: Black terns are not considered threatened. However, some populations have declined due to destruction of wetland habitats, pesticides, and competition with human-introduced fish for food. ■

FOR MORE INFORMATION

Books:

del Hoyo, J., A. Elliott, and J. Sargatal, eds. *Handbook of the Birds of the World.* Vol. 3, *Hoatzin to Auks.* Barcelona: Lynx Edicions, 1996.

Perrins, Christopher, ed. *Firefly Encyclopedia of Birds.* Buffalo, NY: Firefly Books, 2003.

Web sites:

"Family Laridae (Gulls and Terns)." Animal Diversity Web, The University of Michigan Museum of Zoology. http://animaldiversity.ummz.umich.edu/site/accounts/classification/Laridae.html#Laridae (accessed on June 1, 2004).

"Family Rynchopidae (Skimmers)." Animal Diversity Web, The University of Michigan Museum of Zoology. http://animaldiversity.ummz.umich.edu/site/accounts/classification/Rynchopidae.html#Rynchopidae (accessed on June 1, 2004).

"Laridae (Gulls)." The Internet Bird Collection. http://www.hbw.com/ibc/phtml/familia.phtml?idFamilia=66 (accessed on June 1, 2004).

"Rynchopidae (Skimmers)." The Internet Bird Collection. http://www.hbw.com/ibc/phtml/familia.phtml?idFamilia=68 (accessed on June 1, 2004).

"Sternidae (Terns)." The Internet Bird Collection. http://www.hbw.com/ibc/phtml/familia.phtml?idFamilia=67 (accessed on June 1, 2004).

family

CHAPTER

phylum
class
subclass
order
monotypic order
suborder
▲ **family**

PHYSICAL CHARACTERISTICS

Alcids, species in the Alcidae family, range from 6 to 17 inches (12 to 45 centimeters) in length and from 0.17 to 2.4 pounds (0.4 to 1.1 kilograms) in weight. They have narrow, short wings and short tails. Their toes are webbed. Alcids are primarily black, white, and gray in color, although some species have brown feathers during parts of the year. Males and females are similar in coloration. These birds also have a striking upright posture, one of the physical features that makes them well-suited to diving and "flying" underwater. All species are also able to fly in the air, although many need a running start to become airborne.

Bill shape varies a great deal in the group. The razorbill has a long, sharp bill. Puffins have deep bills that are laterally compressed, flattened left to right. The dovekie has a short, pointed bill. Guillemots have straight bills. The parakeet auklet has an unusual bill in which the lower half turns upward at the tip. This bill helps it catch its primary prey, jellyfish.

GEOGRAPHIC RANGE

Auks and their relatives are found in the Northern Hemisphere, in oceanic habitats in the Arctic, North Atlantic, and North Pacific.

HABITAT

Auks and their relatives are found in cold ocean waters. They breed in seashore areas such as shorelines, seaside cliffs, and, in some species, coastal forests.

DIET

Large members of the auk family, including murres, razorbills, puffins, and guillemots, eat primarily small fish. They sometimes also eat invertebrates, animals without backbones, such as squid and crustaceans. Smaller members of the family, such as the dovekie, eat primarily marine invertebrates such as crustaceans and mollusks. Many species fly far out over the ocean in search of food. Auks and their relatives capture food by resting on the surface of the water and then diving down after prey, propelling themselves forward with their wings.

BEHAVIOR AND REPRODUCTION

Auks are capable, but not strong, fliers. Most species require a lengthy running start over water before they are able to take to the air. However, all species are very good swimmers and divers. Auks and their relatives use their wings to propel themselves through the water. Their webbed feet, which are stretched out during swimming, act as a rudder and help them change or maintain direction. Some species have been known to reach depths as great as 600 feet (183 meters).

Auks and their relatives are monogamous (muh-NAH-guh-mus), a single male mates with a single female. However, the same mates are not necessarily kept from one breeding season to the next. Many individuals do, however, return to the same nesting site year after year. Eight of the twenty-three auk species mate on the open ocean. Both parents help incubate, or sit on, eggs, and both help feed and protect the young once they hatch. In most species, the female lays only one large egg which may represent 10 to 20 percent of the female's total weight. Chicks are covered with dense down at birth and are able to see. In several species, chicks leave the nest after two or three weeks and go with their fathers to live on the open ocean until they become independent.

AUKS, PUFFINS, MURRES, AND PEOPLE

Several species are hunted in large numbers in parts of Greenland, Canada, and Alaska.

MATING AT SEA

Eight species in the auk family mate at sea, an unusual breeding strategy. There are several possible reasons why this may be advantageous. Mating at sea may help auks avoid land predators. It may help male auks avoid competition and interference from other males of the same species. Finally, some biologists believe that female auks may use sea mating to figure out which males are healthiest and strongest, and would therefore make the best mates.

CONSERVATION STATUS

The great auk became Extinct, died out, around 1844 C.E. due to hunting by humans. Several currently existing auk species are considered Vulnerable, facing a high risk of extinction in the wild in the medium-term future, including Xantus's murrelet and the marbled murrelet. Xantus's murrelets are threatened by habitat damage in their breeding grounds in Baja California and on islands off the coast of Southern California. They have also been affected by predators associated with humans such as cats and rats. Marbled murrelets, which occur in areas of the United States, have been affected primarily by habitat loss. Both species are listed as Threatened by the U.S. Fish and Wildlife Service. Other members of the auk family are affected by habitat destruction and damage as well as by oil spills and fishing nets.

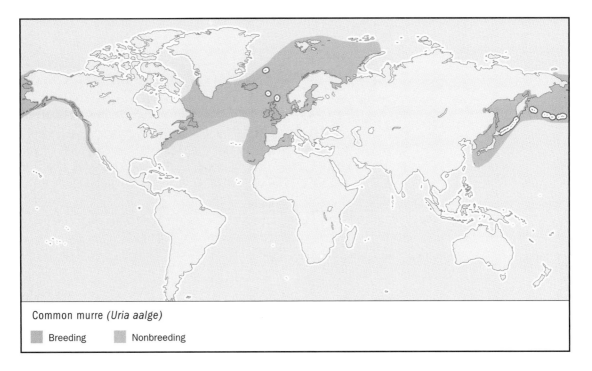

Common murre (*Uria aalge*)

■ Breeding   ■ Nonbreeding

COMMON MURRE
Uria aalge

Physical characteristics: Common murres have black-brown heads and backs. Their bellies are white. They have long, slender, pointed black bills.

Geographic range: Common murres are found from California to Alaska on the western coast of North America. On the eastern coast of North America they can be seen from New England to Labrador. They are also range from Siberia to Japan and Korea.

Habitat: Common murres inhabit rocky seashore areas during the breeding season, but spend most of the rest of the time on the open ocean.

Diet: Common murres eat primarily fish. They also eat some marine invertebrates.

Behavior and reproduction: Common murres are fast, able fliers often found in large flocks. Their calls sound like the purr of a cat.

During the breeding season, common murres nest in large colonies, which may include other species of birds. The female lays a single egg on bare rock. Parents are able to recognize their egg visually by its markings, and can find their own egg if it happens to roll away. Eggs hatch after thirty-two to thirty-five days. The chick leaves the nest after twenty to twenty-two days. Chicks follow their fathers to open ocean and are cared for until they become independent.

Common murres and people: Common murres are hunted in large numbers in Newfoundland.

Conservation status: Common murres are not considered threatened at this time. However, populations have been affected by habitat disturbance and hunting. ■

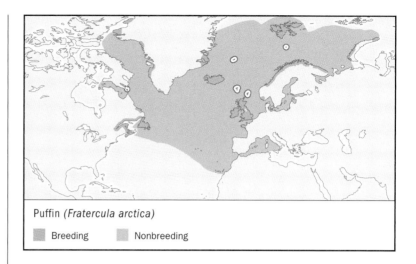

Puffin (*Fratercula arctica*)

■ Breeding ■ Nonbreeding

PUFFIN
Fratercula arctica

Physical characteristics: Puffins have a very distinctive large, yellow and orange bill with a blue-gray base. Their faces are white to gray with a thick black band from the forehead back. Their backs are black and their bellies white. Their legs and feet are orange.

Geographic range: Puffins breed on seashore areas of North America and Europe. They spend the winter in the waters of the North Atlantic.

Habitat: Puffins inhabit rocky seashore areas and islands during the breeding season. They spend the winter at sea.

Diet: Puffins primarily eat fish. When feeding young, adults are known to carry dozens of fish back at a time in their large bills.

Behavior and reproduction: Puffins are strong fliers and spend most of their time at sea, except during the breeding season. At sea, puffins may be found in flocks with other species such as murres and razorbills. Puffins also mate at sea. Courtship, behavior that leads to mating, involves the male and female tapping their bills together. Puffins build nests at the end of long burrows which they dig in the ground. The female lays a single egg. The chick hatches with a thick coat of down and is able to leave the nest after thirty-six to forty-seven days.

Puffins and people: No significant interactions between puffins and people are known.

Conservation status: Puffins are not considered threatened at this time. ■

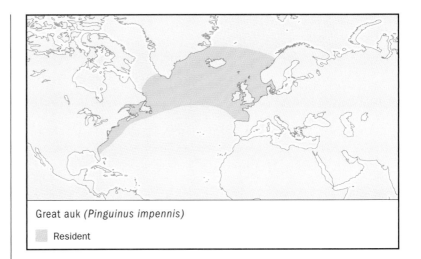

Great auk (*Pinguinus impennis*)

▨ Resident

GREAT AUK
Pinguinus impennis

Physical characteristics: Great auks were the largest members of the auk family, measuring 30.5 inches (78 centimeters) in length and 11 pounds (5 kilograms) in weight. They had black heads and backs, black wings, black feet, and white bellies.

Geographic range: Great auks were once found in the North Atlantic, between the Arctic Circle, New England, and the British Isles.

Habitat: Great auks were found in rocky seashore areas as well as in adjacent open ocean.

Diet: Great auks ate mainly fish.

Behavior and reproduction: Great auks were unable to fly. They spent the winter primarily at sea. During the breeding season, great auks were found in huge colonies on a small number of islands. Females laid a single egg on bare rock. Eggs had unique markings which likely allowed parents to recognize their own egg.

Great auks and people: Great auks were driven to extinction by human hunting. Because they were unable to fly and gathered in large numbers during the breeding season, they were extremely easy to hunt.

Their feathers were collected and their bodies were boiled to extract valuable oil. Their eggs were also collected.

Conservation status: Great auks went extinct sometime around 1844 C.E. due to human hunting and egg collection. ■

FOR MORE INFORMATION

Books:

del Hoyo, J., A. Elliott, and J. Sargatal, eds. *Handbook of the Birds of the World.* Vol. 3, *Hoatzin to Auks.* Barcelona: Lynx Edicions, 1996.

Fuller, E. *The Great Auk.* New York: Harry N. Abrams, 1999.

Perrins, Christopher, ed. *Firefly Encyclopedia of Birds.* Buffalo, NY: Firefly Books, 2003.

Web sites:

"Alcidae (Auks)." *The Internet Bird Collection.* http://www.hbw.com/ibc/phtml/familia.phtml?idFamilia=69 (accessed on June 8, 2004).

"Family Alcidae (Auks)." *Animal Diversity Web, The University of Michigan Museum of Zoology.* http://animaldiversity.ummz.umich.edu/site/accounts/classification/Alcidae.html#Alcidae (accessed on June 8, 2004).

Great auks were unable to fly, which made them easy to hunt. They went extinct in the 1800s due to human hunting and egg collection. (Illustration by Patricia Ferrer. Reproduced by permission.)

Species List by Biome

CONIFEROUS FOREST

African broadbill
African pitta
American cliff swallow
American goldfinch
American robin
Anna's hummingbird
Barn swallow
Barred eagle-owl
Belted kingfisher
Black-and-red broadbill
Black-and-white warbler
Black-capped chickadee
Black-capped vireo
Black-crowned barwing
Blue-gray gnatcatcher
Bornean bristlehead
Brown creeper
Brown kiwi
Cedar waxwing
Chaffinch
Chimney swift
Crag martin
Cuban tody
Dollarbird
Dunnock
Dusky woodswallow
Eastern bluebird
Eastern screech-owl
Emu

Fan-tailed berrypecker
Fiery minivet
Fire-breasted flowerpecker
Gray butcherbird
Gray nightjar
Gray parrot
Gray potoo
Green magpie
House sparrow
House wren
Ivory-billed woodpecker
Japanese white-eye
Kirtland's warbler
Kokako
Laughing kookaburra
Little slaty flycatcher
Malaysian honeyguide
Northern bobwhite quail
Northern wryneck
Nuthatch
Oilbird
Orange-breasted trogon
Osprey
Palmchat
Peregrine falcon
Red crossbill
Red-breasted nuthatch
Red-cockaded woodpecker
Resplendent quetzal
Rifleman

Rose-throated becard
Rufous treecreeper
Rufous-browed peppershrike
Rufous-capped nunlet
Rufous-tailed jacamar
Satyr tragopan
Scarlet macaw
Sparkling violet-ear
Spotted nutcracker
Striated pardalote
Whip-poor-will
White-necked puffbird
White-throated fantail
Winter wren
Wrentit
Yellow-bellied sapsucker
Yellow-breasted chat

CONTINENTAL MARGIN

Blue-footed booby
Brown pelican
Great cormorant
Northern gannet

DECIDUOUS FOREST

African broadbill
African pitta
American cliff swallow
American goldfinch

American robin
Anna's hummingbird
Arctic warbler
Asian fairy-bluebird
Australian magpie-lark
Baltimore oriole
Bar-breasted mousebird
Barn owl
Barn swallow
Baywing
Black bulbul
Black guan
Black-and-white warbler
Black-capped chickadee
Black-capped vireo
Blue jay
Blue-crowned motmot
Blue-gray gnatcatcher
Brown creeper
Brown kiwi
Bushtit
Cedar waxwing
Chaffinch
Chimney swift
Coppersmith barbet
Crag martin
Crested tree swift
Cuban tody
Dollarbird
Dunnock
Dusky woodswallow
Eastern bluebird
Eastern screech-owl
Emu
Eurasian golden oriole
European bee-eater
European roller
Fire-breasted flowerpecker
Gray catbird
Gray nightjar
Gray-crowned babbler
Great tit
House sparrow
House wren
Ivory-billed woodpecker
Jacky winter

Japanese white-eye
Leaf-love
Northern wryneck
Nuthatch
Orange-breasted trogon
Osprey
Painted buttonquail
Peregrine falcon
Peruvian plantcutter
Plain chachalaca
Red-breasted nuthatch
Red-cockaded woodpecker
Rifleman
Rose-ringed parakeet
Rufous scrub-bird
Rufous vanga
Rufous-capped nunlet
Rufous-tailed jacamar
Satyr tragopan
Scarlet macaw
Southern scrub robin
Spotted flycatcher
Striated pardalote
Tawny frogmouth
Toucan barbet
Whip-poor-will
White-breasted mesite
White-helmet shrike
White-necked puffbird
Wild turkey
Willie wagtail
Willow ptarmigan
Winter wren
Wood duck
Yellow-bellied sapsucker
Yellow-breasted chat
Yellow-fronted tinkerbird
Yellowhead
Yellow-rumped thornbill

DESERT

American cliff swallow
American mourning dove
Barn swallow
Cactus wren

California condor
Collared pratincole
Crab plover
Crested caracara
Crimson chat
Egyptian vulture
Emu
Gray catbird
Gray hypocolius
Greater hoopoe-lark
Greater roadrunner
Harris's hawk
House sparrow
Malleefowl
Namaqua sandgrouse
Northern lapwing
Ostrich
Pallas's sandgrouse
Peregrine falcon
Peruvian plantcutter
Rock pigeon
Snow finch
Splendid fairy-wren
Striated grasswren
Verdin
Western scrub-jay
Willie wagtail

GRASSLAND

African broadbill
African palm swift
African paradise-flycatcher
American cliff swallow
American mourning dove
American robin
Anna's hummingbird
Arctic skua
Australasian lark
Australian magpie-lark
Australian pratincole
Bar-breasted mousebird
Barn owl
Barn swallow
Baya weaver
Baywing

Black rail
Black-capped chickadee
Black-capped vireo
Black-crowned barwing
Black-faced sheathbill
Blue bustard
Blue jay
Blue-black grassquit
California condor
Cape sugarbird
Cattle egret
Cedar waxwing
Collared pratincole
Common cuckoo
Common myna
Common waxbill
Corncrake
Crag martin
Crested caracara
Crimson chat
Dollarbird
Eastern phoebe
Eclectus parrot
Egyptian vulture
Emu
Eurasian bittern
European bee-eater
European roller
European starling
European white stork
Fan-tailed berrypecker
Golden-winged sunbird
Gray go-away-bird
Gray hypocolius
Gray potoo
Gray woodpecker
Gray-crowned crane
Great blue heron
Great bustard
Great kiskadee
Green woodhoopoe
Gyrfalcon
Hammerhead
Harris's hawk
Helmeted guineafowl
Hoopoe

Horned lark
House sparrow
Jacky winter
Killdeer
King vulture
Laysan finch
Lesser rhea
Loggerhead shrike
Long-billed curlew
Malleefowl
Northern bobwhite quail
Northern lapwing
Northern raven
Northern wryneck
Ostrich
Painted buttonquail
Pallas's sandgrouse
Palmchat
Peregrine falcon
Peruvian plantcutter
Purple sunbird
Rainbow lorikeet
Red-billed oxpecker
Red-legged seriema
Red-winged blackbird
Rock pigeon
Roseate spoonbill
Rose-ringed parakeet
Rosy-breasted longclaw
Rufous-capped nunlet
Sacred ibis
Sandhill crane
Savanna sparrow
Secretary bird
Shoebill
Small buttonquail
Snowy owl
Song sparrow
Southern ground-hornbill
Southern red bishop
Southern scrub robin
Spotted munia
Sprague's pipit
Stonechat
Tawny frogmouth
Village weaver

White-helmet shrike
White-necked puffbird
Wild turkey
Wrentit
Yellow-fronted tinkerbird
Yellow-rumped thornbill
Zebra finch

LAKE AND POND
African jacana
American anhinga
American cliff swallow
American white pelican
Australian magpie-lark
Barn swallow
Baya weaver
Belted kingfisher
Black tern
Black-and-red broadbill
Black-capped donacobius
Canada goose
Chaffinch
Common iora
Common loon
Crag martin
Eurasian bittern
Gray wagtail
Great blue heron
Great cormorant
Great crested grebe
Greater flamingo
Greater thornbird
Hammerhead
Hoatzin
Mallard
Mute swan
Northern wryneck
Osprey
Peregrine falcon
Pheasant-tailed jacana
Red-throated loon
Roseate spoonbill
Rosy-breasted longclaw
Rufous hornero
Sacred ibis

Shoebill
Song sparrow
Sunbittern
Sungrebe
Village weaver
Western grebe
Wood duck
Yellow-breasted chat
Zebra finch

OCEAN

Arctic skua
Blue-footed booby
Chatham mollymawk
Common diving-petrel
Common iora
Common loon
Common murre
Emperor penguin
Great auk
King eider
Laysan albatross
Laysan finch
Macaroni penguin
Magellanic penguin
Magnificent frigatebird
Manx shearwater
Northern fulmar
Northern gannet
Puffin
Red-throated loon
White-tailed tropicbird
Wilson's storm-petrel

RAINFOREST

African paradise-flycatcher
African pitta
Albert's lyrebird
Amazonian umbrellabird
American cliff swallow
Apapane
Arctic warbler
Asian fairy-bluebird
Australasian figbird
Baltimore oriole

Barn owl
Barn swallow
Barred antshrike
Bishop's oo
Black-naped monarch
Blue-crowned motmot
Bornean bristlehead
Buff-spotted flufftail
Cape batis
Common bulbul
Common cuckoo
Common iora
Common sunbird-asity
Common trumpeter
Coppery-chested jacamar
Crag martin
Cuban tody
Dodo
Eclectus parrot
Fan-tailed berrypecker
Feline owlet-nightjar
Fiery minivet
Golden whistler
Golden-winged sunbird
Gray antbird
Gray nightjar
Gray potoo
Gray-breasted mountain-
    toucan
Gray-necked picathartes
Great blue turaco
Greater racket-tailed drongo
Greater thornbird
Guianan cock-of-the-rock
Hairy hermit
Helmeted hornbill
Highland tinamou
Hooded pitta
House sparrow
Kagu
King bird of paradise
King vulture
Kokako
Little slaty flycatcher
Long-tailed manakin
Luzon bleeding heart

Lyre-tailed honeyguide
Malaysian honeyguide
Maleo
Mauritius cuckoo-shrike
Osprey
Peregrine falcon
Purple sunbird
Purple-bearded bee-eater
Rainbow lorikeet
Red-billed scythebill
Ribbon-tailed astrapia
Roseate spoonbill
Rose-ringed parakeet
Ruby-cheeked sunbird
Rufous scrub-bird
Rufous vanga
Rufous-collared kingfisher
Rusty-belted tapaculo
Satin bowerbird
Sharpbill
Southern cassowary
Southern logrunner
Spangled cotinga
Spotted quail-thrush
Square-tailed drongo
Striated pardalote
Stripe-headed rhabdornis
Sulawesi red-knobbed
    hornbill
Sunbittern
Toco toucan
Toucan barbet
Variable pitohui
Victoria's riflebird
Wattled curassow
White-breasted mesite
Willie wagtail
Wire-tailed manakin

RIVER AND STREAM

African broadbill
African pitta
American anhinga
American cliff swallow
American dipper
American white pelican

Australian magpie-lark
Baltimore oriole
Barn swallow
Baya weaver
Black-and-red broadbill
Black-capped donacobius
Canada goose
Cedar waxwing
Chaffinch
Common loon
Crag martin
Crested caracara
Cuban tody
Dusky woodswallow
Eurasian dipper
European bee-eater
European roller
Gray catbird
Gray hypocolius
Gray wagtail
Gray woodpecker
Great blue heron
Great cormorant
Great crested grebe
Green woodhoopoe
Gyrfalcon
Hoatzin
Mute swan
Northern wryneck
Peregrine falcon
Red-breasted nuthatch
Red-throated loon
Roseate spoonbill
Rosy-breasted longclaw
Rufous-capped nunlet
Rufous hornero
Rufous-tailed jacamar
Sacred ibis
Shoebill
Snow bunting
Song sparrow
Southern red bishop
Spotted bowerbird
Striped honeyeater
Sunbittern
Sungrebe

Village weaver
Wood duck
Yellow-breasted chat
Yellow-fronted tinkerbird

SEASHORE

American cliff swallow
American white pelican
Arctic warbler
Australian magpie-lark
Barn swallow
Beach thick-knee
Belted kingfisher
Black tern
Black-faced sheathbill
Blue-footed booby
Brown pelican
Cactus wren
California condor
Collared pratincole
Common iora
Common murre
Crab plover
Crag martin
Cuban tody
Fiery minivet
Golden whistler
Gray wagtail
Great auk
Great blue heron
Great cormorant
Greater flamingo
Gyrfalcon
Hood mockingbird
Horned lark
Magnificent frigatebird
Northern gannet
Osprey
Peregrine falcon
Puffin
Roseate spoonbill
Ruddy turnstone
Sacred ibis
Saunder's gull
Snow bunting

Song sparrow
Splendid fairy-wren
Stonechat
Variable oystercatcher
Victoria's riflebird
White-tailed tropicbird

TUNDRA

American robin
Arctic skua
Arctic warbler
Canada goose
Common loon
Gyrfalcon
Horned lark
Northern raven
Peregrine falcon
Red-throated loon
Ruddy turnstone
Savanna sparrow
Snow bunting
Snowy owl
Willow ptarmigan

WETLAND

African jacana
African snipe
American anhinga
American avocet
American cliff swallow
American white pelican
Australasian lark
Australian magpie-lark
Baltimore oriole
Barn swallow
Black rail
Black tern
Black-faced sheathbill
Black-winged stilt
Canada goose
Cattle egret
Common bulbul
Common iora
Crag martin
Crested caracara

Eurasian bittern
European white stork
Gray wagtail
Gray-crowned crane
Great blue heron
Great cormorant
Greater flamingo
Greater painted snipe
Hairy hermit
Hammerhead
Harris's hawk
Horned screamer
House sparrow
Killdeer

King eider
Leaf-love
Limpkin
Long-billed curlew
Mallard
Mute swan
Northern lapwing
Osprey
Peregrine falcon
Pheasant-tailed jacana
Red-crowned crane
Red-winged blackbird
Roseate spoonbill
Rosy-breasted longclaw

Ruddy turnstone
Rufous-bellied seedsnipe
Sacred ibis
Sandhill crane
Saunder's gull
Shoebill
Sunbittern
Village weaver
Wood duck
Wood stork
Yellow-breasted chat
Zebra finch
Zitting cisticola

Species List by Geographic Range

AFGHANISTAN
Barn swallow
Chaffinch
Common myna
Crag martin
Egyptian vulture
Eurasian golden oriole
European bee-eater
European roller
European starling
Gray hypocolius
Great cormorant
Great crested grebe
Great tit
Greater hoopoe-lark
Hoopoe
House sparrow
Mute swan
Northern lapwing
Northern raven
Peregrine falcon
Rock pigeon
Snow finch
Spotted flycatcher
Spotted nutcracker
Winter wren

ALBANIA
Barn swallow
Chaffinch

Common cuckoo
Corncrake
Crag martin
Dunnock
Egyptian vulture
Eurasian dipper
Eurasian golden oriole
European bee-eater
European roller
European starling
Gray wagtail
Great cormorant
Great crested grebe
Great tit
Hoopoe
Horned lark
House sparrow
Mallard
Northern gannet
Northern lapwing
Northern raven
Northern wryneck
Nuthatch
Peregrine falcon
Red crossbill
Rock pigmeon
Snow bunting
Spotted flycatcher
Stonechat
Winter wren

Zitting cisticola

ALGERIA
Barn swallow
Black-winged stilt
Chaffinch
Common bulbul
Common cuckoo
Common murre
Corncrake
Crag martin
Dunnock
Egyptian vulture
Eurasian bittern
Eurasian golden oriole
European bee-eater
European roller
European starling
Gray wagtail
Great cormorant
Great crested grebe
Greater hoopoe-lark
Hoopoe
House sparrow
Mallard
Northern gannet
Northern lapwing
Northern raven
Northern wryneck
Peregrine falcon

Rock pigeon
Ruddy turnstone
Small buttonquail
Spotted flycatcher
Stonechat
Winter wren
Zitting cisticola

ANDORRA

Great cormorant
Peregrine falcon

ANGOLA

African jacana
African palm swift
African paradise-flycatcher
African snipe
Bar-breasted mousebird
Barn swallow
Black tern
Black-winged stilt
Buff-spotted flufftail
Cattle egret
Collared pratincole
Common bulbul
Common cuckoo
Common waxbill
Eurasian golden oriole
European bee-eater
European roller
European white stork
Gray go-away-bird
Great cormorant
Greater painted snipe
Green woodhoopoe
Hammerhead
Helmeted guineafowl
Hoopoe
House sparrow
Lyre-tailed honeyguide
Namaqua sandgrouse
Osprey
Ostrich
Peregrine falcon
Red-billed oxpecker

Rock pigeon
Rosy-breasted longclaw
Ruddy turnstone
Sacred ibis
Secretary bird
Small buttonquail
Southern ground-hornbill
Southern red bishop
Spotted flycatcher
Square-tailed drongo
Stonechat
Village weaver
White-helmet shrike
Wilson's storm-petrel
Yellow-fronted tinkerbird
Zitting cisticola

ANTARCTICA

Black-faced sheathbill
Emperor penguin
Macaroni penguin
Wilson's storm-petrel

ARGENTINA

American anhinga
American cliff swallow
Arctic skua
Barn owl
Barn swallow
Barred antshrike
Baywing
Black rail
Black-capped donacobius
Black-winged stilt
Blue-black grassquit
Cattle egret
Common diving-petrel
Crested caracara
Emperor penguin
Gray potoo
Great kiskadee
Greater thornbird
Harris's hawk
House sparrow
King vulture
Lesser rhea

Limpkin
Macaroni penguin
Magellanic penguin
Manx shearwater
Peregrine falcon
Red-billed scythebill
Red-legged seriema
Rock pigeon
Roseate spoonbill
Ruddy turnstone
Rufous hornero
Rufous-bellied seedsnipe
Rufous-browed peppershrike
Rufous-tailed jacamar
Sharpbill
Sparkling violet-ear
Sungrebe
Toco toucan
Wilson's storm-petrel
Wood stork

ARMENIA

Barn swallow
Chaffinch
Common cuckoo
Dunnock
Egyptian vulture
Eurasian dipper
Eurasian golden oriole
European bee-eater
European roller
European starling
Great cormorant
Great crested grebe
Great tit
Hoopoe
Horned lark
House sparrow
Northern lapwing
Northern raven
Nuthatch
Peregrine falcon
Red crossbill
Rock pigeon
Snow finch
Stonechat

Winter wren

ASCENSION
White-tailed tropicbird

AUSTRALIA
Albert's lyrebird
Arctic skua
Australasian figbird
Australasian lark
Australian magpie-lark
Australian pratincole
Beach thick-knee
Black-winged stilt
Cattle egret
Common diving-petrel
Crimson chat
Dollarbird
Dusky woodswallow
Eclectus parrot
Emu
European starling
Golden whistler
Gray butcherbird
Gray-crowned babbler
Great cormorant
Great crested grebe
Greater painted snipe
House sparrow
Jacky winter
Laughing kookaburra
Mallard
Malleefowl
Mute swan
Osprey
Painted buttonquail
Peregrine falcon
Rainbow lorikeet
Rock pigeon
Ruddy turnstone
Rufous scrub-bird
Rufous treecreeper
Satin bowerbird
Southern cassowary
Southern logrunner
Southern scrub robin

Splendid fairy-wren
Spotted bowerbird
Spotted quail-thrush
Striated grasswren
Striated pardalote
Striped honeyeater
Tawny frogmouth
Victoria's riflebird
Willie wagtail
Wilson's storm-petrel
Yellow-rumped thornbill
Zebra finch
Zitting cisticola

AUSTRIA
Barn swallow
Black tern
Chaffinch
Collared pratincole
Common cuckoo
Corncrake
Crag martin
Dunnock
Eurasian golden oriole
European bee-eater
European roller
European starling
European white stork
Gray wagtail
Great cormorant
Great crested grebe
Great tit
Hoopoe
House sparrow
Mallard
Mute swan
Northern lapwing
Northern raven
Northern wryneck
Nuthatch
Peregrine falcon
Red crossbill
Rock pigeon
Snow bunting
Snow finch
Spotted flycatcher

Spotted nutcracker
Stonechat
Winter wren

AZERBAIJAN
Barn swallow
Cattle egret
Chaffinch
Common cuckoo
Dunnock
Egyptian vulture
Eurasian dipper
Eurasian golden oriole
European bee-eater
European roller
European starling
European white stork
Great cormorant
Great crested grebe
Great tit
Hoopoe
Horned lark
House sparrow
Mallard
Northern lapwing
Northern raven
Nuthatch
Peregrine falcon
Red crossbill
Red-throated loon
Rock pigeon
Snow finch
Spotted flycatcher
Winter wren

BAHAMAS
American avocet
American mourning dove
American robin
Barn owl
Belted kingfisher
Black-and-white warbler
Black-winged stilt
Blue-gray gnatcatcher
Brown pelican
Cattle egret

Crested caracara
European starling
Gray catbird
House sparrow
Killdeer
Kirtland's warbler
Osprey
Peregrine falcon
Rock pigeon
Ruddy turnstone
White-tailed tropicbird
Wood stork
Yellow-bellied sapsucker

BANGLADESH

Barn swallow
Baya weaver
Black bulbul
Black-naped monarch
Black-winged stilt
Cattle egret
Common cuckoo
Common iora
Common myna
Coppersmith barbet
Crested tree swift
Dollarbird
Eurasian bittern
European white stork
Gray nightjar
Gray wagtail
Great cormorant
Great crested grebe
Great tit
Greater painted snipe
Greater racket-tailed drongo
Green magpie
Hooded pitta
Hoopoe
House sparrow
Mallard
Northern wryneck
Osprey
Peregrine falcon
Pheasant-tailed jacana
Purple sunbird

Rock pigeon
Rose-ringed parakeet
Ruby-cheeked sunbird
Ruddy turnstone
Small buttonquail
Spotted munia
Stonechat
White-throated fantail
Zitting cisticola

BELARUS

Barn swallow
Black tern
Chaffinch
Common cuckoo
Corncrake
Dunnock
Eurasian bittern
Eurasian golden oriole
European roller
European starling
European white stork
Great cormorant
Great crested grebe
Great tit
Hoopoe
House sparrow
Mallard
Northern lapwing
Northern raven
Northern wryneck
Nuthatch
Peregrine falcon
Red crossbill
Rock pigeon
Spotted flycatcher
Spotted nutcracker
Winter wren

BELGIUM

Barn swallow
Black tern
Chaffinch
Common cuckoo
Common murre
Corncrake

Dunnock
Eurasian golden oriole
European roller
European starling
European white stork
Gray wagtail
Great auk
Great cormorant
Great crested grebe
Great tit
Hoopoe
House sparrow
Mallard
Manx shearwater
Mute swan
Northern fulmar
Northern gannet
Northern lapwing
Northern wryneck
Nuthatch
Peregrine falcon
Puffin
Red-throated loon
Rock pigeon
Ruddy turnstone
Spotted flycatcher
Stonechat
Winter wren

BELIZE

American anhinga
American mourning dove
Baltimore oriole
Barn owl
Barred antshrike
Belted kingfisher
Black rail
Black-and-white warbler
Black-winged stilt
Blue-black grassquit
Blue-crowned motmot
Blue-gray gnatcatcher
Brown pelican
Cattle egret
Cedar waxwing
Crested caracara

Gray catbird
Great blue heron
Great kiskadee
Harris's hawk
House sparrow
Killdeer
King vulture
Limpkin
Magnificent frigatebird
Northern raven
Osprey
Peregrine falcon
Plain chachalaca
Rock pigeon
Rose-throated becard
Ruddy turnstone
Rufous-browed peppershrike
Rufous-tailed jacamar
Savanna sparrow
Scarlet macaw
Sungrebe
Whip-poor-will
White-necked puffbird
Wood stork
Yellow-bellied sapsucker
Yellow-breasted chat

BENIN

African jacana
African palm swift
African paradise-flycatcher
Barn swallow
Black tern
Black-winged stilt
Cattle egret
Collared pratincole
Common bulbul
Eurasian bittern
European bee-eater
European roller
Gray parrot
Gray woodpecker
Great blue turaco
Greater painted snipe
Green woodhoopoe
Hammerhead

Helmeted guineafowl
Hoopoe
Leaf-love
Northern wryneck
Osprey
Peregrine falcon
Rose-ringed parakeet
Ruddy turnstone
Sacred ibis
Secretary bird
Small buttonquail
Spotted flycatcher
Square-tailed drongo
Village weaver
White-helmet shrike
Wilson's storm-petrel
Yellow-fronted tinkerbird
Zitting cisticola

BERMUDA

European starling
Gray catbird
House sparrow
White-tailed tropicbird

BHUTAN

Asian fairy-bluebird
Barn swallow
Black-naped monarch
Cattle egret
Common cuckoo
Coppersmith barbet
Crested tree swift
Dollarbird
Eurasian bittern
European white stork
Fire-breasted flowerpecker
Gray nightjar
Great cormorant
Great crested grebe
Greater painted snipe
Hooded pitta
Hoopoe
House sparrow
Northern wryneck
Osprey

Pheasant-tailed jacana
Purple sunbird
Rock pigeon
Rose-ringed parakeet
Satyr tragopan
Small buttonquail
Snow finch
Spotted munia
Spotted nutcracker
Stonechat
White-throated fantail
Zitting cisticola

BOLIVIA

Amazonian umbrellabird
American anhinga
Barn owl
Barn swallow
Barred antshrike
Baywing
Black-capped donacobius
Black-winged stilt
Blue-black grassquit
Blue-crowned motmot
Cattle egret
Chimney swift
Crested caracara
Gray antbird
Gray potoo
Great kiskadee
Greater thornbird
Hairy hermit
Harris's hawk
Horned screamer
House sparrow
Killdeer
King vulture
Lesser rhea
Limpkin
Oilbird
Peregrine falcon
Red-billed scythebill
Red-legged seriema
Roseate spoonbill
Rufous hornero
Rufous-bellied seedsnipe

Rufous-browed peppershrike
Rufous-capped nunlet
Rufous-tailed jacamar
Scarlet macaw
Sharpbill
Spangled cotinga
Sparkling violet-ear
Sunbittern
Sungrebe
Toco toucan
Wattled curassow
White-necked puffbird
Wood stork

BOSNIA AND HERZEGOVINA
Barn swallow
Chaffinch
Common cuckoo
Corncrake
Dunnock
Eurasian dipper
Eurasian golden oriole
European bee-eater
European roller
European starling
European white stork
Gray wagtail
Great cormorant
Great crested grebe
Great tit
Hoopoe
House sparrow
Mallard
Northern lapwing
Northern raven
Northern wryneck
Nuthatch
Peregrine falcon
Red crossbill
Rock pigeon
Snow bunting
Snow finch
Spotted flycatcher
Stonechat
Winter wren

Zitting cisticola

BOTSWANA
African jacana
African palm swift
African paradise-flycatcher
African snipe
Bar-breasted mousebird
Barn swallow
Black-winged stilt
Cattle egret
Common bulbul
Common waxbill
Corncrake
Eurasian golden oriole
European roller
European white stork
Gray go-away-bird
Great cormorant
Greater painted snipe
Green woodhoopoe
Hammerhead
Helmeted guineafowl
Hoopoe
House sparrow
Namaqua sandgrouse
Osprey
Ostrich
Peregrine falcon
Red-billed oxpecker
Rock pigeon
Rosy-breasted longclaw
Sacred ibis
Secretary bird
Small buttonquail
Southern ground-hornbill
Southern red bishop
Spotted flycatcher
Stonechat
Village weaver
White-helmet shrike
Yellow-fronted tinkerbird
Zitting cisticola

BRAZIL
Amazonian umbrellabird

American anhinga
American cliff swallow
Barn owl
Barn swallow
Barred antshrike
Baywing
Black-capped donacobius
Black-winged stilt
Blue-black grassquit
Blue-crowned motmot
Brown pelican
Cattle egret
Chimney swift
Common trumpeter
Coppery-chested jacamar
Crested caracara
Gray antbird
Gray potoo
Great kiskadee
Greater thornbird
Guianan cock-of-the-rock
Hairy hermit
Harris's hawk
Hoatzin
Horned screamer
House sparrow
King vulture
Limpkin
Magellanic penguin
Magnificent frigatebird
Manx shearwater
Oilbird
Osprey
Peregrine falcon
Red-billed scythebill
Red-legged seriema
Rock pigeon
Roseate spoonbill
Ruddy turnstone
Rufous hornero
Rufous-browed peppershrike
Rufous-capped nunlet
Rufous-tailed jacamar
Rusty-belted tapaculo
Scarlet macaw

Sharpbill
Spangled cotinga
Sparkling violet-ear
Sunbittern
Sungrebe
Toco toucan
Wattled curassow
White-necked puffbird
Wilson's storm-petrel
Wire-tailed manakin
Wood stork

BULGARIA

Barn swallow
Black-winged stilt
Chaffinch
Common cuckoo
Corncrake
Dunnock
Egyptian vulture
Eurasian bittern
Eurasian golden oriole
European bee-eater
European roller
European starling
European white stork
Gray wagtail
Great cormorant
Great crested grebe
Great tit
Hoopoe
House sparrow
Mallard
Mute swan
Northern lapwing
Northern raven
Northern wryneck
Nuthatch
Peregrine falcon
Red crossbill
Red-throated loon
Rock pigeon
Snow bunting
Spotted flycatcher
Stonechat
Winter wren

Zitting cisticola

BURKINA FASO

African jacana
African palm swift
Barn swallow
Black-winged stilt
Cattle egret
Collared pratincole
Common bulbul
Egyptian vulture
Eurasian bittern
European bee-eater
European roller
European white stork
Gray woodpecker
Greater painted snipe
Green woodhoopoe
Hammerhead
Helmeted guineafowl
Hoopoe
Northern wryneck
Osprey
Peregrine falcon
Rose-ringed parakeet
Sacred ibis
Secretary bird
Small buttonquail
Village weaver
White-helmet shrike
Yellow-fronted tinkerbird

BURUNDI

African jacana
African palm swift
African paradise-flycatcher
African pitta
African snipe
Bar-breasted mousebird
Barn swallow
Black-winged stilt
Buff-spotted flufftail
Cattle egret
Collared pratincole
Common bulbul
Common cuckoo

Common waxbill
Corncrake
Eurasian golden oriole
European bee-eater
European roller
European white stork
Gray parrot
Gray-crowned crane
Great blue turaco
Great cormorant
Great crested grebe
Green woodhoopoe
Hammerhead
Helmeted guineafowl
Hoopoe
Osprey
Ostrich
Peregrine falcon
Red-billed oxpecker
Sacred ibis
Small buttonquail
Southern ground-hornbill
Southern red bishop
Spotted flycatcher
Stonechat
Village weaver
Yellow-fronted tinkerbird
Zitting cisticola

CAMBODIA

Arctic warbler
Asian fairy-bluebird
Australasian lark
Barn swallow
Baya weaver
Black-naped monarch
Black-winged stilt
Cattle egret
Common cuckoo
Common iora
Common myna
Coppersmith barbet
Crested tree swift
Dollarbird
Fire-breasted flowerpecker
Gray nightjar

Gray wagtail
Great cormorant
Great tit
Greater painted snipe
Greater racket-tailed drongo
Green magpie
Hoopoe
Northern wryneck
Orange-breasted trogon
Osprey
Peregrine falcon
Pheasant-tailed jacana
Purple sunbird
Rock pigeon
Ruby-cheeked sunbird
Ruddy turnstone
Small buttonquail
Spotted munia
Stonechat
White-throated fantail
Zitting cisticola

CAMEROON

African broadbill
African jacana
African palm swift
African paradise-flycatcher
African pitta
Bar-breasted mousebird
Barn swallow
Black tern
Black-winged stilt
Buff-spotted flufftail
Cattle egret
Collared pratincole
Common bulbul
Common waxbill
Eurasian bittern
Eurasian golden oriole
European roller
European white stork
Gray parrot
Gray woodpecker
Gray-necked picathartes
Great blue turaco
Great cormorant

Green woodhoopoe
Hammerhead
Helmeted guineafowl
Hoopoe
Leaf-love
Lyre-tailed honeyguide
Northern wryneck
Osprey
Peregrine falcon
Rose-ringed parakeet
Ruddy turnstone
Sacred ibis
Secretary bird
Small buttonquail
Spotted flycatcher
Square-tailed drongo
Stonechat
Village weaver
White-helmet shrike
Wilson's storm-petrel
Yellow-fronted tinkerbird
Zitting cisticola

CANADA

American cliff swallow
American dipper
American goldfinch
American mourning dove
American robin
American white pelican
Anna's hummingbird
Arctic skua
Baltimore oriole
Barn owl
Barn swallow
Belted kingfisher
Black tern
Black-and-white warbler
Black-capped chickadee
Blue jay
Brown creeper
Bushtit
Canada goose
Cattle egret
Cedar waxwing
Chimney swift

Common loon
Common murre
Eastern bluebird
Eastern phoebe
Eastern screech-owl
European starling
Gray catbird
Great auk
Great blue heron
Great cormorant
Gyrfalcon
Horned lark
House sparrow
House wren
Killdeer
King eider
Loggerhead shrike
Long-billed curlew
Mallard
Manx shearwater
Northern fulmar
Northern gannet
Northern raven
Osprey
Peregrine falcon
Puffin
Red crossbill
Red-breasted nuthatch
Red-throated loon
Red-winged blackbird
Rock pigeon
Ruddy turnstone
Sandhill crane
Savanna sparrow
Snow bunting
Snowy owl
Song sparrow
Sprague's pipit
Western grebe
Whip-poor-will
Willow ptarmigan
Wilson's storm-petrel
Winter wren
Wood duck
Yellow-bellied sapsucker
Yellow-breasted chat

CENTRAL AFRICAN REPUBLIC

African broadbill
African jacana
African palm swift
African paradise-flycatcher
Bar-breasted mousebird
Barn swallow
Black-winged stilt
Buff-spotted flufftail
Cattle egret
Collared pratincole
Common bulbul
Common waxbill
Eurasian bittern
Eurasian golden oriole
European white stork
Gray parrot
Gray woodpecker
Great blue turaco
Great cormorant
Green woodhoopoe
Hammerhead
Helmeted guineafowl
Hoopoe
Leaf-love
Lyre-tailed honeyguide
Northern wryneck
Osprey
Ostrich
Peregrine falcon
Red-billed oxpecker
Rose-ringed parakeet
Sacred ibis
Secretary bird
Shoebill
Small buttonquail
Spotted flycatcher
Square-tailed drongo
Village weaver
White-helmet shrike
Yellow-fronted tinkerbird

CHAD

African jacana
African palm swift

African paradise-flycatcher
Barn swallow
Black-winged stilt
Cattle egret
Collared pratincole
Common bulbul
Egyptian vulture
Eurasian bittern
European white stork
Gray woodpecker
Great cormorant
Green woodhoopoe
Hammerhead
Helmeted guineafowl
Hoopoe
Northern wryneck
Osprey
Ostrich
Peregrine falcon
Rock pigeon
Rose-ringed parakeet
Sacred ibis
Secretary bird
Small buttonquail
Square-tailed drongo
Village weaver
White-helmet shrike
Yellow-fronted tinkerbird

CHILE

Arctic skua
Barn owl
Barn swallow
Black rail
Black-winged stilt
Blue-black grassquit
Brown pelican
Cattle egret
Chimney swift
Common diving-petrel
Crested caracara
Emperor penguin
Harris's hawk
House sparrow
Killdeer

Lesser rhea
Macaroni penguin
Magellanic penguin
Osprey
Peregrine falcon
Rock pigeon
Ruddy turnstone
Rufous-bellied seedsnipe
Sparkling violet-ear
Wilson's storm-petrel

CHINA

Arctic warbler
Asian fairy-bluebird
Barn swallow
Baya weaver
Black bulbul
Black tern
Black-naped monarch
Black-winged stilt
Cattle egret
Chaffinch
Common cuckoo
Common iora
Common murre
Common myna
Coppersmith barbet
Crag martin
Crested tree swift
Dollarbird
Eurasian bittern
Eurasian dipper
Eurasian golden oriole
European roller
European starling
Fire-breasted flowerpecker
Gray nightjar
Gray wagtail
Great bustard
Great cormorant
Great crested grebe
Great tit
Greater painted snipe
Greater racket-tailed drongo
Green magpie

Hooded pitta
Hoopoe
Horned lark
House sparrow
Japanese white-eye
Mallard
Mute swan
Northern lapwing
Northern raven
Northern wryneck
Nuthatch
Orange-breasted trogon
Osprey
Pallas's sandgrouse
Peregrine falcon
Pheasant-tailed jacana
Purple sunbird
Red crossbill
Red-crowned crane
Red-throated loon
Rock pigeon
Rose-ringed parakeet
Ruby-cheeked sunbird
Ruddy turnstone
Satyr tragopan
Saunder's gull
Small buttonquail
Snow bunting
Snow finch
Spotted flycatcher
Spotted munia
Spotted nutcracker
Stonechat
White-throated fantail
Willow ptarmigan
Winter wren
Zitting cisticola

COLOMBIA
Amazonian umbrellabird
American anhinga
Baltimore oriole
Barn owl
Barn swallow
Barred antshrike

Belted kingfisher
Black tern
Black-and-white warbler
Black-capped donacobius
Black-winged stilt
Blue-black grassquit
Blue-crowned motmot
Blue-footed booby
Brown pelican
Cattle egret
Common trumpeter
Coppery-chested jacamar
Crested caracara
Gray antbird
Gray potoo
Gray-breasted mountain-
   toucan
Great blue heron
Great kiskadee
Greater flamingo
Guianan cock-of-the-rock
Hairy hermit
Harris's hawk
Highland tinamou
Hoatzin
Horned lark
Horned screamer
House sparrow
Killdeer
King vulture
Limpkin
Magnificent frigatebird
Oilbird
Osprey
Peregrine falcon
Red-billed scythebill
Roseate spoonbill
Ruddy turnstone
Rufous-browed peppershrike
Rufous-tailed jacamar
Rusty-belted tapaculo
Scarlet macaw
Spangled cotinga
Sparkling violet-ear
Sunbittern
Sungrebe

Toucan barbet
Wattled curassow
White-necked puffbird
Wilson's storm-petrel
Wire-tailed manakin
Wood stork

COMOROS
White-tailed tropicbird

CONGO
African jacana
African palm swift
African paradise-flycatcher
African pitta
Bar-breasted mousebird
Barn swallow
Black tern
Black-winged stilt
Buff-spotted flufftail
Cattle egret
Collared pratincole
Common bulbul
Common cuckoo
Common waxbill
Eurasian golden oriole
Gray parrot
Great blue turaco
Great cormorant
Greater painted snipe
Hammerhead
Helmeted guineafowl
Hoopoe
Leaf-love
Lyre-tailed honeyguide
Osprey
Peregrine falcon
Ruddy turnstone
Sacred ibis
Small buttonquail
Spotted flycatcher
Square-tailed drongo
Stonechat
Village weaver
Zitting cisticola

COSTA RICA

American anhinga
American dipper
American mourning dove
Baltimore oriole
Barn owl
Barn swallow
Barred antshrike
Belted kingfisher
Black guan
Black rail
Black tern
Black-and-white warbler
Black-winged stilt
Blue-black grassquit
Blue-crowned motmot
Blue-footed booby
Brown pelican
Cattle egret
Cedar waxwing
Crested caracara
Gray catbird
Gray potoo
Great blue heron
Great kiskadee
Harris's hawk
Highland tinamou
House sparrow
Killdeer
King vulture
Limpkin
Long-tailed manakin
Magnificent frigatebird
Oilbird
Osprey
Peregrine falcon
Plain chachalaca
Resplendent quetzal
Rock pigeon
Roseate spoonbill
Rose-throated becard
Ruddy turnstone
Rufous-browed peppershrike
Rufous-tailed jacamar
Scarlet macaw
Sharpbill

Sunbittern
Sungrebe
White-necked puffbird
Wood stork
Yellow-bellied sapsucker
Yellow-breasted chat

CROATIA

Barn swallow
Chaffinch
Collared pratincole
Common cuckoo
Corncrake
Dunnock
Eurasian bittern
Eurasian dipper
Eurasian golden oriole
European bee-eater
European roller
European starling
European white stork
Gray wagtail
Great cormorant
Great crested grebe
Great tit
Hoopoe
House sparrow
Mallard
Northern lapwing
Northern raven
Northern wryneck
Nuthatch
Peregrine falcon
Red crossbill
Red-throated loon
Rock pigeon
Snow bunting
Snow finch
Spotted flycatcher
Stonechat
Winter wren
Zitting cisticola

CUBA

American avocet
American mourning dove

Barn owl
Belted kingfisher
Black rail
Black-and-white warbler
Black-winged stilt
Blue-gray gnatcatcher
Brown pelican
Crested caracara
Cuban tody
Gray catbird
Greater flamingo
House sparrow
Ivory-billed woodpecker
Killdeer
Limpkin
Magnificent frigatebird
Northern bobwhite quail
Osprey
Peregrine falcon
Rock pigeon
Roseate spoonbill
Ruddy turnstone
Whip-poor-will
White-tailed tropicbird
Wood duck
Wood stork
Yellow-bellied sapsucker

CYPRUS

European roller
Great cormorant
Northern gannet
Peregrine falcon
Zitting cisticola

CZECH REPUBLIC

Barn swallow
Black tern
Chaffinch
Common cuckoo
Corncrake
Dunnock
Eurasian dipper
Eurasian golden oriole
European roller
European starling

European white stork
Gray wagtail
Great cormorant
Great crested grebe
Great tit
Hoopoe
House sparrow
Mallard
Mute swan
Northern lapwing
Northern raven
Northern wryneck
Nuthatch
Peregrine falcon
Red crossbill
Rock pigeon
Snow bunting
Spotted flycatcher
Spotted nutcracker
Stonechat
Winter wren

DEMOCRATIC REPUBLIC OF THE CONGO

African broadbill
African jacana
African palm swift
African paradise-flycatcher
African pitta
African snipe
Barn swallow
Black tern
Black-winged stilt
Buff-spotted flufftail
Cattle egret
Collared pratincole
Common bulbul
Common cuckoo
Common waxbill
Corncrake
Egyptian vulture
Eurasian bittern
Eurasian golden oriole
European bee-eater
European roller

European white stork
Golden-winged sunbird
Gray go-away-bird
Gray parrot
Gray woodpecker
Gray-crowned crane
Great blue turaco
Great cormorant
Great crested grebe
Greater painted snipe
Green woodhoopoe
Hammerhead
Helmeted guineafowl
Hoopoe
House sparrow
Leaf-love
Lyre-tailed honeyguide
Northern wryneck
Osprey
Peregrine falcon
Red-billed oxpecker
Ruddy turnstone
Sacred ibis
Secretary bird
Shoebill
Small buttonquail
Southern ground-hornbill
Southern red bishop
Spotted flycatcher
Square-tailed drongo
Stonechat
Village weaver
White-helmet shrike
Yellow-fronted tinkerbird
Zitting cisticola

DENMARK

Barn swallow
Canada goose
Chaffinch
Common cuckoo
Common murre
Corncrake
Dunnock
Eurasian bittern
European roller

European starling
Great auk
Great cormorant
Great crested grebe
Great tit
House sparrow
Mallard
Manx shearwater
Mute swan
Northern fulmar
Northern gannet
Northern lapwing
Northern wryneck
Nuthatch
Peregrine falcon
Puffin
Red crossbill
Red-throated loon
Rock pigeon
Snow bunting
Spotted flycatcher
Stonechat
Winter wren

DJIBOUTI

African paradise-flycatcher
African snipe
Bar-breasted mousebird
Cattle egret
Collared pratincole
Common bulbul
Corncrake
Crab plovers
Egyptian vulture
European roller
Great cormorant
Greater flamingo
Greater hoopoe-lark
Green woodhoopoe
Hammerhead
Hoopoe
Osprey
Ostrich
Peregrine falcon
Red-billed oxpecker
Ruddy turnstone

Sacred ibis
Secretary bird
Small buttonquail
Stonechat
Wilson's storm-petrel

DOMINICAN REPUBLIC

American mourning dove
Barn owl
Belted kingfisher
Black rail
Black-and-white warbler
Black-winged stilt
Brown pelican
Cattle egret
Crested caracara
Greater flamingo
House sparrow
Killdeer
Limpkin
Magnificent frigatebird
Osprey
Palmchat
Peregrine falcon
Rock pigeon
Roseate spoonbill
Ruddy turnstone
White-tailed tropicbird
Wilson's storm-petrel
Wood stork
Yellow-bellied sapsucker

ECUADOR

Amazonian umbrellabird
American anhinga
Barn owl
Barn swallow
Barred antshrike
Black tern
Black-winged stilt
Blue-black grassquit
Blue-crowned motmot
Blue-footed booby
Brown pelican
Cattle egret
Chimney swift

Common trumpeter
Coppery-chested jacamar
Crested caracara
Gray antbird
Gray potoo
Gray-breasted mountain-
  toucan
Great kiskadee
Greater flamingo
Harris's hawk
Highland tinamou
Hood mockingbird
Horned screamer
House sparrow
Killdeer
King vulture
Limpkin
Magnificent frigatebird
Oilbird
Osprey
Peregrine falcon
Red-billed scythebill
Roseate spoonbill
Ruddy turnstone
Rufous-bellied seedsnipe
Rufous-browed peppershrike
Rufous-tailed jacamar
Rusty-belted tapaculo
Scarlet macaw
Sharpbill
Spangled cotinga
Sparkling violet-ear
Sunbittern
Sungrebe
Toucan barbet
White-necked puffbird
Wilson's storm-petrel
Wire-tailed manakin

EGYPT

Barn swallow
Black tern
Black-winged stilt
Cattle egret
Common bulbul
Corncrake

Egyptian vulture
Eurasian bittern
European roller
Gray wagtail
Great cormorant
Great crested grebe
Greater flamingo
Greater hoopoe-lark
Greater painted snipe
Hoopoe
House sparrow
Mallard
Northern gannet
Northern lapwing
Northern raven
Osprey
Peregrine falcon
Rock pigeon
Ruddy turnstone
Stonechat
Zitting cisticola

EL SALVADOR

American anhinga
American mourning dove
Baltimore oriole
Barn owl
Barred antshrike
Belted kingfisher
Black rail
Black tern
Black-and-white warbler
Black-winged stilt
Blue-black grassquit
Blue-crowned motmot
Blue-footed booby
Blue-gray gnatcatcher
Brown creeper
Brown pelican
Cattle egret
Cedar waxwing
Crested caracara
Great blue heron
Great kiskadee
Harris's hawk
House sparrow

Killdeer
King vulture
Limpkin
Long-tailed manakin
Magnificent frigatebird
Northern raven
Osprey
Peregrine falcon
Rock pigeon
Roseate spoonbill
Rose-throated becard
Ruddy turnstone
Rufous-browed peppershrike
Rufous-tailed jacamar
Sunbittern
Sungrebe
Whip-poor-will
White-necked puffbird
Wood stork
Yellow-bellied sapsucker
Yellow-breasted chat

EQUATORIAL GUINEA
African jacana
African palm swift
African paradise-flycatcher
African pitta
Barn swallow
Black tern
Black-winged stilt
Cattle egret
Collared pratincole
Common bulbul
Common waxbill
Gray parrot
Gray-necked picathartes
Great blue turaco
Great cormorant
Great crested grebe
Hammerhead
Helmeted guineafowl
Leaf-love
Lyre-tailed honeyguide
Osprey
Peregrine falcon
Ruddy turnstone

Sacred ibis
Spotted flycatcher
Village weaver
Wilson's storm-petrel
Zitting cisticola

ERITREA
African paradise-flycatcher
African snipe
Bar-breasted mousebird
Cattle egret
Collared pratincole
Common bulbul
Corncrake
Crab plovers
Egyptian vulture
Eurasian bittern
European roller
European white stork
Gray woodpecker
Greater flamingo
Greater hoopoe-lark
Greater painted snipe
Green woodhoopoe
Hammerhead
Helmeted guineafowl
Hoopoe
Osprey
Ostrich
Peregrine falcon
Red-billed oxpecker
Rock pigeon
Rose-ringed parakeet
Ruddy turnstone
Sacred ibis
Secretary bird
Small buttonquail
Stonechat
White-helmet shrike
Wilson's storm-petrel
Zitting cisticola

ESTONIA
Barn swallow
Black tern
Chaffinch

Common cuckoo
Common murre
Corncrake
Dunnock
Eurasian bittern
Eurasian dipper
Eurasian golden oriole
European roller
European starling
European white stork
Great cormorant
Great crested grebe
Great tit
Hoopoe
House sparrow
Mallard
Northern fulmar
Northern gannet
Northern lapwing
Northern raven
Northern wryneck
Nuthatch
Osprey
Red crossbill
Rock pigeon
Spotted flycatcher
Willow ptarmigan
Winter wren

ETHIOPIA
African jacana
African palm swift
African paradise-flycatcher
African snipe
Bar-breasted mousebird
Barn swallow
Black-winged stilt
Buff-spotted flufftail
Cattle egret
Collared pratincole
Common bulbul
Common waxbill
Corncrake
Egyptian vulture
Eurasian bittern
European roller

European white stork
Gray wagtail
Gray woodpecker
Great cormorant
Great crested grebe
Greater painted snipe
Green woodhoopoe
Hammerhead
Helmeted guineafowl
Hoopoe
Northern wryneck
Osprey
Ostrich
Peregrine falcon
Red-billed oxpecker
Rose-ringed parakeet
Sacred ibis
Secretary bird
Small buttonquail
Stonechat
Village weaver
White-helmet shrike
Yellow-fronted tinkerbird
Zitting cisticola

FALKLAND ISLANDS
Arctic skua
Crested caracara
Emperor penguin
House sparrow
Macaroni penguin
Magellanic penguin
Peregrine falcon

FIJI
European starling
Golden whistler
White-tailed tropicbird

FINLAND
Arctic warbler
Barn swallow
Chaffinch
Common cuckoo
Common murre

Corncrake
Dunnock
Eurasian bittern
Eurasian dipper
European roller
European starling
Gray wagtail
Great cormorant
Great crested grebe
Great tit
Gyrfalcon
Horned lark
House sparrow
Mute swan
Northern fulmar
Northern gannet
Northern lapwing
Northern raven
Northern wryneck
Osprey
Peregrine falcon
Puffin
Red crossbill
Red-throated loon
Rock pigeon
Ruddy turnstone
Spotted flycatcher
Spotted nutcracker
Willow ptarmigan
Winter wren

FRANCE
Barn swallow
Black tern
Black-winged stilt
Cattle egret
Chaffinch
Common cuckoo
Common loon
Common murre
Corncrake
Dunnock
Eurasian bittern
Eurasian dipper
Eurasian golden oriole
European bee-eater

European roller
European starling
European white stork
Gray wagtail
Great auk
Great cormorant
Great crested grebe
Great tit
Greater flamingo
Hoopoe
House sparrow
Mallard
Manx shearwater
Mute swan
Northern fulmar
Northern gannet
Northern lapwing
Northern raven
Northern wryneck
Nuthatch
Osprey
Peregrine falcon
Puffin
Red crossbill
Red-throated loon
Rock pigeon
Ruddy turnstone
Snow finch
Spotted flycatcher
Stonechat
Wilson's storm-petrel
Winter wren
Zitting cisticola

FRENCH GUIANA
American anhinga
Barn owl
Barn swallow
Barred antshrike
Black tern
Black-capped donacobius
Black-winged stilt
Blue-black grassquit
Blue-crowned motmot
Brown pelican
Cattle egret

Common trumpeter
Crested caracara
Gray antbird
Gray potoo
Great kiskadee
Guianan cock-of-the-rock
Hairy hermit
Hoatzin
King vulture
Limpkin
Magnificent frigatebird
Osprey
Peregrine falcon
Roseate spoonbill
Ruddy turnstone
Rufous-browed peppershrike
Rufous-tailed jacamar
Scarlet macaw
Spangled cotinga
Sunbittern
Sungrebe
White-necked puffbird
Wilson's storm-petrel
Wood stork

GABON
African broadbill
African jacana
African palm swift
African paradise-flycatcher
African pitta
Bar-breasted mousebird
Barn swallow
Black tern
Black-winged stilt
Buff-spotted flufftail
Cattle egret
Collared pratincole
Common bulbul
Common cuckoo
Common waxbill
Eurasian golden oriole
Gray parrot
Gray-necked picathartes
Great blue turaco
Great cormorant

Greater painted snipe
Hammerhead
Helmeted guineafowl
Hoopoe
Leaf-love
Lyre-tailed honeyguide
Osprey
Peregrine falcon
Ruddy turnstone
Sacred ibis
Small buttonquail
Spotted flycatcher
Square-tailed drongo
Stonechat
Village weaver
Wilson's storm-petrel
Zitting cisticola

GAMBIA
African palm swift
African paradise-flycatcher
Black tern
Black-winged stilt
Cattle egret
Collared pratincole
Common bulbul
Egyptian vulture
Eurasian bittern
Gray woodpecker
Greater flamingo
Green woodhoopoe
Hammerhead
Helmeted guineafowl
Hoopoe
Leaf-love
Magnificent frigatebird
Northern wryneck
Osprey
Peregrine falcon
Rose-ringed parakeet
Ruddy turnstone
Sacred ibis
Secretary bird
Small buttonquail
Village weaver
White-helmet shrike

Wilson's storm-petrel
Yellow-fronted tinkerbird

GEORGIA
Barn swallow
Chaffinch
Common cuckoo
Corncrake
Dunnock
Egyptian vulture
Eurasian dipper
Eurasian golden oriole
European bee-eater
European roller
European starling
Gray wagtail
Great cormorant
Great crested grebe
Great tit
Hoopoe
Horned lark
House sparrow
Northern raven
Northern wryneck
Nuthatch
Peregrine falcon
Red crossbill
Rock pigeon
Snow finch
Spotted flycatcher
Stonechat
Winter wren

GERMANY
Barn swallow
Black tern
Canada goose
Chaffinch
Common cuckoo
Common murre
Corncrake
Dunnock
Eurasian bittern
Eurasian dipper
Eurasian golden oriole

European roller
European starling
European white stork
Gray wagtail
Great auk
Great bustard
Great cormorant
Great crested grebe
Great tit
Hoopoe
House sparrow
Mallard
Manx shearwater
Mute swan
Northern fulmar
Northern gannet
Northern lapwing
Northern raven
Northern wryneck
Nuthatch
Peregrine falcon
Puffin
Red crossbill
Red-throated loon
Rock pigeon
Ruddy turnstone
Snow bunting
Snow finch
Spotted flycatcher
Spotted nutcracker
Stonechat
Winter wren

GHANA

African broadbill
African jacana
African palm swift
African paradise-flycatcher
African pitta
Barn swallow
Black tern
Black-winged stilt
Cattle egret
Collared pratincole
Common bulbul
Eurasian bittern

European bee-eater
European roller
Gray parrot
Gray woodpecker
Great blue turaco
Greater painted snipe
Green woodhoopoe
Hammerhead
Helmeted guineafowl
Hoopoe
Leaf-love
Northern wryneck
Osprey
Peregrine falcon
Rose-ringed parakeet
Ruddy turnstone
Sacred ibis
Secretary bird
Small buttonquail
Spotted flycatcher
Square-tailed drongo
Village weaver
White-helmet shrike
Wilson's storm-petrel
Yellow-fronted tinkerbird
Zitting cisticola

GREECE

Barn swallow
Chaffinch
Common cuckoo
Corncrake
Crag martin
Dunnock
Egyptian vulture
Eurasian bittern
Eurasian dipper
Eurasian golden oriole
European bee-eater
European roller
European starling
Gray wagtail
Great cormorant
Great crested grebe
Great tit
Hoopoe

Horned lark
House sparrow
Mallard
Mute swan
Northern gannet
Northern lapwing
Northern raven
Northern wryneck
Peregrine falcon
Red crossbill
Rock pigeon
Spotted flycatcher
Stonechat
Winter wren
Zitting cisticola

GREENLAND

Arctic skua
Common loon
Common murre
Great auk
Great cormorant
Gyrfalcon
King eider
Mallard
Manx shearwater
Northern fulmar
Northern gannet
Northern raven
Peregrine falcon
Puffin
Red-throated loon
Ruddy turnstone
Snow bunting
Snowy owl

GUATEMALA

American anhinga
American dipper
American mourning dove
American robin
Baltimore oriole
Barn owl
Barred antshrike
Belted kingfisher
Black rail

Black tern
Black-and-white warbler
Black-capped vireo
Black-winged stilt
Blue-black grassquit
Blue-crowned motmot
Blue-footed booby
Blue-gray gnatcatcher
Brown creeper
Brown pelican
Cattle egret
Cedar waxwing
Crested caracara
Gray catbird
Great blue heron
Great kiskadee
Harris's hawk
House sparrow
Killdeer
King vulture
Limpkin
Long-tailed manakin
Magnificent frigatebird
Northern raven
Osprey
Peregrine falcon
Plain chachalaca
Resplendent quetzal
Rock pigeon
Roseate spoonbill
Rose-throated becard
Ruddy turnstone
Rufous-browed peppershrike
Rufous-tailed jacamar
Savanna sparrow
Scarlet macaw
Sunbittern
Sungrebe
Whip-poor-will
White-necked puffbird
Wood stork
Yellow-bellied sapsucker
Yellow-breasted chat

GUINEA

African palm swift

African paradise-flycatcher
Barn swallow
Black tern
Black-winged stilt
Buff-spotted flufftail
Cattle egret
Collared pratincole
Common bulbul
Common waxbill
Eurasian bittern
European bee-eater
European roller
Gray parrot
Gray woodpecker
Great blue turaco
Green woodhoopoe
Hammerhead
Helmeted guineafowl
Hoopoe
Leaf-love
Northern wryneck
Osprey
Peregrine falcon
Rock pigeon
Rose-ringed parakeet
Ruddy turnstone
Sacred ibis
Small buttonquail
Square-tailed drongo
Stonechat
Village weaver
White-helmet shrike
Wilson's storm-petrel
Yellow-fronted tinkerbird

GUINEA-BISSAU

African palm swift
African paradise-flycatcher
Barn swallow
Black tern
Black-winged stilt
Cattle egret
Collared pratincole
Common bulbul
Common waxbill
Egyptian vulture

Eurasian bittern
Gray parrot
Gray woodpecker
Green woodhoopoe
Hammerhead
Helmeted guineafowl
Hoopoe
Leaf-love
Magnificent frigatebird
Northern wryneck
Osprey
Peregrine falcon
Rose-ringed parakeet
Ruddy turnstone
Sacred ibis
Small buttonquail
Square-tailed drongo
Village weaver
Wilson's storm-petrel

GUYANA

American anhinga
Barn owl
Barn swallow
Barred antshrike
Belted kingfisher
Black tern
Black-capped donacobius
Black-winged stilt
Blue-black grassquit
Blue-crowned motmot
Brown pelican
Cattle egret
Common trumpeter
Crested caracara
Gray antbird
Gray potoo
Great kiskadee
Greater flamingo
Guianan cock-of-the-rock
Hairy hermit
Hoatzin
King vulture
Limpkin
Magnificent frigatebird
Oilbird

Osprey
Peregrine falcon
Roseate spoonbill
Ruddy turnstone
Rufous-browed peppershrike
Rufous-tailed jacamar
Scarlet macaw
Sharpbill
Spangled cotinga
Sparkling violet-ear
Sunbittern
Sungrebe
White-necked puffbird
Wilson's storm-petrel
Wood stork

HAITI
American mourning dove
Barn owl
Belted kingfisher
Black-and-white warbler
Black-winged stilt
Brown pelican
Cattle egret
Crested caracara
Greater flamingo
House sparrow
Killdeer
Limpkin
Magnificent frigatebird
Osprey
Palmchat
Peregrine falcon
Rock pigeon
Roseate spoonbill
Ruddy turnstone
White-tailed tropicbird
Wood stork
Yellow-bellied sapsucker

HONDURAS
American anhinga
American mourning dove
Baltimore oriole
Barn owl
Barred antshrike

Belted kingfisher
Black tern
Black-and-white warbler
Black-winged stilt
Blue-black grassquit
Blue-crowned motmot
Blue-footed booby
Blue-gray gnatcatcher
Brown creeper
Brown pelican
Cattle egret
Cedar waxwing
Crested caracara
Gray catbird
Great blue heron
Great kiskadee
Harris's hawk
House sparrow
Killdeer
King vulture
Limpkin
Long-tailed manakin
Magnificent frigatebird
Northern raven
Osprey
Peregrine falcon
Plain chachalaca
Resplendent quetzal
Rock pigeon
Roseate spoonbill
Rose-throated becard
Ruddy turnstone
Rufous-browed peppershrike
Rufous-tailed jacamar
Scarlet macaw
Sunbittern
Sungrebe
Whip-poor-will
White-necked puffbird
Wood stork
Yellow-bellied sapsucker
Yellow-breasted chat

HUNGARY
Barn swallow
Black tern

Chaffinch
Collared pratincole
Common cuckoo
Corncrake
Dunnock
Eurasian golden oriole
European bee-eater
European roller
European starling
European white stork
Gray wagtail
Great bustard
Great cormorant
Great crested grebe
Great tit
Hoopoe
House sparrow
Mallard
Northern lapwing
Northern raven
Northern wryneck
Nuthatch
Peregrine falcon
Red crossbill
Rock pigeon
Snow bunting
Spotted flycatcher
Stonechat
Winter wren

ICELAND
Arctic skua
Common loon
Common murre
European starling
Great auk
Great cormorant
Gyrfalcon
King eider
Mallard
Manx shearwater
Northern fulmar
Northern gannet
Northern raven
Puffin
Red-throated loon

Snow bunting

INDIA
Asian fairy-bluebird
Barn swallow
Baya weaver
Black bulbul
Black-naped monarch
Black-winged stilt
Cattle egret
Chaffinch
Collared pratincole
Common cuckoo
Common iora
Common myna
Coppersmith barbet
Crab plovers
Crag martin
Crested tree swift
Dollarbird
Egyptian vulture
Eurasian bittern
Eurasian golden oriole
European bee-eater
European roller
European starling
European white stork
Fire-breasted flowerpecker
Gray hypocolius
Gray nightjar
Gray wagtail
Great cormorant
Great crested grebe
Great tit
Greater flamingo
Greater painted snipe
Greater racket-tailed drongo
Green magpie
Hooded pitta
Hoopoe
House sparrow
Mallard
Northern lapwing
Northern raven
Northern wryneck
Osprey

Peregrine falcon
Pheasant-tailed jacana
Purple sunbird
Rock pigeon
Rose-ringed parakeet
Ruby-cheeked sunbird
Ruddy turnstone
Satyr tragopan
Small buttonquail
Spotted munia
Spotted nutcracker
Stonechat
White-throated fantail
Wilson's storm-petrel
Zitting cisticola

INDONESIA
Arctic warbler
Asian fairy-bluebird
Australasian figbird
Australasian lark
Australian magpie-lark
Australian pratincole
Barn swallow
Barred eagle-owl
Baya weaver
Beach thick-knee
Black-and-red broadbill
Black-naped monarch
Black-winged stilt
Bornean bristlehead
Cattle egret
Common iora
Coppersmith barbet
Dollarbird
Eclectus parrot
Fan-tailed berrypecker
Feline owlet-nightjar
Fiery minivet
Fire-breasted flowerpecker
Golden whistler
Gray nightjar
Gray wagtail
Gray-crowned babbler
Great cormorant
Great tit

Greater painted snipe
Greater racket-tailed drongo
Green magpie
Helmeted hornbill
Hooded pitta
King bird of paradise
Malaysian honeyguide
Maleo
Orange-breasted trogon
Osprey
Peregrine falcon
Pheasant-tailed jacana
Purple-bearded bee-eater
Rainbow lorikeet
Rock pigeon
Ruby-cheeked sunbird
Ruddy turnstone
Rufous-collared kingfisher
Small buttonquail
Southern cassowary
Spotted munia
Sulawesi red-knobbed
  hornbill
Variable pitohui
White-throated fantail
Willie wagtail
Wilson's storm-petrel
Zebra finch
Zitting cisticola

IRAN
Barn swallow
Black-winged stilt
Cattle egret
Chaffinch
Common cuckoo
Common myna
Corncrake
Crab plovers
Crag martin
Dunnock
Egyptian vulture
Eurasian dipper
Eurasian golden oriole
European bee-eater
European roller

European starling
European white stork
Gray hypocolius
Gray wagtail
Great bustard
Great cormorant
Great crested grebe
Great tit
Greater flamingo
Greater hoopoe-lark
Hoopoe
Horned lark
House sparrow
Mallard
Mute swan
Northern lapwing
Northern raven
Nuthatch
Osprey
Peregrine falcon
Purple sunbird
Red-throated loon
Rock pigeon
Ruddy turnstone
Snow finch
Spotted flycatcher
Stonechat
Wilson's storm-petrel
Winter wren

IRAQ
Black-winged stilt
Cattle egret
Chaffinch
Collared pratincole
Corncrake
Dunnock
Egyptian vulture
Eurasian bittern
European bee-eater
European roller
European starling
Gray hypocolius
Gray wagtail
Great cormorant
Great crested grebe

Greater hoopoe-lark
Hoopoe
House sparrow
Mallard
Northern lapwing
Nuthatch
Osprey
Peregrine falcon
Rock pigeon
Spotted flycatcher
Stonechat

IRELAND
Barn owl
Barn swallow
Canada goose
Chaffinch
Common cuckoo
Common loon
Common murre
Corncrake
Dunnock
Eurasian dipper
European starling
Gray wagtail
Great auk
Great cormorant
Great crested grebe
Great tit
House sparrow
Mallard
Manx shearwater
Mute swan
Northern gannet
Northern lapwing
Northern raven
Peregrine falcon
Puffin
Red-throated loon
Rock pigeon
Ruddy turnstone
Spotted flycatcher
Stonechat
Willow ptarmigan
Winter wren

ISRAEL
Black-winged stilt
Cattle egret
Collared pratincole
Common cuckoo
Egyptian vulture
European bee-eater
European roller
Great cormorant
Greater flamingo
Hoopoe
Horned lark
House sparrow
Mallard
Northern gannet
Northern lapwing
Peregrine falcon
Rock pigeon
Stonechat
Winter wren
Zitting cisticola

ITALY
Barn swallow
Black tern
Black-winged stilt
Cattle egret
Chaffinch
Common cuckoo
Corncrake
Crag martin
Dunnock
Egyptian vulture
Eurasian dipper
Eurasian golden oriole
European bee-eater
European roller
European starling
Gray wagtail
Great cormorant
Great crested grebe
Great tit
Greater flamingo
Hoopoe
House sparrow
Mallard

Mute swan
Northern gannet
Northern lapwing
Northern raven
Northern wryneck
Nuthatch
Peregrine falcon
Red crossbill
Rock pigeon
Snow finch
Spotted flycatcher
Stonechat
Winter wren
Zitting cisticola

IVORY COAST
African broadbill
African jacana
African palm swift
African paradise-flycatcher
African pitta
Barn swallow
Black tern
Black-winged stilt
Cattle egret
Collared pratincole
Common bulbul
Common waxbill
Eurasian bittern
European bee-eater
European roller
Gray parrot
Gray woodpecker
Great blue turaco
Green woodhoopoe
Hammerhead
Hoopoe
Leaf-love
Lyre-tailed honeyguide
Northern wryneck
Osprey
Peregrine falcon
Rose-ringed parakeet
Ruddy turnstone
Sacred ibis
Small buttonquail

Spotted flycatcher
Square-tailed drongo
Village weaver
White-helmet shrike
Wilson's storm-petrel
Yellow-fronted tinkerbird
Zitting cisticola

JAMAICA
American mourning dove
Barn owl
Belted kingfisher
Black rail
Black-and-white warbler
Brown pelican
Cattle egret
Crested caracara
European starling
Gray catbird
House sparrow
Killdeer
Magnificent frigatebird
Osprey
Peregrine falcon
Rock pigeon
Ruddy turnstone
White-tailed tropicbird
Wood stork

JAPAN
Arctic warbler
Barn swallow
Cattle egret
Common murre
Dollarbird
Eurasian bittern
Gray nightjar
Gray wagtail
Great cormorant
Great tit
Greater painted snipe
Hoopoe
Japanese white-eye
Laysan albatross
Mallard
Mute swan

Northern fulmar
Northern lapwing
Northern raven
Nuthatch
Osprey
Peregrine falcon
Red crossbill
Red-crowned crane
Red-throated loon
Rock pigeon
Saunder's gull
Spotted nutcracker
Stonechat
Willow ptarmigan
Winter wren

JORDAN
Black-winged stilt
Cattle egret
Collared pratincole
Common bulbul
Egyptian vulture
European bee-eater
European roller
Gray wagtail
Great cormorant
Hoopoe
House sparrow
Northern gannet
Northern lapwing
Peregrine falcon
Rock pigeon
Stonechat
Winter wren

KAZAKHSTAN
Barn swallow
Black tern
Black-winged stilt
Chaffinch
Collared pratincole
Common cuckoo
Common myna
Corncrake
Egyptian vulture
Eurasian bittern

Eurasian golden oriole
European bee-eater
European roller
European starling
European white stork
Great cormorant
Great crested grebe
Great tit
Greater flamingo
Hoopoe
Horned lark
House sparrow
Mallard
Mute swan
Northern raven
Pallas's sandgrouse
Peregrine falcon
Red crossbill
Red-throated loon
Rock pigeon
Snow bunting
Spotted flycatcher
Spotted nutcracker
Stonechat
Willow ptarmigan
Winter wren

KENYA
African broadbill
African jacana
African palm swift
African paradise-flycatcher
African snipe
Bar-breasted mousebird
Barn swallow
Black-winged stilt
Buff-spotted flufftail
Cattle egret
Collared pratincole
Common bulbul
Common cuckoo
Common waxbill
Corncrake
Crab plovers
Egyptian vulture
Eurasian golden oriole

European bee-eater
European roller
European white stork
Golden-winged sunbird
Gray parrot
Gray wagtail
Gray woodpecker
Gray-crowned crane
Great blue turaco
Great cormorant
Great crested grebe
Greater flamingo
Greater painted snipe
Green woodhoopoe
Hammerhead
Helmeted guineafowl
Hoopoe
Northern wryneck
Osprey
Ostrich
Peregrine falcon
Red-billed oxpecker
Rock pigeon
Rosy-breasted longclaw
Ruddy turnstone
Sacred ibis
Secretary bird
Shoebill
Small buttonquail
Southern ground-hornbill
Southern red bishop
Spotted flycatcher
Square-tailed drongo
Stonechat
Village weaver
White-helmet shrike
Wilson's storm-petrel
Zitting cisticola

KUWAIT
Black-winged stilt
Cattle egret
Chaffinch
Collared pratincole
Crab plovers
Eurasian bittern

European roller
Gray wagtail
Great cormorant
Great crested grebe
Greater hoopoe-lark
House sparrow
Mallard
Northern lapwing
Nuthatch
Osprey
Peregrine falcon
Rock pigeon
Ruddy turnstone
Spotted flycatcher
Wilson's storm-petrel
Zitting cisticola

KYRGYZSTAN
Barn swallow
Chaffinch
Common cuckoo
Crag martin
Egyptian vulture
Eurasian bittern
Eurasian golden oriole
European roller
European starling
Gray wagtail
Great cormorant
Great crested grebe
Great tit
Hoopoe
House sparrow
Mallard
Northern raven
Pallas's sandgrouse
Peregrine falcon
Rock pigeon
Snow finch
Spotted flycatcher
Stonechat
Winter wren

LAOS
Asian fairy-bluebird
Australasian lark

Barn swallow
Baya weaver
Black bulbul
Black-and-red broadbill
Black-crowned barwing
Black-naped monarch
Black-winged stilt
Cattle egret
Common cuckoo
Common iora
Common myna
Coppersmith barbet
Crested tree swift
Dollarbird
Eurasian bittern
Fire-breasted flowerpecker
Gray nightjar
Gray wagtail
Great cormorant
Greater painted snipe
Greater racket-tailed drongo
Green magpie
Hoopoe
Northern wryneck
Orange-breasted trogon
Peregrine falcon
Pheasant-tailed jacana
Purple sunbird
Rock pigeon
Ruby-cheeked sunbird
Small buttonquail
Spotted munia
Stonechat
White-throated fantail
Zitting cisticola

LATVIA
Barn swallow
Black tern
Chaffinch
Common cuckoo
Common murre
Corncrake
Dunnock
Eurasian bittern
Eurasian dipper

Eurasian golden oriole
European roller
European starling
European white stork
Great cormorant
Great crested grebe
Great tit
Hoopoe
House sparrow
Mallard
Northern fulmar
Northern gannet
Northern lapwing
Northern raven
Northern wryneck
Nuthatch
Red crossbill
Rock pigeon
Spotted flycatcher
Spotted nutcracker
Willow ptarmigan
Winter wren

LEBANON
Black-winged stilt
Cattle egret
Collared pratincole
Common bulbul
Common cuckoo
Dunnock
Egyptian vulture
European bee-eater
European roller
Great cormorant
Greater flamingo
Hoopoe
Horned lark
House sparrow
Mallard
Northern gannet
Northern lapwing
Nuthatch
Peregrine falcon
Rock pigeon
Spotted flycatcher
Stonechat

Winter wren

LESOTHO
African jacana
African snipe
Barn swallow
Black-winged stilt
Blue bustard
Cattle egret
Common cuckoo
Common waxbill
Corncrake
European roller
European white stork
Great cormorant
Great crested grebe
Greater painted snipe
Green woodhoopoe
Hammerhead
Helmeted guineafowl
Hoopoe
House sparrow
Osprey
Peregrine falcon
Sacred ibis
Secretary bird
Small buttonquail
Southern red bishop
Spotted flycatcher
Stonechat
Village weaver
Zitting cisticola

LESSER ANTILLES
Barn owl
Belted kingfisher
Brown pelican
Cattle egret
Crested caracara
Greater flamingo
House sparrow
Killdeer
Magnificent frigatebird
Osprey
Peregrine falcon
Rock pigeon

Ruddy turnstone
White-tailed tropicbird
Wood stork

LIBERIA

African broadbill
African palm swift
African paradise-flycatcher
African pitta
Barn swallow
Black tern
Black-winged stilt
Buff-spotted flufftail
Cattle egret
Collared pratincole
Common bulbul
Common waxbill
Eurasian bittern
Gray parrot
Gray woodpecker
Great blue turaco
Hammerhead
Leaf-love
Lyre-tailed honeyguide
Northern wryneck
Osprey
Peregrine falcon
Ruddy turnstone
Sacred ibis
Small buttonquail
Spotted flycatcher
Village weaver
Wilson's storm-petrel

LIBYA

Barn swallow
Black-winged stilt
Common bulbul
Crag martin
Egyptian vulture
Eurasian bittern
Gray wagtail
Greater hoopoe-lark
House sparrow
Mallard
Northern gannet

Northern lapwing
Northern raven
Peregrine falcon
Rock pigeon
Ruddy turnstone
Stonechat
Winter wren

LIECHTENSTEIN

Barn swallow
Black tern
Chaffinch
Common cuckoo
Corncrake
Dunnock
Eurasian golden oriole
European roller
European starling
Gray wagtail
Great cormorant
Great crested grebe
Great tit
Hoopoe
House sparrow
Mallard
Mute swan
Northern lapwing
Northern raven
Northern wryneck
Nuthatch
Peregrine falcon
Red crossbill
Rock pigeon
Snow finch
Spotted flycatcher
Stonechat
Winter wren

LITHUANIA

Barn swallow
Black tern
Chaffinch
Common cuckoo
Common murre
Corncrake
Dunnock

Eurasian bittern
Eurasian dipper
Eurasian golden oriole
European roller
European starling
European white stork
Great cormorant
Great crested grebe
Great tit
Hoopoe
House sparrow
Mallard
Northern fulmar
Northern gannet
Northern lapwing
Northern raven
Northern wryneck
Nuthatch
Red crossbill
Rock pigeon
Spotted flycatcher
Spotted nutcracker
Winter wren

LUXEMBOURG

Barn swallow
Black tern
Chaffinch
Common cuckoo
Corncrake
Dunnock
Eurasian golden oriole
European roller
European starling
European white stork
Gray wagtail
Great cormorant
Great crested grebe
Great tit
Hoopoe
House sparrow
Mallard
Mute swan
Northern lapwing
Northern raven
Northern wryneck

Nuthatch
Peregrine falcon
Red crossbill
Rock pigeon
Spotted flycatcher
Stonechat
Winter wren

MACEDONIA

Barn swallow
Chaffinch
Common cuckoo
Corncrake
Crag martin
Dunnock
Egyptian vulture
Eurasian dipper
Eurasian golden oriole
European bee-eater
European roller
European starling
European white stork
Gray wagtail
Great cormorant
Great crested grebe
Great tit
Hoopoe
Horned lark
House sparrow
Mallard
Northern lapwing
Northern raven
Northern wryneck
Nuthatch
Peregrine falcon
Red crossbill
Rock pigeon
Snow bunting
Spotted flycatcher
Stonechat
Winter wren

MADAGASCAR

African palm swift
Black-winged stilt
Cattle egret

Common sunbird-asity
Crab plovers
Greater flamingo
Greater painted snipe
Hammerhead
Hoopoe
Peregrine falcon
Ruddy turnstone
Rufous vanga
Sacred ibis
Stonechat
White-breasted mesite
Wilson's storm-petrel

MALAWI

African broadbill
African jacana
African palm swift
African paradise-flycatcher
African pitta
African snipe
Bar-breasted mousebird
Barn swallow
Black-winged stilt
Buff-spotted flufftail
Cape batis
Cattle egret
Collared pratincole
Common bulbul
Common cuckoo
Common waxbill
Corncrake
Eurasian golden oriole
European bee-eater
European roller
European white stork
Gray go-away-bird
Gray-crowned crane
Great cormorant
Greater painted snipe
Green woodhoopoe
Hammerhead
Helmeted guineafowl
Hoopoe
House sparrow
Osprey

Peregrine falcon
Red-billed oxpecker
Rock pigeon
Sacred ibis
Secretary bird
Small buttonquail
Southern ground-hornbill
Southern red bishop
Spotted flycatcher
Square-tailed drongo
Stonechat
Village weaver
White-helmet shrike
Yellow-fronted tinkerbird
Zitting cisticola

MALAYSIA

Arctic warbler
Asian fairy-bluebird
Barn swallow
Barred eagle-owl
Baya weaver
Black-and-red broadbill
Black-naped monarch
Black-winged stilt
Common iora
Common myna
Coppersmith barbet
Dollarbird
Fiery minivet
Fire-breasted flowerpecker
Gray nightjar
Gray wagtail
Great cormorant
Greater painted snipe
Greater racket-tailed drongo
Green magpie
Helmeted hornbill
Hooded pitta
Malaysian honeyguide
Orange-breasted trogon
Osprey
Peregrine falcon
Pheasant-tailed jacana
Rock pigeon
Ruby-cheeked sunbird

Ruddy turnstone
Rufous-collared kingfisher
Spotted munia
White-throated fantail
Zitting cisticola

MALI
African jacana
African palm swift
African paradise-flycatcher
Barn swallow
Black-winged stilt
Cattle egret
Collared pratincole
Common bulbul
Egyptian vulture
Eurasian bittern
European bee-eater
European roller
European white stork
Gray wagtail
Gray woodpecker
Greater hoopoe-lark
Greater painted snipe
Green woodhoopoe
Hammerhead
Helmeted guineafowl
Hoopoe
Leaf-love
Northern wryneck
Osprey
Ostrich
Peregrine falcon
Rock pigeon
Rose-ringed parakeet
Sacred ibis
Secretary bird
Small buttonquail
Stonechat
Village weaver
White-helmet shrike
Yellow-fronted tinkerbird
Zitting cisticola

MAURITANIA
Barn swallow

Black-winged stilt
Cattle egret
Collared pratincole
Common bulbul
Crag martin
Egyptian vulture
Eurasian bittern
European roller
European white stork
Gray woodpecker
Greater flamingo
Greater hoopoe-lark
Greater painted snipe
Green woodhoopoe
Hammerhead
Helmeted guineafowl
Hoopoe
Magnificent frigatebird
Manx shearwater
Northern gannet
Osprey
Ostrich
Peregrine falcon
Rock pigeon
Rose-ringed parakeet
Ruddy turnstone
Secretary bird
Small buttonquail
Wilson's storm-petrel
Zitting cisticola

MAURITIUS
Dodo
Mauritius cuckoo-shrike

MEXICO
American anhinga
American avocet
American cliff swallow
American dipper
American goldfinch
American mourning dove
American robin
American white pelican
Anna's hummingbird
Baltimore oriole

Barn owl
Barn swallow
Barred antshrike
Belted kingfisher
Black rail
Black tern
Black-and-white warbler
Black-capped vireo
Black-winged stilt
Blue jay
Blue-black grassquit
Blue-crowned motmot
Blue-footed booby
Blue-gray gnatcatcher
Brown creeper
Brown pelican
Bushtit
Cactus wren
Canada goose
Cattle egret
Cedar waxwing
Common loon
Crested caracara
Eastern bluebird
Eastern phoebe
Eastern screech-owl
European starling
Gray catbird
Great blue heron
Great kiskadee
Greater roadrunner
Harris's hawk
Horned lark
House sparrow
House wren
Killdeer
King vulture
Limpkin
Loggerhead shrike
Long-billed curlew
Long-tailed manakin
Magnificent frigatebird
Mallard
Northern bobwhite quail
Northern gannet
Northern raven

Osprey
Peregrine falcon
Plain chachalaca
Red-throated loon
Red-winged blackbird
Resplendent quetzal
Rock pigeon
Roseate spoonbill
Rose-throated becard
Ruddy turnstone
Rufous-browed peppershrike
Rufous-tailed jacamar
Sandhill crane
Savanna sparrow
Scarlet macaw
Song sparrow
Sprague's pipit
Sungrebe
Verdin
Western grebe
Western scrub-jay
Whip-poor-will
White-necked puffbird
Wild turkey
Wilson's storm-petrel
Winter wren
Wood duck
Wood stork
Wrentit
Yellow-bellied sapsucker
Yellow-breasted chat

MOLDOVA
Barn swallow
Black tern
Chaffinch
Collared pratincole
Common cuckoo
Corncrake
Dunnock
Eurasian bittern
Eurasian golden oriole
European bee-eater
European roller
European starling
European white stork

Great cormorant
Great crested grebe
Great tit
Hoopoe
House sparrow
Mallard
Northern lapwing
Northern raven
Northern wryneck
Nuthatch
Peregrine falcon
Rock pigeon
Snow bunting
Spotted flycatcher
Stonechat
Winter wren

MONACO
Greater flamingo
Northern gannet

MONGOLIA
Barn swallow
Black tern
Black-winged stilt
Common cuckoo
Crag martin
Eurasian bittern
Gray wagtail
Great bustard
Great cormorant
Great crested grebe
Hoopoe
Horned lark
House sparrow
Mallard
Mute swan
Northern raven
Northern wryneck
Nuthatch
Pallas's sandgrouse
Peregrine falcon
Red crossbill
Rock pigeon
Snow bunting
Snow finch

Spotted flycatcher
Spotted nutcracker
Stonechat

MOROCCO
Barn swallow
Black-winged stilt
Cattle egret
Chaffinch
Collared pratincole
Common bulbul
Common cuckoo
Common murre
Corncrake
Crag martin
Dunnock
Egyptian vulture
Eurasian dipper
Eurasian golden oriole
European bee-eater
European roller
European starling
Gray wagtail
Great bustard
Great cormorant
Great crested grebe
Greater flamingo
Greater hoopoe-lark
Hoopoe
Horned lark
House sparrow
Magnificent frigatebird
Mallard
Manx shearwater
Northern gannet
Northern raven
Ostrich
Peregrine falcon
Rock pigeon
Ruddy turnstone
Small buttonquail
Spotted flycatcher
Stonechat
Wilson's storm-petrel
Winter wren
Zitting cisticola

MOZAMBIQUE

African broadbill
African jacana
African palm swift
African paradise-flycatcher
African pitta
African snipe
Bar-breasted mousebird
Barn swallow
Black-winged stilt
Buff-spotted flufftail
Cape batis
Cattle egret
Collared pratincole
Common bulbul
Common cuckoo
Common waxbill
Corncrake
Crab plovers
Eurasian golden oriole
European bee-eater
European roller
European white stork
Gray go-away-bird
Gray-crowned crane
Great cormorant
Greater painted snipe
Green woodhoopoe
Hammerhead
Helmeted guineafowl
Hoopoe
House sparrow
Osprey
Ostrich
Peregrine falcon
Rock pigeon
Rosy-breasted longclaw
Ruddy turnstone
Sacred ibis
Secretary bird
Small buttonquail
Southern ground-hornbill
Southern red bishop
Spotted flycatcher
Square-tailed drongo
Stonechat

Village weaver
White-helmet shrike
Wilson's storm-petrel
Yellow-fronted tinkerbird
Zitting cisticola

MYANMAR

Asian fairy-bluebird
Australasian lark
Barn swallow
Barred eagle-owl
Baya weaver
Black bulbul
Black-and-red broadbill
Black-naped monarch
Black-winged stilt
Cattle egret
Common cuckoo
Common iora
Common myna
Coppersmith barbet
Crested tree swift
Dollarbird
Fiery minivet
Fire-breasted flowerpecker
Gray nightjar
Gray wagtail
Great cormorant
Great crested grebe
Great tit
Greater painted snipe
Greater racket-tailed drongo
Green magpie
Helmeted hornbill
Hooded pitta
Hoopoe
House sparrow
Mallard
Northern wryneck
Orange-breasted trogon
Osprey
Peregrine falcon
Pheasant-tailed jacana
Purple sunbird
Rock pigeon
Rose-ringed parakeet

Rose-ringed parakeet
Ruby-cheeked sunbird
Ruddy turnstone
Rufous-collared kingfisher
Small buttonquail
Spotted munia
Stonechat
White-throated fantail
Winter wren
Zitting cisticola

NAMIBIA

African jacana
African palm swift
African paradise-flycatcher
Arctic skua
Barn swallow
Black tern
Black-winged stilt
Cattle egret
Common cuckoo
Common waxbill
Egyptian vulture
Eurasian golden oriole
European roller
European white stork
Gray go-away-bird
Great cormorant
Great crested grebe
Greater painted snipe
Green woodhoopoe
Hammerhead
Helmeted guineafowl
Hoopoe
House sparrow
Namaqua sandgrouse
Osprey
Ostrich
Peregrine falcon
Rock pigeon
Ruddy turnstone
Sacred ibis
Secretary bird
Small buttonquail
Southern ground-hornbill
Southern red bishop

Spotted flycatcher
White-helmet shrike
Wilson's storm-petrel
Yellow-fronted tinkerbird
Zitting cisticola

NEPAL
Asian fairy-bluebird
Barn swallow
Black-naped monarch
Cattle egret
Common cuckoo
Coppersmith barbet
Crested tree swift
Dollarbird
Egyptian vulture
Eurasian bittern
Eurasian golden oriole
European roller
European white stork
Fire-breasted flowerpecker
Gray nightjar
Gray wagtail
Great cormorant
Great crested grebe
Greater painted snipe
Hooded pitta
Hoopoe
House sparrow
Northern wryneck
Osprey
Peregrine falcon
Pheasant-tailed jacana
Purple sunbird
Rock pigeon
Rose-ringed parakeet
Ruby-cheeked sunbird
Satyr tragopan
Small buttonquail
Snow finch
Spotted munia
Spotted nutcracker
Stonechat
White-throated fantail
Winter wren

Zitting cisticola

NETHERLANDS
Barn swallow
Black tern
Chaffinch
Common cuckoo
Common murre
Corncrake
Dunnock
Eurasian golden oriole
European roller
European starling
European white stork
Great auk
Great cormorant
Great crested grebe
Great tit
House sparrow
Mallard
Manx shearwater
Mute swan
Northern fulmar
Northern gannet
Northern lapwing
Northern wryneck
Nuthatch
Peregrine falcon
Puffin
Red-throated loon
Rock pigeon
Ruddy turnstone
Spotted flycatcher
Stonechat
Winter wren

NEW CALEDONIA
Beach thick-knee
Black-winged stilt
House sparrow
Kagu
Osprey
Painted buttonquail
Peregrine falcon
Rainbow lorikeet

White-tailed tropicbird

NEW ZEALAND
Arctic skua
Black-winged stilt
Brown kiwi
Canada goose
Cattle egret
Chatham mollymawk
Common diving-petrel
Emperor penguin
European starling
Great cormorant
Great crested grebe
House sparrow
Kokako
Laughing kookaburra
Mallard
Mute swan
Rifleman
Rock pigeon
Ruddy turnstone
Variable oystercatcher
Wilson's storm-petrel
Yellowhead

NICARAGUA
American anhinga
American dipper
American mourning dove
Baltimore oriole
Barn owl
Barred antshrike
Belted kingfisher
Black tern
Black-and-white warbler
Black-winged stilt
Blue-black grassquit
Blue-crowned motmot
Blue-footed booby
Brown creeper
Brown pelican
Cattle egret
Cedar waxwing
Crested caracara

Gray catbird
Gray potoo
Great blue heron
Great kiskadee
Harris's hawk
House sparrow
Killdeer
King vulture
Limpkin
Long-tailed manakin
Magnificent frigatebird
Northern raven
Osprey
Peregrine falcon
Plain chachalaca
Resplendent quetzal
Rock pigeon
Roseate spoonbill
Rose-throated becard
Ruddy turnstone
Rufous-browed peppershrike
Rufous-tailed jacamar
Scarlet macaw
Sunbittern
Sungrebe
White-necked puffbird
Wood stork
Yellow-bellied sapsucker
Yellow-breasted chat

NIGER
African jacana
African palm swift
African paradise-flycatcher
Barn swallow
Black-winged stilt
Cattle egret
Collared pratincole
Common bulbul
Egyptian vulture
Eurasian bittern
European white stork
Gray woodpecker
Greater hoopoe-lark
Greater painted snipe
Green woodhoopoe

Hammerhead
Helmeted guineafowl
Hoopoe
Northern wryneck
Osprey
Ostrich
Peregrine falcon
Rock pigeon
Rose-ringed parakeet
Sacred ibis
Secretary bird
Small buttonquail
Village weaver
Yellow-fronted tinkerbird
Zitting cisticola

NIGERIA
African jacana
African palm swift
African paradise-flycatcher
African pitta
Bar-breasted mousebird
Barn swallow
Black tern
Black-winged stilt
Buff-spotted flufftail
Cattle egret
Collared pratincole
Common bulbul
Common waxbill
Eurasian bittern
European roller
European white stork
Gray parrot
Gray woodpecker
Gray-necked picathartes
Great blue turaco
Greater painted snipe
Green woodhoopoe
Hammerhead
Helmeted guineafowl
Hoopoe
Leaf-love
Lyre-tailed honeyguide
Northern wryneck
Osprey

Peregrine falcon
Rose-ringed parakeet
Ruddy turnstone
Sacred ibis
Secretary bird
Small buttonquail
Spotted flycatcher
Square-tailed drongo
White-helmet shrike
Wilson's storm-petrel
Yellow-fronted tinkerbird
Zitting cisticola

NORTH KOREA
Arctic warbler
Barn swallow
Common cuckoo
Common murre
Dollarbird
Eurasian bittern
Gray nightjar
Gray wagtail
Great bustard
Great cormorant
Great tit
Greater painted snipe
Hoopoe
Mute swan
Nuthatch
Red crossbill
Red-crowned crane
Red-throated loon
Rock pigeon
Saunder's gull
Stonechat
Winter wren

NORWAY
Arctic skua
Arctic warbler
Barn swallow
Chaffinch
Common cuckoo
Common loon
Common murre

Corncrake
Dunnock
Eurasian dipper
European starling
Gray wagtail
Great auk
Great cormorant
Great crested grebe
Great tit
Gyrfalcon
Horned lark
House sparrow
King eider
Manx shearwater
Northern fulmar
Northern gannet
Northern lapwing
Northern raven
Northern wryneck
Nuthatch
Osprey
Peregrine falcon
Puffin
Red crossbill
Red-throated loon
Rock pigeon
Ruddy turnstone
Snow bunting
Snowy owl
Spotted flycatcher
Spotted nutcracker
Willow ptarmigan
Winter wren

OMAN
Crab plovers
Egyptian vulture
European roller
Gray wagtail
Greater hoopoe-lark
Hoopoe
House sparrow
Osprey
Peregrine falcon
Purple sunbird
Rock pigeon

Ruddy turnstone
Wilson's storm-petrel

PAKISTAN
Barn swallow
Baya weaver
Black bulbul
Black-winged stilt
Cattle egret
Chaffinch
Collared pratincole
Common cuckoo
Common myna
Coppersmith barbet
Crab plovers
Crag martin
Egyptian vulture
Eurasian bittern
Eurasian golden oriole
European bee-eater
European roller
European starling
European white stork
Gray hypocolius
Gray wagtail
Great cormorant
Great crested grebe
Great tit
Greater flamingo
Greater hoopoe-lark
Greater painted snipe
Hoopoe
House sparrow
Mallard
Mute swan
Northern lapwing
Northern raven
Osprey
Peregrine falcon
Pheasant-tailed jacana
Purple sunbird
Rock pigeon
Rose-ringed parakeet
Ruddy turnstone
Small buttonquail
Snow finch

Spotted flycatcher
Spotted nutcracker
Stonechat
White-throated fantail
Wilson's storm-petrel

PANAMA
American anhinga
American dipper
American mourning dove
Baltimore oriole
Barn owl
Barn swallow
Barred antshrike
Belted kingfisher
Black guan
Black rail
Black tern
Black-and-white warbler
Black-capped donacobius
Black-winged stilt
Blue-black grassquit
Blue-crowned motmot
Blue-footed booby
Brown pelican
Cattle egret
Crested caracara
Gray catbird
Gray potoo
Great blue heron
Great kiskadee
Hairy hermit
Harris's hawk
Highland tinamou
House sparrow
Killdeer
King vulture
Limpkin
Magnificent frigatebird
Oilbird
Osprey
Peregrine falcon
Red-billed scythebill
Resplendent quetzal
Rock pigeon
Roseate spoonbill

Rose-throated becard
Ruddy turnstone
Rufous-browed peppershrike
Rufous-tailed jacamar
Scarlet macaw
Sharpbill
Sunbittern
Sungrebe
White-necked puffbird
Wood stork
Yellow-bellied sapsucker

PAPUA NEW GUINEA
Australasian figbird
Australasian lark
Australian magpie-lark
Australian pratincole
Barn swallow
Beach thick-knee
Black-winged stilt
Cattle egret
Dollarbird
Eclectus parrot
Fan-tailed berrypecker
Feline owlet-nightjar
Golden whistler
Gray wagtail
Gray-crowned babbler
Hooded pitta
Jacky winter
King bird of paradise
Osprey
Peregrine falcon
Rainbow lorikeet
Ribbon-tailed astrapia
Ruddy turnstone
Southern cassowary
Variable pitohui
White-tailed tropicbird
Willie wagtail
Wilson's storm-petrel
Zitting cisticola

PARAGUAY
American anhinga
American cliff swallow

Barn owl
Barn swallow
Barred antshrike
Baywing
Black-capped donacobius
Black-winged stilt
Blue-black grassquit
Blue-crowned motmot
Cattle egret
Crested caracara
Gray potoo
Great kiskadee
Greater thornbird
Hairy hermit
Harris's hawk
House sparrow
King vulture
Limpkin
Peregrine falcon
Red-billed scythebill
Red-legged seriema
Roseate spoonbill
Rufous hornero
Rufous-browed peppershrike
Rufous-tailed jacamar
Sharpbill
Sungrebe
Toco toucan
Wood stork

PERU
Amazonian umbrellabird
American anhinga
Arctic skua
Barn owl
Barn swallow
Barred antshrike
Black rail
Black tern
Black-capped donacobius
Black-winged stilt
Blue-black grassquit
Blue-crowned motmot
Blue-footed booby
Brown pelican
Cattle egret

Chimney swift
Common trumpeter
Coppery-chested jacamar
Crested caracara
Gray antbird
Gray potoo
Gray-breasted mountain-
   toucan
Great kiskadee
Hairy hermit
Harris's hawk
Highland tinamou
Hoatzin
Horned screamer
House sparrow
Killdeer
King vulture
Lesser rhea
Limpkin
Magellanic penguin
Oilbird
Osprey
Peregrine falcon
Peruvian plantcutter
Red-billed scythebill
Rock pigeon
Roseate spoonbill
Ruddy turnstone
Rufous-bellied seedsnipe
Rufous-browed peppershrike
Rufous-capped nunlet
Rufous-tailed jacamar
Rusty-belted tapaculo
Scarlet macaw
Sharpbill
Spangled cotinga
Sparkling violet-ear
Sunbittern
Sungrebe
Wattled curassow
White-necked puffbird
Wilson's storm-petrel
Wire-tailed manakin
Wood stork

PHILIPPINES
Arctic warbler

Asian fairy-bluebird
Australasian lark
Barn swallow
Beach thick-knee
Black-naped monarch
Black-winged stilt
Cattle egret
Coppersmith barbet
Dollarbird
Fiery minivet
Fire-breasted flowerpecker
Gray nightjar
Gray wagtail
Greater painted snipe
Hooded pitta
Japanese white-eye
Little slaty flycatcher
Luzon bleeding heart
Osprey
Peregrine falcon
Pheasant-tailed jacana
Rock pigeon
Ruddy turnstone
Small buttonquail
Spotted munia
Stripe-headed rhabdornis
Zitting cisticola

POLAND

Barn swallow
Black tern
Chaffinch
Common cuckoo
Common murre
Corncrake
Dunnock
Eurasian bittern
Eurasian dipper
Eurasian golden oriole
European roller
European starling
European white stork
Gray wagtail
Great cormorant
Great crested grebe
Great tit

Hoopoe
House sparrow
Mallard
Northern fulmar
Northern gannet
Northern lapwing
Northern raven
Northern wryneck
Nuthatch
Osprey
Peregrine falcon
Puffin
Red crossbill
Rock pigeon
Snow bunting
Snow finch
Spotted flycatcher
Spotted nutcracker
Winter wren

PORTUGAL

Barn swallow
Black-winged stilt
Chaffinch
Collared pratincole
Common cuckoo
Common loon
Common murre
Crag martin
Dunnock
Egyptian vulture
Eurasian dipper
Eurasian golden oriole
European bee-eater
European roller
European white stork
Gray wagtail
Great bustard
Great cormorant
Great crested grebe
Great tit
Hoopoe
House sparrow
Mallard
Manx shearwater
Northern gannet

Northern lapwing
Northern raven
Northern wryneck
Nuthatch
Osprey
Peregrine falcon
Red crossbill
Red-throated loon
Rock pigeon
Ruddy turnstone
Spotted flycatcher
Stonechat
Wilson's storm-petrel
Winter wren
Zitting cisticola

PUERTO RICO

American mourning dove
Barn owl
Belted kingfisher
Brown pelican
Cattle egret
Crested caracara
European starling
Greater flamingo
House sparrow
Killdeer
Magnificent frigatebird
Osprey
Peregrine falcon
Rock pigeon
Ruddy turnstone
White-tailed tropicbird
Wood stork
Yellow-bellied sapsucker

QATAR

European roller
Greater hoopoe-lark
Hoopoe
House sparrow
Stonechat

ROMANIA

Barn swallow

Black tern
Black-winged stilt
Chaffinch
Collared pratincole
Common cuckoo
Corncrake
Dunnock
Egyptian vulture
Eurasian bittern
Eurasian dipper
Eurasian golden oriole
European bee-eater
European roller
European starling
European white stork
Gray wagtail
Great cormorant
Great crested grebe
Great tit
Hoopoe
House sparrow
Mallard
Northern lapwing
Northern raven
Northern wryneck
Nuthatch
Peregrine falcon
Red crossbill
Red-throated loon
Rock pigeon
Snow bunting
Spotted flycatcher
Stonechat
Winter wren

RUSSIA
Arctic skua
Arctic warbler
Barn swallow
Black tern
Black-winged stilt
Cattle egret
Chaffinch
Collared pratincole
Common cuckoo

Common murre
Corncrake
Crag martin
Dollarbird
Dunnock
Eurasian bittern
Eurasian dipper
Eurasian golden oriole
European bee-eater
European starling
European white stork
Gray nightjar
Gray wagtail
Great bustard
Great cormorant
Great crested grebe
Great tit
Greater painted snipe
Gyrfalcon
Hoopoe
Horned lark
House sparrow
King eider
Mallard
Mute swan
Northern fulmar
Northern gannet
Northern lapwing
Northern raven
Northern wryneck
Nuthatch
Osprey
Pallas's sandgrouse
Peregrine falcon
Puffin
Red crossbill
Red-crowned crane
Red-throated loon
Rock pigeon
Ruddy turnstone
Sandhill crane
Snow bunting
Snow finch
Snowy owl
Spotted flycatcher
Spotted nutcracker

Stonechat
Willow ptarmigan
Winter wren

RWANDA
African jacana
African palm swift
African paradise-flycatcher
African pitta
African snipe
Bar-breasted mousebird
Barn swallow
Black-winged stilt
Buff-spotted flufftail
Cattle egret
Collared pratincole
Common bulbul
Common cuckoo
Common waxbill
Corncrake
Eurasian golden oriole
European bee-eater
European roller
European white stork
Gray parrot
Gray woodpecker
Gray-crowned crane
Great blue turaco
Great cormorant
Great crested grebe
Green woodhoopoe
Hammerhead
Helmeted guineafowl
Hoopoe
Osprey
Ostrich
Peregrine falcon
Red-billed oxpecker
Sacred ibis
Shoebill
Small buttonquail
Southern red bishop
Spotted flycatcher
Stonechat
Village weaver

Yellow-fronted tinkerbird
Zitting cisticola

SÃO TOMÉ AND PRÍNCIPE
White-tailed tropicbird

SAUDI ARABIA
African palm swift
Black-winged stilt
Cattle egret
Crab plovers
Crag martin
Egyptian vulture
European roller
Gray hypocolius
Gray wagtail
Great cormorant
Greater hoopoe-lark
Hammerhead
Hoopoe
House sparrow
Mallard
Northern lapwing
Osprey
Peregrine falcon
Rock pigeon
Ruddy turnstone
Stonechat
Wilson's storm-petrel

SENEGAL
African palm swift
African paradise-flycatcher
Black tern
Black-winged stilt
Cattle egret
Collared pratincole
Common bulbul
Common waxbill
Egyptian vulture
Eurasian bittern
European roller
European white stork
Gray wagtail

Gray woodpecker
Greater flamingo
Greater hoopoe-lark
Greater painted snipe
Green woodhoopoe
Hammerhead
Helmeted guineafowl
Hoopoe
Leaf-love
Magnificent frigatebird
Northern wryneck
Osprey
Peregrine falcon
Rose-ringed parakeet
Ruddy turnstone
Sacred ibis
Secretary bird
Small buttonquail
Village weaver
White-helmet shrike
Wilson's storm-petrel
Yellow-fronted tinkerbird
Zitting cisticola

SEYCHELLES
White-tailed tropicbird

SIERRA LEONE
African broadbill
African palm swift
African paradise-flycatcher
African pitta
Barn swallow
Black tern
Black-winged stilt
Buff-spotted flufftail
Cattle egret
Collared pratincole
Common bulbul
Common waxbill
Eurasian bittern
Gray parrot
Gray woodpecker
Great blue turaco
Hammerhead
Leaf-love

Lyre-tailed honeyguide
Northern wryneck
Osprey
Peregrine falcon
Rose-ringed parakeet
Ruddy turnstone
Sacred ibis
Small buttonquail
Spotted flycatcher
Square-tailed drongo
Village weaver
Wilson's storm-petrel

SINGAPORE
Baya weaver

SLOVAKIA
Barn swallow
Black tern
Chaffinch
Collared pratincole
Common cuckoo
Corncrake
Dunnock
Eurasian golden oriole
European bee-eater
European roller
European starling
European white stork
Gray wagtail
Great cormorant
Great crested grebe
Great tit
Hoopoe
House sparrow
Mallard
Northern lapwing
Northern raven
Northern wryneck
Nuthatch
Peregrine falcon
Red crossbill
Rock pigeon
Snow bunting
Snow finch
Spotted flycatcher

Stonechat
Winter wren

SLOVENIA
Barn swallow
Black tern
Chaffinch
Collared pratincole
Common cuckoo
Corncrake
Dunnock
Eurasian dipper
Eurasian golden oriole
European bee-eater
European roller
European starling
Gray wagtail
Great cormorant
Great crested grebe
Great tit
Hoopoe
House sparrow
Mallard
Northern lapwing
Northern raven
Northern wryneck
Nuthatch
Peregrine falcon
Rock pigeon
Snow bunting
Snow finch
Spotted flycatcher
Stonechat
Winter wren
Zitting cisticola

SOMALIA
African jacana
African palm swift
African paradise-flycatcher
Bar-breasted mousebird
Barn swallow
Black-winged stilt
Cattle egret
Collared pratincole
Common bulbul

Corncrake
Crab plovers
Egyptian vulture
European roller
European white stork
Gray wagtail
Great cormorant
Greater hoopoe-lark
Green woodhoopoe
Hammerhead
Hoopoe
Ostrich
Peregrine falcon
Red-billed oxpecker
Rose-ringed parakeet
Ruddy turnstone
Sacred ibis
Small buttonquail
Spotted flycatcher
Square-tailed drongo
Stonechat
White-helmet shrike
Wilson's storm petrel

SOUTH AFRICA
African jacana
African palm swift
African paradise-flycatcher
African snipe
Arctic skua
Bar-breasted mousebird
Barn swallow
Black tern
Black-winged stilt
Blue bustard
Buff-spotted flufftail
Cape batis
Cape sugarbird
Cattle egret
Collared pratincole
Common bulbul
Common cuckoo
Common waxbill
Corncrake
Crab plovers
Eurasian golden oriole

European bee-eater
European roller
European starling
European white stork
Gray-crowned crane
Great cormorant
Great crested grebe
Greater flamingo
Greater painted snipe
Green woodhoopoe
Hammerhead
Helmeted guineafowl
Hoopoe
House sparrow
Manx shearwater
Mute swan
Namaqua sandgrouse
Osprey
Ostrich
Peregrine falcon
Red-billed oxpecker
Rock pigeon
Rosy-breasted longclaw
Ruddy turnstone
Sacred ibis
Secretary bird
Small buttonquail
Southern ground-hornbill
Southern red bishop
Spotted flycatcher
Square-tailed drongo
Stonechat
Village weaver
White-helmet shrike
Wilson's storm-petrel
Yellow-fronted tinkerbird
Zitting cisticola

SOUTH KOREA
Arctic warbler
Barn swallow
Cattle egret
Common cuckoo
Common murre
Dollarbird
Eurasian bittern

Gray nightjar
Gray wagtail
Great cormorant
Great tit
Greater painted snipe
Japanese white-eye
Mallard
Mute swan
Northern lapwing
Nuthatch
Red crossbill
Red-throated loon
Rock pigeon
Saunder's gull
Stonechat
Winter wren

SPAIN
Barn swallow
Black-winged stilt
Chaffinch
Collared pratincole
Common cuckoo
Common loon
Common murre
Corncrake
Crag martin
Dunnock
Egyptian vulture
Eurasian bittern
Eurasian dipper
Eurasian golden oriole
European bee-eater
European roller
European white stork
Gray wagtail
Great auk
Great bustard
Great cormorant
Great crested grebe
Great tit
Greater flamingo
Hoopoe
House sparrow
Mallard
Manx shearwater

Northern fulmar
Northern gannet
Northern lapwing
Northern raven
Northern wryneck
Nuthatch
Peregrine falcon
Red crossbill
Red-throated loon
Rock pigeon
Ruddy turnstone
Small buttonquail
Snow finch
Spotted flycatcher
Stonechat
Wilson's storm-petrel
Winter wren
Zitting cisticola

SRI LANKA
Baya weaver
Black bulbul
Common iora
Common myna
Coppersmith barbet
Crested tree swift
Dollarbird
Eurasian golden oriole
Gray nightjar
Great tit
Greater racket-tailed drongo
House sparrow
Pheasant-tailed jacana
Purple sunbird
Rose-ringed parakeet
Spotted munia
White-throated fantail
Wilson's storm-petrel

SUDAN
African jacana
African palm swift
African paradise-flycatcher
Bar-breasted mousebird
Barn swallow

Black tern
Black-winged stilt
Buff-spotted flufftail
Cattle egret
Collared pratincole
Common bulbul
Common waxbill
Corncrake
Crab plovers
Crag martin
Egyptian vulture
Eurasian bittern
European roller
European white stork
Gray wagtail
Gray woodpecker
Great blue turaco
Great cormorant
Greater flamingo
Greater hoopoe-lark
Greater painted snipe
Green woodhoopoe
Hammerhead
Helmeted guineafowl
Hoopoe
Leaf-love
Northern wryneck
Osprey
Ostrich
Peregrine falcon
Red-billed oxpecker
Rock pigeon
Rose-ringed parakeet
Ruddy turnstone
Sacred ibis
Secretary bird
Shoebill
Small buttonquail
Spotted flycatcher
Square-tailed drongo
Stonechat
Village weaver
White-helmet shrike
Wilson's storm-petrel
Yellow-fronted tinkerbird
Zitting cisticola

SURINAME

American anhinga
Barn owl
Barn swallow
Barred antshrike
Black tern
Black-capped donacobius
Black-winged stilt
Blue-black grassquit
Blue-crowned motmot
Brown pelican
Cattle egret
Common trumpeter
Crested caracara
Gray antbird
Gray potoo
Great kiskadee
Guianan cock-of-the-rock
Hairy hermit
Hoatzin
King vulture
Limpkin
Magnificent frigatebird
Osprey
Peregrine falcon
Roseate spoonbill
Ruddy turnstone
Rufous-browed peppershrike
Scarlet macaw
Sharpbill
Spangled cotinga
Sunbittern
Sungrebe
White-necked puffbird
Wilson's storm-petrel
Wood stork

SWAZILAND

African jacana
African palm swift
African paradise-flycatcher
African snipe
Barn swallow
Black-winged stilt
Buff-spotted flufftail
Cape batis

Cattle egret
Collared pratincole
Common bulbul
Common cuckoo
Common waxbill
Corncrake
European bee-eater
European roller
European white stork
Great cormorant
Greater painted snipe
Green woodhoopoe
Hammerhead
Helmeted guineafowl
Hoopoe
House sparrow
Osprey
Peregrine falcon
Sacred ibis
Secretary bird
Small buttonquail
Southern ground-hornbill
Southern red bishop
Spotted flycatcher
Stonechat
Village weaver
White-helmet shrike
Zitting cisticola

SWEDEN

Barn swallow
Chaffinch
Common cuckoo
Common murre
Corncrake
Dunnock
Eurasian bittern
Eurasian dipper
European roller
European starling
Gray wagtail
Great auk
Great cormorant
Great crested grebe
Great tit
Gyrfalcon

Hoopoe
Horned lark
House sparrow
Mute swan
Northern fulmar
Northern gannet
Northern lapwing
Northern raven
Northern wryneck
Nuthatch
Osprey
Peregrine falcon
Puffin
Red crossbill
Red-throated loon
Rock pigeon
Ruddy turnstone
Snow bunting
Spotted flycatcher
Spotted nutcracker
Willow ptarmigan
Winter wren

SWITZERLAND

Barn swallow
Black tern
Chaffinch
Common cuckoo
Corncrake
Dunnock
Eurasian dipper
Eurasian golden oriole
European roller
European starling
European white stork
Gray wagtail
Great cormorant
Great crested grebe
Great tit
Hoopoe
House sparrow
Mallard
Mute swan
Northern lapwing
Northern raven
Northern wryneck

Nuthatch
Peregrine falcon
Red crossbill
Rock pigeon
Snow finch
Spotted flycatcher
Spotted nutcracker
Stonechat
Winter wren

SYRIA
Black-winged stilt
Cattle egret
Chaffinch
Collared pratincole
Common bulbul
Common cuckoo
Corncrake
Crag martin
Dunnock
Egyptian vulture
European bee-eater
European roller
European starling
Great bustard
Great cormorant
Greater flamingo
Hoopoe
House sparrow
Mallard
Northern gannet
Northern lapwing
Nuthatch
Peregrine falcon
Red crossbill
Rock pigeon
Spotted flycatcher
Stonechat
Winter wren

TAJIKISTAN
Barn swallow
Chaffinch
Common cuckoo
Crag martin
Egyptian vulture

Eurasian golden oriole
European roller
European starling
Great bustard
Great cormorant
Great crested grebe
Great tit
Hoopoe
House sparrow
Mallard
Northern raven
Peregrine falcon
Rock pigeon
Snow finch
Spotted flycatcher
Stonechat
Winter wren

TANZANIA
African broadbill
African jacana
African palm swift
African paradise-flycatcher
African pitta
African snipe
Bar-breasted mousebird
Barn swallow
Black-winged stilt
Buff-spotted flufftail
Cattle egret
Collared pratincole
Common bulbul
Common waxbill
Corncrake
Crab plovers
Eurasian golden oriole
European bee-eater
European roller
European white stork
Golden-winged sunbird
Gray go-away-bird
Gray wagtail
Gray woodpecker
Great cormorant
Great crested grebe
Greater flamingo

Greater painted snipe
Green woodhoopoe
Hammerhead
Helmeted guineafowl
Hoopoe
House sparrow
Leaf-love
Osprey
Ostrich
Peregrine falcon
Red-billed oxpecker
Rock pigeon
Rosy-breasted longclaw
Ruddy turnstone
Sacred ibis
Secretary bird
Shoebill
Small buttonquail
Southern ground-hornbill
Southern red bishop
Spotted flycatcher
Square-tailed drongo
Stonechat
Village weaver
White-helmet shrike
Wilson's storm-petrel
Yellow-fronted tinkerbird
Zitting cisticola

THAILAND
Arctic warbler
Asian fairy-bluebird
Australasian lark
Barn swallow
Barred eagle-owl
Baya weaver
Black bulbul
Black-and-red broadbill
Black-naped monarch
Black-winged stilt
Cattle egret
Common cuckoo
Common iora
Common myna
Coppersmith barbet
Crested tree swift

Dollarbird
Fiery minivet
Fire-breasted flowerpecker
Gray nightjar
Gray wagtail
Great cormorant
Greater painted snipe
Greater racket-tailed drongo
Green magpie
Helmeted hornbill
Hooded pitta
Hoopoe
Malaysian honeyguide
Northern lapwing
Northern wryneck
Orange-breasted trogon
Osprey
Peregrine falcon
Pheasant-tailed jacana
Purple sunbird
Rock pigeon
Ruby-cheeked sunbird
Ruddy turnstone
Rufous-collared kingfisher
Small buttonquail
Spotted munia
Stonechat
White-throated fantail
Zitting cisticola

TOGO

African jacana
African palm swift
African paradise-flycatcher
Barn swallow
Black tern
Black-winged stilt
Cattle egret
Collared pratincole
Common bulbul
Eurasian bittern
European bee-eater
European roller
Gray parrot
Gray woodpecker
Great blue turaco

Greater painted snipe
Green woodhoopoe
Hammerhead
Helmeted guineafowl
Hoopoe
Leaf-love
Northern wryneck
Osprey
Peregrine falcon
Rose-ringed parakeet
Ruddy turnstone
Sacred ibis
Secretary bird
Small buttonquail
Spotted flycatcher
Square-tailed drongo
Village weaver
White-helmet shrike
Wilson's storm-petrel
Yellow-fronted tinkerbird
Zitting cisticola

TRINIDAD AND TOBAGO

Blue-crowned motmot
Gray potoo
Hairy hermit
Oilbird
Rufous-tailed jacamar

TUNISIA

Barn swallow
Black-winged stilt
Collared pratincole
Common bulbul
Corncrake
Crag martin
Dunnock
Egyptian vulture
Eurasian bittern
European bee-eater
European roller
European starling
Gray wagtail
Great cormorant
Great crested grebe

Greater flamingo
Greater hoopoe-lark
Hoopoe
House sparrow
Northern gannet
Northern lapwing
Northern raven
Northern wryneck
Peregrine falcon
Rock pigeon
Ruddy turnstone
Small buttonquail
Spotted flycatcher
Stonechat
Winter wren
Zitting cisticola

TURKEY

Barn swallow
Black tern
Cattle egret
Chaffinch
Collared pratincole
Common bulbul
Common cuckoo
Corncrake
Crag martin
Dunnock
Egyptian vulture
Eurasian bittern
Eurasian dipper
Eurasian golden oriole
European bee-eater
European roller
European starling
Gray wagtail
Great bustard
Great cormorant
Great crested grebe
Great tit
Greater flamingo
Hoopoe
Horned lark
House sparrow
Mallard
Mute swan

Northern gannet
Northern lapwing
Northern raven
Northern wryneck
Nuthatch
Peregrine falcon
Red crossbill
Red-throated loon
Rock pigeon
Snow finch
Spotted flycatcher
Stonechat
Winter wren
Zitting cisticola

TURKMENISTAN

Barn swallow
Black-winged stilt
Cattle egret
Chaffinch
Collared pratincole
Common cuckoo
Common myna
Crag martin
Egyptian vulture
Eurasian bittern
Eurasian golden oriole
European bee-eater
European roller
European starling
Gray hypocolius
Great cormorant
Great crested grebe
Great tit
Hoopoe
Horned lark
House sparrow
Mallard
Northern lapwing
Northern raven
Nuthatch
Peregrine falcon
Red-throated loon
Rock pigeon
Spotted flycatcher

Winter wren

UGANDA

African broadbill
African jacana
African palm swift
African paradise-flycatcher
African pitta
African snipe
Bar-breasted mousebird
Barn swallow
Black-winged stilt
Buff-spotted flufftail
Cattle egret
Collared pratincole
Common bulbul
Common cuckoo
Common waxbill
Corncrake
Egyptian vulture
Eurasian golden oriole
European roller
European white stork
Golden-winged sunbird
Gray parrot
Gray woodpecker
Gray-crowned crane
Great blue turaco
Great cormorant
Great crested grebe
Greater painted snipe
Green woodhoopoe
Hammerhead
Helmeted guineafowl
Hoopoe
Leaf-love
Northern wryneck
Osprey
Ostrich
Peregrine falcon
Red-billed oxpecker
Rose-ringed parakeet
Sacred ibis
Secretary bird
Shoebill

Small buttonquail
Southern red bishop
Spotted flycatcher
Village weaver
White-helmet shrike
Yellow-fronted tinkerbird
Zitting cisticola

UKRAINE

Barn swallow
Black tern
Black-winged stilt
Chaffinch
Collared pratincole
Common cuckoo
Corncrake
Dunnock
Eurasian bittern
Eurasian golden oriole
European bee-eater
European roller
European starling
European white stork
Gray wagtail
Great bustard
Great cormorant
Great crested grebe
Great tit
Hoopoe
Horned lark
House sparrow
Mallard
Mute swan
Northern lapwing
Northern raven
Northern wryneck
Nuthatch
Osprey
Peregrine falcon
Red crossbill
Red-throated loon
Rock pigeon
Snow bunting
Spotted flycatcher
Spotted nutcracker

Stonechat
Winter wren

UNITED ARAB EMIRATES

Crab plovers
Egyptian vulture
European roller
Greater hoopoe-lark
Hoopoe
House sparrow
Northern lapwing
Osprey
Purple sunbird
Rock pigeon
Ruddy turnstone
Stonechat
Wilson's storm-petrel

UNITED KINGDOM

Barn owl
Barn swallow
Canada goose
Chaffinch
Common cuckoo
Common loon
Common murre
Corncrake
Dunnock
Eurasian bittern
Eurasian dipper
Eurasian golden oriole
European roller
European starling
Gray wagtail
Great auk
Great cormorant
Great crested grebe
Great tit
House sparrow
Mallard
Manx shearwater
Mute swan
Northern gannet
Northern lapwing

Northern raven
Northern wryneck
Nuthatch
Osprey
Peregrine falcon
Puffin
Red crossbill
Red-throated loon
Rock pigeon
Ruddy turnstone
Snow bunting
Spotted flycatcher
Stonechat
Willow ptarmigan
Winter wren

UNITED STATES

American anhinga
American avocet
American cliff swallow
American dipper
American goldfinch
American mourning dove
American robin
American white pelican
Anna's hummingbird
Apapane
Arctic skua
Arctic warbler
Baltimore oriole
Barn owl
Barn swallow
Belted kingfisher
Bishop's oo
Black rail
Black tern
Black-and-white warbler
Black-capped chickadee
Black-capped vireo
Black-winged stilt
Blue jay
Blue-gray gnatcatcher
Brown creeper
Brown pelican
Bushtit

Cactus wren
California condor
Canada goose
Cattle egret
Cedar waxwing
Chimney swift
Common loon
Common murre
Crested caracara
Eastern bluebird
Eastern phoebe
Eastern screech-owl
European starling
Gray catbird
Great auk
Great blue heron
Great cormorant
Great kiskadee
Greater roadrunner
Gyrfalcon
Harris's hawk
Hawaiian honeycreepers
Horned lark
House sparrow
House wren
Ivory-billed woodpecker
Killdeer
King eider
Kirtland's warbler
Laysan albatross
Laysan finch
Limpkin
Loggerhead shrike
Long-billed curlew
Magnificent frigatebird
Mallard
Manx shearwater
Mute swan
Northern bobwhite quail
Northern fulmar
Northern gannet
Northern raven
Osprey
Peregrine falcon
Plain chachalaca
Puffin

Red crossbill
Red-breasted nuthatch
Red-cockaded woodpecker
Red-throated loon
Red-winged blackbird
Rock pigeon
Roseate spoonbill
Rose-throated becard
Ruddy turnstone
Sandhill crane
Savanna sparrow
Snow bunting
Song sparrow
Sprague's pipit
Verdin
Western grebe
Western scrub-jay
Whip-poor-will
White-tailed tropicbird
Wild turkey
Willow ptarmigan
Wilson's storm-petrel
Winter wren
Wood duck
Wood stork
Wrentit
Yellow-bellied sapsucker
Yellow-breasted chat

URUGUAY
American anhinga
American cliff swallow
Barn owl
Baywing
Black-winged stilt
Cattle egret
Crested caracara
Gray potoo
Great kiskadee
Greater thornbird
Harris's hawk
House sparrow
King vulture
Limpkin
Magellanic penguin
Manx shearwater

Peregrine falcon
Red-legged seriema
Rock pigeon
Roseate spoonbill
Ruddy turnstone
Rufous hornero
Wilson's storm-petrel
Wood stork

UZBEKISTAN
Barn swallow
Black-winged stilt
Chaffinch
Collared pratincole
Common cuckoo
Common myna
Crag martin
Egyptian vulture
Eurasian bittern
Eurasian dipper
Eurasian golden oriole
European bee-eater
European roller
European starling
Great bustard
Great cormorant
Great crested grebe
Great tit
Hoopoe
Horned lark
House sparrow
Mallard
Northern raven
Pallas's sandgrouse
Peregrine falcon
Rock pigeon

VENEZUELA
Amazonian umbrellabird
American anhinga
Baltimore oriole
Barn owl
Barn swallow
Barred antshrike
Belted kingfisher
Black tern

Black-and-white warbler
Black-capped donacobius
Black-winged stilt
Blue-black grassquit
Blue-crowned motmot
Brown pelican
Cattle egret
Common trumpeter
Crested caracara
Gray antbird
Gray potoo
Great kiskadee
Greater flamingo
Guianan cock-of-the-rock
Hairy hermit
Harris's hawk
Highland tinamou
Hoatzin
Horned screamer
King vulture
Limpkin
Magnificent frigatebird
Oilbird
Osprey
Peregrine falcon
Red-billed scythebill
Roseate spoonbill
Ruddy turnstone
Rufous-browed peppershrike
Rufous-tailed jacamar
Scarlet macaw
Sharpbill
Spangled cotinga
Sparkling violet-ear
Sunbittern
Sungrebe
White-necked puffbird
Wilson's storm-petrel
Wire-tailed manakin
Wood stork

VIETNAM
Arctic warbler
Asian fairy-bluebird
Australasian lark
Barn swallow

Baya weaver
Black bulbul
Black-and-red broadbill
Black-crowned barwing
Black-naped monarch
Black-winged stilt
Cattle egret
Common cuckoo
Common iora
Common myna
Coppersmith barbet
Crag martin
Crested tree swift
Dollarbird
Eurasian bittern
Fire-breasted flowerpecker
Gray nightjar
Gray wagtail
Great cormorant
Great tit
Greater painted snipe
Greater racket-tailed drongo
Green magpie
Hoopoe
Northern wryneck
Orange-breasted trogon
Osprey
Peregrine falcon
Pheasant-tailed jacana
Purple sunbird
Rock pigeon
Ruby-cheeked sunbird
Ruddy turnstone
Saunder's gull
Small buttonquail
Spotted munia
Stonechat
White-throated fantail
Zitting cisticola

YEMEN

African palm swift
Cattle egret
Crab plovers
Crag martin
Egyptian vulture

European roller
Gray wagtail
Greater hoopoe-lark
Hammerhead
Hoopoe
House sparrow
Osprey
Peregrine falcon
Rock pigeon
Ruddy turnstone
Stonechat
Wilson's storm-petrel

YUGOSLAVIA

Common cuckoo
Corncrake
Crag martin
Egyptian vulture
Eurasian dipper
European bee-eater
European roller
European white stork
Gray wagtail
Great cormorant
Great crested grebe
Hoopoe
Horned lark
Mallard
Northern lapwing
Peregrine falcon
Rock pigeon
Snow bunting
Zitting cisticola

ZAMBIA

African broadbill
African jacana
African palm swift
African paradise-flycatcher
African pitta
African snipe
Bar-breasted mousebird
Barn swallow
Black-winged stilt
Buff-spotted flufftail

Cattle egret
Collared pratincole
Common bulbul
Common cuckoo
Common waxbill
Corncrake
Eurasian golden oriole
European bee-eater
European roller
European white stork
Gray go-away-bird
Gray-crowned crane
Great cormorant
Greater flamingo
Greater painted snipe
Green woodhoopoe
Hammerhead
Helmeted guineafowl
Hoopoe
House sparrow
Osprey
Ostrich
Peregrine falcon
Red-billed oxpecker
Rosy-breasted longclaw
Sacred ibis
Secretary bird
Shoebill
Small buttonquail
Southern ground-hornbill
Southern red bishop
Spotted flycatcher
Square-tailed drongo
Stonechat
Village weaver
White-helmet shrike
Yellow-fronted tinkerbird
Zitting cisticola

ZIMBABWE

African broadbill
African palm swift
African paradise-flycatcher
African pitta
African snipe
Bar-breasted mousebird

Barn swallow
Black-winged stilt
Buff-spotted flufftail
Cape batis
Cattle egret
Collared pratincole
Common bulbul
Common cuckoo
Common waxbill
Corncrake
Eurasian golden oriole
European bee-eater
European roller
European white stork

Gray go-away-bird
Gray-crowned crane
Great cormorant
Greater painted snipe
Green woodhoopoe
Hammerhead
Helmeted guineafowl
Hoopoe
House sparrow
Osprey
Ostrich
Peregrine falcon
Red-billed oxpecker
Rock pigeon

Rosy-breasted longclaw
Sacred ibis
Secretary bird
Shoebill
Small buttonquail
Southern ground-hornbill
Southern red bishop
Spotted flycatcher
Stonechat
Village weaver
White-helmet shrike
Yellow-fronted tinkerbird
Zitting cisticola

Index

Italic type indicates volume number; **boldface** type indicates entries and their pages; (ill.) indicates illustrations.

Australian pelicans, *1:* 98, 134
Australian pratincoles, *2:* 436, 437, 442–43, 442 (ill.), 443 (ill.)
Australian robins, *5:* **1123–29**
Australian warblers, *4:* **1079–86**
Australian whipbirds, *4:* 1099, 1101
Avocets, *2:* **423–30**

B

Babblers, *4:* **1025–35**
  See also Pseudo babblers
Bachman's warblers, *5:* 1260
Bahama swallows, *4:* 915
Balaeniceps rex. See Shoebills
Balaenicipitidae. See Shoebills
Bald eagles, *1:* 209; *2:* 295
Balearica regulorum. See Gray crowned cranes
Baltimore orioles, *5:* 1270–71, 1270 (ill.), 1271 (ill.)
Banded cotingas, *4:* 874
Banded stilts, *2:* 423
Banded wattle-eyes, *4:* 1062
Banding birds, *4:* 852
Bannerman's turacos, *3:* 539
Bar-breasted mousebirds, *3:* 639, 641–43, 641 (ill.), 642 (ill.)
Barbados yellow warblers, *5:* 1260
Barbets, *3:* 708–9, 725–29, 747–56, 766, 768
Barn owls, *3:* **557–63**, 564, 565
Barn swallows, *4:* 913, 916–18, 916 (ill.), 917 (ill.)
Barred antshrikes, *4:* 836, 840–41, 840 (ill.), 841 (ill.)
Barred buttonquails, *2:* 317
Barred eagle-owls, *3:* 570–71, 570 (ill.), 571 (ill.)
Barrow, Mary Reid, *2:* 247
Bates' sunbirds, *5:* 1209
Batis capensis. See Cape batises
Batrachostomus. See Asian frogmouths

Bay-winged cowbirds. *See* Baywings
Baya weavers, *5:* 1313–14, 1313 (ill.), 1314 (ill.)
Baybirds, *5:* 1269
Baywings, *5:* 1275–76, 1275 (ill.), 1276 (ill.)
Beach thick-knees, *2:* 431, 432, 434–35, 434 (ill.), 435 (ill.)
Beaks. *See* Bills and beaks
Bearded reedlings, *4:* 1026, 1027
Bearded wood-partridge, *2:* 305
Becards, rose-throated, *4:* 854–55, 854 (ill.), 855 (ill.)
Bee-eaters, *3:* 653, 654, 655–56, **682–90**, 768
Bee hummingbirds, *3:* 630
Bellbirds, *4:* 872; *5:* 1131, 1132
Belted kingfishers, *3:* 654, 666–68, 666 (ill.), 667 (ill.)
Bengal florican bustards, *2:* 319
Bernier's vangas, *4:* 972, 975
Berrypeckers, *5:* 1194–95
  crested, *5:* 1196
  fan-tailed, *5:* 1199–1201, 1199 (ill.), 1200 (ill.)
  scarlet-collared, *5:* 1196
  Visayan, *5:* 1196
Bewick's wrens, *4:* 1037
Bhai tapaculos, *4:* 847
Biak gerygones, *4:* 1081
Bills and beaks, *1:* 146
  See also specific species
BirdLife International, *1:* 62
Birds of paradise, *4:* 789; *5:* **1389–97**
Birds of prey, diurnal, *1:* **207–11**; *3:* 555; *5:* 1346
Bishops, *5:* 1306
  red, *5:* 1309
  southern red, *5:* 1315–16, 1315 (ill.), 1316 (ill.)
  yellow-crowned, *5:* 1309

Bishop's oos, *5:* 1229–30, 1229 (ill.), 1230 (ill.)
Bitterns, *1:* 143, 146, **149–59**
Black-and-red broadbills, *4:* 798–800, 798 (ill.), 799 (ill.)
Black-and-white warblers, *5:* 1263–64, 1263 (ill.), 1264 (ill.)
Black-bellied dippers, *4:* 1010
Black-bellied plovers, *2:* 446
Black-belted flowerpeckers, *5:* 1196
Black-billed wood ducks, *2:* 259
Black-breasted buttonquails, *2:* 328
Black bulbuls, *4:* 945, 952–53, 952 (ill.), 953 (ill.)
Black-capped chickadees, *5:* 1167–69, 1167 (ill.), 1168 (ill.)
Black-capped donacobius, *4:* 1047–49, 1047 (ill.), 1048 (ill.)
Black-capped vireos, *5:* 1238–40, 1238 (ill.), 1239 (ill.)
Black catbirds, *4:* 998
Black-cinnamon fantails, *4:* 1105
Black-crowned barwings, *4:* 1028–29, 1028 (ill.), 1029 (ill.)
Black cuckoos. *See* Anis
Black-faced sheathbills, *2:* 469, 472–73, 472 (ill.), 473 (ill.)
Black guans, *2:* 284–85, 284 (ill.), 285 (ill.)
Black-headed weavers. *See* Village weavers
Black herons, *1:* 150
Black larks, *4:* 903
Black-legged seriemas, *2:* 383
Black-naped monarchs, *5:* 1120–22, 1120 (ill.), 1121 (ill.)
Black-necked cranes, *2:* 319

Black pillows. *See* Black-naped monarchs

Black rails, *2*: 356, 362 (ill.), 363, 363 (ill.)

Black sicklebills, *5*: 1390

Black stilts, *2*: 424, 425

Black storks, *1*: 166

Black-tailed native-hens, *2*: 358

Black-tailed treecreepers, *5*: 1147

Black terns, *2*: 483–84, 483 (ill.), 484 (ill.)

Black tinamous, *1*: 7

Black vultures, *1*: 175

Black-winged stilts, *2*: 424, 425, 426–27, 426 (ill.), 427 (ill.)

Black woodpeckers, *3*: 728

Blackbirds, New World, *4*: 1013; *5*: **1268–77**

Blue birds of paradise, *5*: 1390

Blue-black grassquits, *5*: 1253–54, 1253 (ill.), 1254 (ill.)

Blue bustards, *2*: 392–94, 392 (ill.), 393 (ill.)

Blue cranes, *2*: 319

Blue-crowned motmots, *3*: 679–81, 679 (ill.), 680 (ill.)

Blue fairies of the forest. *See* Black-naped monarchs

Blue-footed boobies, *1*: 130–31, 130 (ill.), 131 (ill.)

Blue-gray gnatcatchers, *4*: 1051, 1055–57, 1055 (ill.), 1056 (ill.)

Blue-headed picathartes. *See* Gray-necked picathartes

Blue jays, *5*: 1398, 1401–2, 1401 (ill.), 1402 (ill.)

Blue-naped mousebirds, *3*: 639

Blue swallows, *4*: 915

Blue-throated motmots, *3*: 677

Blue toucans, *3*: 728, 759

Blue vangas, *4*: 972, 973

Blue wattled crows. *See* Kokakos

Bluebirds
eastern, *4*: 1017–19, 1017 (ill.), 1018 (ill.)
fairy, *4*: **955–61**

Boat-billed herons, *1*: 149

Bobwhites, *2*: 303, 304
masked, *2*: 308
northern, *2*: 306–8, 306 (ill.), 307 (ill.)

Bombycilla cedrorum. See Cedar waxwings

Bombycillidae. See Silky flycatchers; Waxwings

Bonaparte's nightjars, *3*: 577, 604

Boobies, *1*: 99, 100, **125–33**

Boreal owls, *3*: 565

Bornean bristleheads, *5*: 1374, 1375–76, 1375 (ill.), 1376 (ill.)

Bornean frogmouths, *3*: 587

Botaurus stellaris. See Eurasian bitterns

Botha's larks, *4*: 905

Boubous, *4*: 963

Bowerbirds, *5*: 1146, **1380–88**

Branta canadensis. See Canada geese

Breeding, communal, *5*: 1140
See also specific species

Bristle-thighed curlews, *2*: 456

Bristlebirds, *4*: 1080

Bristlefronts, Streseman's, *4*: 847

Bristleheads, *5*: 1372–74

Bristles, whisker-like, *3*: 603

Broad-billed rollers, *3*: 655

Broad-billed todies, *3*: 669

Broadbills, *4*: **793–800**

Bronze-cuckoos, *4*: 1071, 1080, 1089

Brood parasitism, *5*: 1259
See also specific species

Brown creepers, *5*: 1184–86, 1184 (ill.), 1185 (ill.)

Brown-eared bulbuls, *4*: 945

Brown flycatchers. *See* Jacky winters

Brown-headed cowbirds, *5*: 1249, 1259

Brown kiwis, *1*: 30, 32–34, 32 (ill.), 33 (ill.)

Brown mesites, *2*: 320–21, 322

Brown pelicans, *1*: 101, 134, 135, 136–38, 136 (ill.), 137 (ill.)

Brown roatelos. *See* Brown mesites

Brown treecreepers, *5*: 1145, 1146, 1147

Bubo sumatranus. See Barred eagle-owls

Bucconidae. *See* Puffbirds

Bucerotidae. *See* Hornbills

Bucorvus leadbeateri. See Southern ground-hornbills

Buff-breasted buttonquails, *2*: 328

Buff-breasted sandpipers, *2*: 455

Buff-spotted flufftails, *2*: 360–61, 360 (ill.), 361 (ill.)

Buff-throated purpletufts, *4*: 874

Buffalo-weavers, red-billed, *5*: 1307, 1308–9

Bulbuls, *4*: **943–54**

Buphagus erythrorhynchus. See Red-billed oxpeckers

Burhinidae. *See* Thick-knees

Burrowing owls, *3*: 554, 565

Burrows, nest, *2*: 414
See also specific species

Bush-shrikes, *4*: 962, 963, 964

Bush thick-knees, *2*: 433

Bushbirds, Rondonia, *4*: 838

Bushlarks, Sidamo, *4*: 905

Bushtits, *5*: 1151–53, 1154–56, 1154 (ill.), 1155 (ill.)

Bustards, *2*: 315, 316, 318–19, **387–94**

Butcherbirds, *5*: 1372–74, 1377–79, 1377 (ill.), 1378 (ill.)
See also Loggerhead shrikes; Shrikes

Nyctibiidae. *See* Potoos
Nyctibius griseus. See Gray potoos

O

O'Brien, Mark, *2:* 271
Oceanites oceanicus. See Wilson's storm-petrels
Odontophoridae. *See* New World quails
Oil spills, *1:* 91
Oilbirds, *3:* 574–77, **579–84,** 581 (ill.), 582 (ill.)
Old World flycatchers, *4:* **1060–69**
Old World orioles, *5:* **1337–44**
Old World vultures, *1:* 143, 207, 208, 212, 219
Old World warblers, *4:* **1050–59**
Olive sunbirds, *5:* 1209
Opisthocomidae. *See* Hoatzins
Opisthocomiformes. *See* Hoatzins
Opisthocomus hoazin. See Hoatzins
Opportunistic birds, *4:* 1061
  See also specific species
Orange-breasted trogons, *3:* 647–48, 647 (ill.), 648 (ill.)
Orange chats, *4:* 1087, 1088, 1089
Organbirds. *See* Kokakos
Oriental bay owls, *3:* 557
Oriental skylarks, *4:* 904
Oriental white storks, *1:* 166
Orioles, *5:* **1268–77**
  See also Old World orioles
Oriolidae. *See* Figbirds; Old World orioles
Oriolus oriolus. See Eurasian golden orioles
Ortalis vetula. See Plain chachalacas
Orthonychidae. *See* Chowchillas; Logrunners

Orthonyx temminckii. See Southern logrunners
Osprey, *1:* 215–16, 215 (ill.), 216 (ill.)
Ostriches, *1:* 1, 11, **35–40,** 37 (ill.), 38 (ill.)
Otididae. *See* Bustards
Otis tarda. See Great bustards
Otus asio. See Eastern screech-owls
Ouzels. *See* American dippers
Ouzels, ring, *4:* 1015
Ovenbirds, *4:* **821–29**
Owlet-frogmouths. *See* Owlet-nightjars
Owlet-nightjars, *3:* 575, 576
Owls, *3:* **552–56,** 579, 585
  barn, *3:* **557–63,** 564, 565
  typical (Strigidae), *3:* 557, 564–73
Oxpeckers, red-billed, *5:* 1334–36, 1334 (ill.), 1335 (ill.)
Oxyruncidae. *See* Sharpbills
Oxyruncus cristatus. See Sharpbills
Oystercatchers, *2:* **417–22**

P

Pachycephala pectoralis. See Golden whistlers
Pachycephalidae. *See* Whistlers
Pachyramphus aglaiae. See Rose-throated becards
Pacific golden plovers, *2:* 396
Pacific monarchs. *See* Black-naped monarchs
Painted buttonquails, *2:* 331–32, 331 (ill.), 332 (ill.)
Painted snipes, *2:* **407–12**
Palawan tits, *5:* 1166
Pale-billed sicklebills, *5:* 1390
Pale-browed tinamous, *1:* 7
Pale-faced sheathbills, *2:* 469
Pallas's cormorants, *1:* 117
Pallas's sandgrouse, *3:* 501–2, 501 (ill.), 502 (ill.)

Pallid cuckoos, *4:* 1108
Palmchats, *4:* **988–90,** 989 (ill.), 990 (ill.)
Pandion haliaetus. See Osprey
Papuan treecreepers, *5:* 1145
Papuan whipbirds, *4:* 1099
Parabuteo unicinctus. See Harris's hawks
Paradigallas, long-tailed, *5:* 1390
Paradisaeidae. *See* Birds of paradise
Paradise birds. *See* Birds of paradise
Paradise-flycatchers, African, *5:* 1117–19, 1117 (ill.), 1118 (ill.)
Parakeet auklets, *2:* 486
Parakeets, *3:* 523, 524–25, 524 (ill.), 525 (ill.)
Pardalotes, *5:* **1202–7**
Pardalotidae. *See* Pardalotes
Pardalotus striatus. See Striated pardalotes
Paridae. *See* Chickadees; Titmice
Parotias, Wahnes's, *5:* 1390
Parrotbills, *4:* 1025
Parrots, *3:* **522–37**
Partridges, *2:* 269
Parulidae. *See* New World warblers
Parus major. See Great tits
Passenger pigeons, *3:* 505, 510
Passer domesticus. See House sparrows
Passerculus sandwichensis. See Savanna sparrows
Passeridae. *See* Sparrows
Passeriformes. *See* Perching birds
Passerines. *See* Perching birds
Peafowl, green, *2:* 266
Peewees. *See* Australian magpie-larks
Pelecanidae. *See* Pelicans
Pelecaniformes, *1:* **98–102**

Red-backed shrikes, 4: 962

Red-billed buffalo-weavers, 5: 1307, 1308–9

Red-billed oxpeckers, 5: 1334–36, 1334 (ill.), 1335 (ill.)

Red-billed queleas, 5: 1309

Red-billed scythebills, 4: 833–35, 833 (ill.), 834 (ill.)

Red-billed tropicbirds, 1: 103

Red birds of paradise, 5: 1390

Red bishops, 5: 1309

Red-breasted cacklers. See Gray-crowned babblers

Red-breasted nuthatches, 5: 1176–78, 1176 (ill.), 1177 (ill.)

Red-breasted plantcutters, 4: 881–82, 883

Red-breasted pygmy parrots, 3: 522

Red-browed treecreepers, 5: 1145

Red-cockaded woodpeckers, 3: 781–83, 781 (ill.), 782 (ill.)

Red-collared widowbirds, 5: 1306–7

Red crossbills, 5: 1285–87, 1285 (ill.), 1286 (ill.)

Red-crowned cranes, 2: 319, 341–42, 341 (ill.), 342 (ill.)

Red-eyed bulbuls, 4: 944

Red-eyed vireos, 4: 792

Red-faced mousebirds, 3: 639

Red-headed rockfowl. See Gray-necked picathartes

Red-headed weavers, 5: 1308

Red-kneed dotterels, 2: 445

Red larks, 4: 905

Red-legged seriemas, 2: 384–86, 384 (ill.), 385 (ill.)

Red List of Threatened Species. See World Conservation Union (IUCN) Red List of Threatened Species

Red-lored whistlers, 5: 1132

Red-shouldered vangas, 4: 974–75

Red-tailed newtonias, 4: 1062

Red-tailed vangas, 4: 972

Red-throated loons, 1: 85–86, 85 (ill.), 86 (ill.)

Red-vented bulbuls, 4: 944

Red-whiskered bulbuls, 4: 944

Red-winged blackbirds, 5: 1269, 1272–74, 1272 (ill.), 1273 (ill.)

Reed warblers, 4: 1051

Reedlings, bearded, 4: 1026, 1027

Regent bowerbirds, 5: 1380

Remizidae. See Penduline titmice

Resplendent quetzals, 3: 649–51, 649 (ill.), 650 (ill.)

Réunion cuckoo-shrikes, 4: 937

Réunion flightless ibises, 1: 193

Réunion solitaires, 3: 517

Rhabdornis, 5: 1188–93

Rhabdornis mysticalis. See Stripe-headed rhabdornis

Rhabdornithidae. See Philippine creepers

Rheas, 1: 2, 3, **11–17**

Rheidae. See Rheas

Rhinocryptidae. See Tapaculos

Rhinoplax vigil. See Helmeted hornbills

Rhipidura albicollis. See White-throated fantails

Rhipidura leucophrys. See Willie wagtails

Rhipiduridae. See Fantails

Rhynochetidae. See Kagus

Rhynochetos jubatus. See Kagus

Ribbon-tailed astrapias, 5: 1391–92, 1391 (ill.), 1392 (ill.)

Ribbon-tailed birds of paradise, 5: 1390

Riflebirds, Victoria's, 5: 1393–94, 1393 (ill.), 1394 (ill.)

Riflemen, 4: 816, 817–19, 817 (ill.), 818 (ill.)

The Rime of the Ancient Mariner, 1: 46

Ring ouzels, 4: 1015

Rio de Janeiro antwrens, 4: 838

River-martins, white-eyed, 4: 914–15

Roadrunners, 3: **545–51**

Roatelos, 2: **320–25**

Robin accentors, 4: 992

Robins, 4: 1038; 5: 1124

American, 4: 1014, 1015, 1022–23, 1022 (ill.), 1023 (ill.)

Australian, 5: **1123–29**

Rock pigeons, 3: 511–12, 511 (ill.), 512 (ill.)

Rock thrushes, 4: 1014, 1015

Rockfowl, 4: 1025

See also Gray-necked picathartes

Rockwarblers, 4: 1079

Rodrigues solitaires, 3: 517–18

Rollers, 3: 653, 654, 655, **691–99**

Rondonia bushbirds, 4: 838

Rooks, 5: 1398

Rose-ringed parakeets, 3: 524–25, 524 (ill.), 525 (ill.)

Rose-throated becards, 4: 854–55, 854 (ill.), 855 (ill.)

Roseate spoonbills, 1: 196–97, 196 (ill.), 197 (ill.)

Rostratula benghalensis. See Greater painted snipes

Rostratulidae. See Painted snipes

Rosy-breasted longclaws, 4: 930–31, 930 (ill.), 931 (ill.)

Rotten meat, 1: 176

Ruby-cheeked sunbirds, 5: 1211–12, 1211 (ill.), 1212 (ill.)

Rudd's larks, 4: 905

Ruddy turnstones, 2: 461–62, 461 (ill.), 462 (ill.)